TREES
IN THE
MIST

*clear the
mist in
your family*

*Mike
Neif*

TREES IN THE MIST

MIKE NEIL

In honor of my mother, Bobbe Neil
1927–2018

Trees in the Mist is a collaboration between my mother, Barbara Jean Swanson Neil, and me. She was born in Everett, Washington, on February 2, 1927. She and her mother, Louisa, were best friends all their lives.

Bobbe, as her friends knew her, always told me stories about her grandmother Lucy. Even though she never knew her grandmother, she would share with me things her mother had told her. She saved the writing box and the notebook Lucy used to record her trip across the country on the train from Lowell, Massachusetts, in 1906, which provided valuable insights in the writing of this book.

Bobbe married my father, Lloyd Neil, Jr., in 1947. He became an optician and opened his own optical store in 1972 in Fircrest, Washington. Mom was an incredible artist and writer in her own right, and had a dream to one day be published. She would be so proud of this book.

I believe my mother's legacy is best seen in her deep love for her children. We never had any question that the woman loved people, especially her family. She had three children: Pam, her firstborn, me, and our little sister, Melissa, whom we all adopted when I was fifteen years old.

In Mom's obituary, my sister Pam wrote, "She loved babies, little kids, and especially teenagers. We always said she was a 'teenager at heart.' She taught her kids and their friends how to drive, cook, and sew. She encouraged everyone to treat each other fairly, love one another, and do good things in the world. She was the mom every kid could talk to and share their soul."

My father died in early 2007, and Mom lived alone until 2014, when she almost died after falling at home. The doctors gave up hope and put her on hospice care, but she lived another five years in Assisted Living. We would talk every day as I did family research for this book, and I would read the manuscript to her over the phone. Every time I found something new, I couldn't wait to share it.

This book would not exist without my mom's encouragement and the family stories passed down from her mother. It was hard to finish it on my own without her. She died on August 13, 2018, with all of her children at her bedside.

TABLE OF CONTENTS

INTRODUCTION

Trees in the Mist is my story of time travel and discovery. It all began when I published my first novel, *The Miracle of Africa*, in 2014. During the writing process, as I formulated the story and developed the characters, I came to know my fictitious characters intimately. They became old friends. To write their dialogue I had to get to know my characters, their emotions, reactions, and surroundings. In some ways, it was like time travel.

The 2011 movie *Midnight in Paris* captures this phenomenon. An American writer goes to Paris with his fiancée and finds himself able to travel back in time to meet his heroes, Ernest Hemingway and Picasso. As an author, this is precisely what I must do.

Then I thought, *If the writing process brought me so close to my characters, what if it could bring me closer to my own past and heritage? What if I used the magic of writing to time travel back through my family and tell their stories?* This is what I did in writing *Trees in the Mist*.

From boyhood, I have heard the stories about my mother's grandmother, Lucy Cook. My mother was taken by these stories, and her own relationship with her mother and grandmother was strong. My grandmother, Louisa, was a friend of mine. She was the kind of person who loved me down to my soul.

My mother told me a story about how my parents had gone somewhere and left me with my Dad's parents when I was about a year old. My grandmother, Arvella Neil, couldn't get me to stop crying, so she called the other grandmother, Louisa Swanson, for help. As Louisa stood on the porch, she could hear me crying. As soon as I was laid in the arms of my Grandmother Louisa, I stopped crying.

My great-grandfather, James Neil, died when his son, Walter Quantrill Neil, was just a year old; his wife remarried. All of his siblings were Mohneys, but Walter never gave up his last name. There was a story about how, when he was a teenager, his grandfather died, and he traveled to the Appalachians in West Virginia to attend the funeral. They were all Confederates, as noted by the middle name his father had given him. He expected them to embrace their long-lost son like a prodigal come home. Instead, they accused him of trying to get part of the inheritance, so he left and never looked back. What he knew about them he never shared with his children. His children never had a clue as to their origin. Walter died when a runaway team of horses threw him from a wagon, when my father was four years old. It wasn't until I began to research the Neil family ancestry that I found these hidden stories through looking at the government census and marriage and death records.

Trees in the Mist is the story of a family tree, a tree shrouded in a foggy mist of dates. I have found names and places, dates when people were married, and when they were born and died. Some have disappeared only to reappear somewhere else, the stories in between lost in history. In *Trees in the Mist,* I fill in the branches of my own family tree. No longer are my ancestors just names carved in a headstone with a birth and death date separated by a dash. That dash is filled with untold stories, the stories of those who came before me.

To me, that is what this novel represents. It's a story about my family tree. It is about making the dash come alive by traveling back in time to discover people and their stories. But, I also hope this novel does more than that. I hope it inspires you to discover your story and find your roots. When you know where you came from, you can better know where you are going.

I hope you enjoy *Trees in the Mist.* It's about life, love, and loss. It's also about happiness, sadness, hopes and dreams, tragedy and triumph, and making the dash come to life.

—*Mike Neil, 2021*

TREES
IN THE
MIST

Part I—John and Peggy Dowling

Samuel Davis Bryant
Born: July 11, 1736, Scarborough, Cumberland County, Maine
Died: 1810 (age 74), Cutler, Washington County, Maine

Elizabeth Harmon Bryant
Born: May, 1736, Scarborough, Cumberland County, Maine
Died: December 3, 1806 (age 70), Cutler,
Washington County, Maine

John Dowling, Sr.
Born: c.1755, Ireland
Died: c.1816 (around age 61), Whiting,
Washington County, Maine

Margaret (Peggy) Bryant Dowling
Born: August 30, 1761 Scarborough,
Cumberland County, Maine
Died: 1855 (age 94), Marion, Washington County, Maine

Part I

John Dowling, Sr.
1755–1816

Margaret (Peggy) Bryant Dowling
1761–1855

Chapter 1

American Hope

L and ho!"

John Dowling stepped back and took a firm grip of the rail as the boat pitched. The canvas sails of the Voyager bulged, rippling in the wind, and the white-capped waves danced as they smashed against the wooden hull. John focused on the horizon, straining to get his first glimpse of America.

"You haven't changed your mind? You are still planning to land in Boston?" asked Captain Dunlang, stepping beside John.

"I guess I will be, even though I hate city life."

The captain looked earnestly into young John's eyes.

"You don't have to, you know. The crew and I would like you to stay on with us. You know we're headed to West Falls in the upper colony of Massachusetts. We'll be taking on lumber and then trading down the coast."

John gulped, trying to muster up a brave response. He didn't want to leave the only people he knew to step alone into a new city.

"The offer is appreciated. But I'm a farmer, sir. My family has always been farmers. I got it in my head to find land." He tried to stand a little taller to appear older than his thirteen years.

"You going to settle land on your *own*?"

"It's just me in the world. I never planned on leaving Ireland, but after my father dropped over dead last year, and with my mother gone since I was two, this was my only option. I'm determined to find some land." He looked across at the city looming on the horizon. "Although, I think I should like to stay on and see if this place called West Falls might suit me better."

"I don't recommend West Falls," said the captain, shaking his head. "There is nothing in that place."

"Sounds perfect for me," John replied with a grin.

It took three days to cover the two hundred and fifty miles to West Falls. Hour by hour, John's anticipation grew. John stood on the bridge in the brisk morning chill of the late October morning, his satchel and musket beside him. As they finally rounded the point, he spotted a few buildings nestled in the harbor, surrounded by timber.

The captain stepped on the deck behind him to watch as the crew brought the ship in for anchorage. "You are going to regret not staying with us."

John stood firm. He was ready to get off the ship and onto land. He was excited to step foot in America.

"You know the colonies are in for a fight," continued the captain. "They think they can be liberated from the English, but they are all merchants, farmers, and fishermen, and they aren't equipped to take on a trained army from the King of England."

"They are fighting for freedom, and that I agree with."

"A lot of people are going to die here on this soil. The fight is heating up."

"My father fought with the Jacobites in '45. He survived the Battle of Culloden and escaped to Ireland. I have his musket, and, along with that, his courage too. The British have been the enemy of my people for many generations. It would be an honor for me to be found by my father fighting them again."

"You're a good lad, young John. Let's make our ship ready for landfall."

John blew out of his mouth to see his breath. A smoky haze hung over the few small, colorless, wooden houses in the port as wood smoke rose from the chimneys. It wouldn't be long now before this place was covered with snow. John's anxiety grew again as the anchor chain rattled, splashing in the calm waters, and men began to lower the jolly boat* over the side.

"You ready to take land?" the older man queried, still testing.

"As ready as I can be, sir."

"Toss your satchel in the skiff, then," instructed the captain as he headed over the side. John took his bag on his arm and tossed it to the bow of the jolly boat, then grabbed the rope ladder with one hand, trying to hold on to the musket with the other.

"I'll take that thing," shouted a crew member he had come to know. " 'Ere, toss'er down."

"You better catch it and don't let it go into the drink. It belonged to my father!"

John took a deep breath, then pitched his most prized possession. He remembered the way his father's eyes welled whenever he spoke about the gun. The sailor caught it clean, then pretended to lose his grip, making a deep guttural laugh as the musket nearly flew out of his hands.

---

*The jolly boat was a type of ship's boat in use during the 18th and 19th centuries. Used mainly to ferry personnel to and from the ship, or for other small-scale activities, it was, by the 18th century, one of several types of ship's boat. The design evolved throughout its period in service.

"I'm not going to miss your dirty tricks," said John, grinning good naturedly as he went hand over hand down the rope ladder, then stepped onto the deck of the skiff.

"Here you go, Johnny." The sailor stood holding out the musket. "Quite a piece you got there. She's a good one. If you stay on this soil, you'll be needing it for years to come."

John's gaze fell on the musket and his heart warmed as its significance impressed itself on him once again.

"This musket made it through the Battle of Culloden and I plan to pass it down to my children," John replied seriously.

The oarlocks creaked and the paddles splashed; all the time, the houses on shore got bigger. He looked back at the Voyager anchored safely in deep water, her majestic masts standing tall and peaceful. The thought crossed his mind that maybe he should have stayed with these men whom he had come to call friends, but he quickly erased it from his head. The skiff brushed the wharf, and the captain caught the edge.

John paused, remembering an Irish blessing his father had taught him. It seemed appropriate for the moment, and it rolled smoothly off his tongue. "May a rainbow always follow your rainstorms, and may you always count your joys instead of your woes; count your friends instead of your foes."

The captain stepped onto the dock with his hand stretched out while a sailor held the boat. "Don't know when I ever met a young man such as you, John. Are you sure I can't talk you out of this just one more time?"

"My heart is set, sir."

"Like I said, you are a better man than me walking into a strange town, not knowing if you will have a next meal or bed. Do you have a penny to your name, lad?"

"I've got the shirt on my back, my musket in my hand, and the warm jacket you gave me."

"We are here for several days. Don't be shy if you change your mind. Folks won't take to you here. They've got plenty of mouths to feed, and no one will be looking for one more."

"I'll make it, sir, just wait and see." John took a gulp to ease the pit in his stomach as he stepped out on the dock. He walked up the planks with his satchel over his shoulder and the musket weighed heavy in his hand. The locks creaking on the skiff were the only sound on the bay.

"He'll be back, you'll see," whispered the captain.

With a deep breath, John stepped off the boardwalk and into the deserted narrow street. He peered in a window but could see no signs of life. He laid the musket against the wall and sat down on the cobblestones, and, using his worn, brown leather satchel to rest his back, he dozed off.

John awoke with the noise of voices in the street. Unsure of how long he had snoozed, he clambered to his feet. A man passing by gave him a dirty look, as if he were a vagrant.

"Got any work for me, sir?"

The question fell onto the cobblestones like a dead cat. The man acted as if John were invisible. Another passerby approached with a friendlier face.

"Nothing here, boy. You might try that ship in the harbor."

John peered in another shop window and spotted some life behind the counter. He grabbed the latch and opened the door.

"What are you doing in here, young man?" asked the clerk with an unfriendly scowl.

"I just got off the Voyager, and you see, sir . . ." John's words were cut off with swift precision.

"No sense telling your sad story here, boy. This town is full of sad stories, and we don't need to hear one more from the likes of you. Now, if you've got coins in your pocket, I might be obliged to help you find something. Short of that, you can take yourself and that musket out of here before you kill someone."

"What if I told you the captain sent me in to buy provisions?" replied John, standing tall.

"I'll believe that when the captain himself shows up to vouch for you." John shrugged his shoulders and took the advice to vacate the premises.

As he stood outside the shop, trying to decide what to do next, a man exited the shop behind him and began loading things onto a handcart.

"Top of the morning to you, mate; can I lend a hand?" John inquired politely.

"Rightly so, if you are a mind to," responded the stranger as John set his things aside and began to help with the boxes. "Is that your father's musket?"

"Yep."

"Where is he?"

"Six feet underground back in Ireland. My mother is buried with him."

"You're not really here to purchase provisions for the captain, are you?" the stranger asked with a sharp edge that sounded more cautious than unfriendly.

"Guess I wasn't too convincing."

"Looks to me like they tossed you off the ship." John laughed, knowing that his fiery red windblown hair did not help the situation.

"Oh, no, sir. They begged me to stay, but I told them I needed to make a life on land."

"This isn't another one of your stories, is it? If that ship is trading with the British, folks around here won't take too kindly to it."

"That ship, good sir, is an Irish ship, and not likely to trade anything to the likes of a Tory," muttered John under his breath.

"You know anybody here, boy?"

"Let me introduce myself; my name is John Dowling." John smiled broadly as he extended his hand.

"I'm Samuel Davis Bryant of Goldsborough Inlet." Samuel took John's hand and gave it a firm shake. John withdrew his hand from the handshake and grabbed a heavy box. He sized up the well-built fellow with a greying beard and strong chin, who appeared to be some twenty years his senior.

"In answer to your question, sir, so far I only know you. Other than that, I am on my own."

"Can you go back and stay on the ship?"

"I could, I suppose . . . but I've had enough of the sea life. I'll stay under a tree if I have to, but I'm going to need to find a job."

"I can do you better than that, lad. My land is south of here about twenty miles, and I could use a good hand, such as yourself. You are welcome to come along if you like; I have a place in the barn out of the weather, such as it is. If you work hard, you will never go hungry."

"Best offer I've had all day," laughed John.

"Is your family from here?" John asked as he picked up the handles on the cart and began pushing.

"No, my wife Elizabeth and I are from Scarborough. We moved here a while ago with my brother, Bartholomew. I lost both my parents when I was a young lad like you. Hard to lose your parents at such an age, I know what it feels like to be new to a place." Samuel began to push the loaded handcart over the cobblestone road.

"Are we pushing this handcart twenty miles?"

"Oh, heavens, no," chuckled Samuel, "That's my skiff on the shore." John followed Samuel as he pushed the heavy cart off the road and onto a path leading down toward the bay, where the twenty-five-foot skiff had been pulled up and tied to a log.

"I thought we would go by horse and wagon."

"Good idea if I had one. But there are no roads from here to there. Do you know how to row a boat?"

"I've seen it done fair enough, but I've never been on the sticks."

"Well, today you are going to get a lesson on how to row a boat. She's got a sail if we get winds, so say a prayer that we don't have to row twenty miles."

As Samuel spoke, John found himself growing comfortable around the man. He liked the way Samuel held himself. He imagined them becoming close companions, like a father and son. He let himself stay in the thought of it for a while. For the lonely boy, it was a pleasant one.

Chapter 2

A Son and a Brother

Rowing past the Voyager, John felt regret growing in the pit of his stomach. He hoped he had made the right choice and not squandered a good chance to become a sailor. A crewman spotted them as they rowed alongside and beckoned to the other crewmen to join him on the rail.

"Where you off to, Johnny?" shouted the boatswain.*

"A place called Gouldsboro!"† Other men came to the rail as they watched the skiff pass.

"Aye, you take care now," shouted a crewman.

"We'll miss you," yelled another.

"Sounds like you're famous here," commented Samuel as John waved and they watched the ship grow smaller in the distance. The only noise now came from the creaking oarlocks. Each time Samuel pulled to move the skiff forward, it pushed out little whirlpools into the

---

*Most senior member of the crew.

†Now known as Steuben, just on the south edge of Washington County, Maine.

calm water behind the oars. Rounding the point into the open ocean, the chop on the water splashed against the gunnel, and a cool mist blew against John's face.

"We'll have fair winds," said Samuel. "Let's raise the sail and see what we can catch. You take the oars, and I'll hold the rudder."

For several hours, John horsed on the oars as the seabirds played in the whitecaps and the coastline passed by. Then Samuel shouted, "How about it, John, you want to try the rudder? I'll give her a try for a while to give your arms a rest."

"I thought you'd never ask."

"You got to hold it hard against the wind to keep the sail filled. Goldsborough Bay is about another five miles or so." John gladly took the rudder, hoping to fulfill Samuel's expectations.

John had seen the coastline from the Voyager, but from a rowboat, he now had a first-hand look. So many inlets, islands, and bays, too numerous to count, each with their own name. How could he remember them all?

By the time they arrived in Goldsborough, they had rowed for nearly five hours.

John spotted a house perched on a bluff overlooking the bay. He saw a barn and some outbuildings and a covey of children making their way to the shore to meet the boat. There was a woman making her way behind them, carrying a baby in her arms. Samuel pulled eagerly on the oars to quickly traverse the last several hundred yards to the rocky beach as the sail fell limp from the lack of wind.

"Father!" shouted a girl from the shore. She was tall and her long, dark hair fluttered in the breeze. "What did you bring us?"

"That's Elizabeth, my oldest; we call her Lizzie. She just turned eleven last month."

Another girl with fiery hair like John's waded out knee deep, soaking her skirt as she caught the bow of the skiff to keep it from hitting on the rocks.

"Who is this, Father?" she asked, wrinkling her brow. Samuel dropped the oars, and John stepped out into the water, taking the boat from the girl.

"Pull us up, John, and we'll make formal introductions," urged Samuel. "Tie us off on that rock."

"Give me the rope," the girl interjected, "I know how to do it." She grabbed it away from him with an impatient jerk that John found as sisterly as it was impudent. Samuel stepped to the bow of the skiff as John pulled it to a sandy spot, and then Samuel leaped off the skiff to the dry beach.

"Good to have you back, dear," smiled the woman as she embraced him.

"How's our Benjamin?" he asked affectionately, returning her embrace and giving the baby in her arms a big kiss.

"Healthy as a horse," she replied with a grin.

Samuel waved his arm toward John to bring him forward. "Gather 'round, children; this is John Dowling from Ireland. He's going to be lending a hand around here." Turning to John, he added, "This is my wife, Elizabeth, and the children are . . ." Samuel paused as the second oldest daughter spoke up for herself.

"I'm Peggy, and I just turned nine. How old are you?" Peggy picked up the rope and tied it to the rock on the beach.

"Almost fourteen, but I feel a lot older than that after spending three months on a sailing ship."

Peggy pointed to her older sister, the one John had noticed from the shore, "That's Elizabeth. We call her Lizzie, so we don't get her and Momma mixed up."

"I'm Susanna, but they call me Susanne, and I'm eight. This is my brother John, and he's six. He don't like to talk much."

"And that's little Benjy," said Peggy, pointing to her mother holding the baby. "He was just born probably right about when you got on that ship from Ireland."

"Now that we're all acquainted, we have a boat to unload," Samuel interjected with a smile. "Everyone take what you can carry."

John parted out the supplies to the girls, trying to match loads with their abilities. He grabbed a heavy box and headed up the beach as he surreptitiously listened to the conversation between Samuel and Elizabeth.

"Seriously, Samuel, did you have to pick up a stray?" she whispered under her breath, trying to keep her words private.

"I couldn't very well just leave him to fend for himself in Machias," he whispered back.

"I thought you went to West Falls?"

"The natives call it Machias."

"Wherever; it doesn't matter. We don't need one more mouth to feed."

"He's just a boy, dear, and he's got no one. He seems to be a good worker, and God knows I could use another hand."

"He's your responsibility, then. You hear me? I won't raise a child that don't belong to us." Elizabeth looked over her shoulder to see if John had heard the conversation, but he kept a straight face.

John lost track of their conversation as Peggy trotted up beside him. "There's lots of stuff to do here, John. At low tide, we can find lobster just off the shore in shallow water. Ever had lobster?"

"Can't say I have, lass," he replied as they climbed the hill to the house carrying the heavy wooden box.

"Oh, you're going like lobster. And we go swimming too."

"Must be a lake close by."

"We go swimming in the bay, silly."

"The only time you swim in the salt water is if your boat sinks," laughed John. "That water is freezing."

John loved working on the farm,* but even more so, he loved being a part of the Bryant family. Despite Mother Elizabeth's sometimes cold mannerisms, most of the time he felt welcomed, and she appeared to love him as a brother to her other children, like part of the family.

He embraced the daily farm routine of his new life, working in the fields and taking breaks in the summer to swim in the bay. He even learned to love the freezing cold water. On long days after helping Samuel in the fields, he would follow Lizzie, Peggy, and the children down to the bay, where they would splash energetically for as long they could before it was time to clean up for dinner. In the winter, the family would gather around the stone central fireplace. Each day seemingly melted into the next, and the days into years.

Most afternoons, one of the girls would walk out into the field and bring him lunch. The days when he and Samuel worked side by side, they took a break in nearby shade. If Peggy brought them lunch, she would always join them, sitting on the dirt beside them peppering them with questions about their work, or the growing tensions with the British.

Whenever they went into Machias—for now John also called West Falls by its native name—they gathered news about the rising taxes and unrest. The British continued to raise taxes on necessary goods, and corruption was growing rampant.

The farmers, like Samuel, were good men who worked hard. It was they who transformed the land and worked the ground day after day. They did not appreciate their hard-earned money going toward the rich in England. Many, like John's own father, had already fought the British and had left the mainland to find freedom on the shores of America. It was ill advised of the British to threaten American freedom.

John, now passionate about the American cause, appreciated Samuel's cool head, wisdom, and political knowledge. He was eager to use

---

*Sometime before 1772, Samuel Bryant sold his land and moved north to the location now known as Cutler, approximately ten miles due south of Whiting.

his musket against the British if it came to that. Samuel too was fired up for the cause, but he had a family and land to farm. He brought John back down to earth, instilling in him the values of freedom, but also of family and faith. John always looked forward to their daily hour in the shade where he could pick Samuel's brain.

But, increasingly, what John found himself longing for most were the days he worked alone in the field. As he worked, his eyes were constantly drawn toward the house, waiting for the moment the door would open and he could see who was bringing lunch. Peggy was joyful and always brought a good laugh. But now that he was sixteen and Lizzie almost fourteen, he found his heart racing when he saw the Bryants' oldest daughter. She almost never stayed to eat with him—she hated getting dirty—but those few moments alone with her left him daydreaming for the rest of the afternoon. Everyone else was family, but as for Lizzie, he no longer saw her as a sister.

"Can I work with you in the field today?" asked Peggy eagerly, her eleven-year-old legs bouncing as she handed him a cup of tea.

"Such service," he said, smiling as he took a battered tin cup of steaming tea from her hands. "Don't you have laundry to help your mother with?"

"I want to spend the day with you. We hardly ever get to spend time together."

"You'll get your hands dirty."

"I don't care. Lizzie is the one who doesn't like to get her hands dirty. She tries to be a proper lady. She won't even go to the beach. I can't for the life of me see why you are so sweet on her."

"Oh heck . . . I'm not sweet on her." He blushed, wondering how Peggy had noticed.

"You know you are, John. But I'm the one you should be sweet on. You and I love the same things." He laughed at the thought of being sweet toward such a young girl, practically his sister.

"I'm going to be a woman soon and I'll be ready for marriage."

"Oh, hold on there, little girl. Ain't nobody getting married around here." He could not imagine this red-haired, pig-tailed girl growing up into a woman. "You'll always be little Peggy to me."

"You gonna let me tag along with you today or not?" Tears began welling up in her eyes.

"I guess I owe you something, since you brought me tea," laughed John, trying to lighten the mood.

"You know I love you, John."

"And I love you too, little sister. Come on, grab a hoe, and I'll show you how to weed."

Peggy giggled as she took the hoe from John. "If we get done early, let's go find a lobster."

Chapter 3

A Ship in the Harbor

The years passed quickly as John grew in strength, stature, and maturity. After five years, John still slept in his private quarters in the Bryants' barn, but he had long been considered a member of the family. He had gained a fierce love for his new country, and the passion for independence flowed hotly in his veins as one of the faithful sons of liberty*.

"The fight has begun," announced Samuel as John, now eighteen, came in from the field in early May of 1775. Samuel had been down in Machias and John was eager for news.

"They have finally had a belly full of their oppression. Our boys have whipped them for now, but I fear this will be a long fight when the British get their feet under them."

"What happened?" asked John as Elizabeth listened in.

"Seven hundred British troops marched on Lexington two weeks ago, looking for army supplies. They found seventy-seven of our armed

---

*The name given to those willing to fight for the rights of colonies.

men in the town square. The Brits demanded they drop their weapons, but somebody fired a shot that started a firestorm. When the smoke cleared, eight of our fighters lay dead, and ten were wounded."

"I thought you said we whipped 'em?" asked John.

"We did. The Brits marched on to Concord, but by that time, every able man had been warned by some riders. Some two thousand of our boys were waiting for them. That's when the real fight started. We killed about two hundred and fifty of the red-coated scoundrels."

"They'd better not come here," said John. "We'll be ready for 'em too."

John looked around at the table. Lizzie and Peggy were listening intently. Elizabeth was standing at the stove, looking worried.

"Not so fast, John," warned Elizabeth. "If we lose, they will hunt every rebel man down like a dog. They won't care if you are adopted or just close enough to be a son to us. They will burn us out, and they won't care, not one iota, if the children are hiding in the barn. They will burn everything to the ground."

The reality of what might be coming felt thick in the air.

"That's why we have to stick together, dear," said Samuel. "If we do that, America will prevail."

"With your permission, sir, just as soon as we get the crops in, I'm heading for town to see what's brewing," announced John with determination.

"I won't stop you, John, and I won't be far behind," agreed Samuel firmly.

"Samuel . . ." said Elizabeth, her face tight with worry.

"Elizabeth, these are dangerous times that require tough men and even tougher women. The folks in town have already put up a liberty pole at the tavern."

"Oh, for heaven's sake, there ain't gonna be no stopping these chumps now," Elizabeth muttered.

"What's a liberty pole?" asked Peggy.

"It's a cut tree with the limbs removed. In Boston, they had a red Phrygian cap on the top. The cap comes from Homer's *Iliad*, a symbol of defiance and freedom."

"If they come, we'll be ready. As soon as you give me leave to go, I'm headed for town to sign up."

"Why are boys always looking for a fight?" Elizabeth said, gritting her teeth and shaking her head. "No wonder these colonists are going to war. They're all just a bunch of boys."

"Let's give it a couple days," instructed Samuel. "If you want to head for town then, you have my blessing."

♠ ♠ ♠

The night John prepared to leave, he bid everyone in the family goodbye. He settled into his bed in the barn and had just dozed off when he felt a touch on his arm.

"What is it?" John tried to clear his head, squinting to see in the darkness.

"It's me, John . . . Peggy. I'm afraid. I don't want you to go. I'm afraid you'll never come home."

"You know I have to go, sis."

"Is that all I will ever be to you, a little sister?" she choked. "When will you finally realize we are destined to be together?"

"You will always be my little sister, sweet Peg." John didn't have the heart to hurt her feelings again with talk about the more eligible Lizzie, who would be turning fifteen in two weeks.

"Besides, I don't plan on getting killed. With my father's musket, I'm an expert and have brought down many a moose and bear. My skills will play well in a fight with men just the same. It takes me a fifteen count to reload the second ball, and I've taken many moose with a second shot."

"Mother says the British soldiers will win."

In the moonlight that fell through a crack in the board, John could see a tear glistening on her cheek. "She says they are tough and seasoned, and they will overwhelm our forces."

"I respect your mother with all my heart. She is like a mother to me. But your father knows I have to go. Now hug me quickly so I can get some rest."

"I put some supper together for you in a flour sack, just in case you get hungry on your way." Peggy held it out and gave him a hug around his neck. "Don't forget me, John. I am going to marry you one day."

"Oh, you little scamp." John gave her a fist bump on the shoulder. "Now get out of here so I can get some rest."

⇞⇞⇞

Long before sunup, John started out on the seventeen-mile walk for Machias. He had his musket, a half horn of powder, and a pocket full of lead balls. He arrived in the late morning to see the liberty pole, tall and true, in front of Burnham Tavern, just as Samuel had said. Gazing up at it, knowing what it stood for, goosebumps began to crawl up his arms.

There was a group of men milling around outside the tavern as John approached. He could hear shouting, and he wormed his way through the crowd at the doorway to listen to the argument.

"Not a stick of your lumber will leave this harbor, Mister Ichabod Jones," shouted a stern man who appeared to be in his early fifties, dressed in a militia colonel's uniform. "Mark my words, sir."

"Under what authority?" asked Jones, a man around the same age.

"We have received a formal proclamation from the Provincial Congress of Massachusetts," answered the colonel.

Ichabod Jones cleared his throat, "Colonel Foster, you and your provincial congress are nothing but a bunch of outlaws. How are you or anyone else in this room going to stop me? I am going to sell my lumber to the British ship when it comes in, and none of you can do anything about it."

The crowd roared at the mention of the British ship. John guessed that Ichabod Jones must be one of the only people in the town still supporting the British. Jones continued, "The HMS Margaretta is due here any time and, mark my words, she will have her guns at the ready. If this liberty pole is still standing, her captain will be obliged to fire on the town."

The crowd was getting agitated. John recognized some of the prominent families in town and from the surrounding farms: the O'Brien brothers, known for their temper, the Libby brothers, and other heads of families like Hill, Berry, and Larrabee.

Colonel Foster responded to Jones in a stern voice, "If a warship is coming, as you say, Ichabod, we will not let the blood of our brothers shed at Lexington and Concord be forgotten. The presence of a British warship in our harbor will not dampen the spirits of Machians. We don't care if we are in desperate need of provisions. We would rather starve than trade with the British."

"You men are impossible," shouted Jones. "There are plenty of folks in this town who support the crown. Mark my words, cooler heads will prevail. Now, if you will excuse me, I have business to attend to." Jones turned and pushed a man out of his way, disappearing in a huff down the street.

Colonel Foster turned and headed into the tavern. John, guessing he was the man to speak to about enlisting in the militia, followed him inside.

Men stood and sat around the tavern, mugs of ale in their hands, discussing what had just happened outside.

"There is a warship coming . . . you know that," said a tall man with a three-cornered hat.

"Yes, we know," said Colonel Foster. "We spotted them off Foster Island two days ago looking for cannons on the wreck of the Halifax. Little do they know, we got there first and the cannons are now in our possession. I will tell you and everyone in this room, we will not be intimidated."

"Good thing we got those cannons before the British arrived," said another.

"They have the next move," said Colonel Foster. "If this warship comes in our harbor, expecting to trade with us, we will deal with it then."

"What about the families who are on hard times and need help?"

"We will appeal to the Continental Congress for help before we trade with a Tory."

Just as he said it, a man burst into the room out of breath, "There is a warship comin' in!" he shouted.

Shoe heels clamored on the wooden floor as the crowd forced their way through the doorway and men gathered in the street.

"Looks like we will have to deal with this sooner than later," said the colonel, gazing at the Margaretta entering the harbor with full sails.

"I see no carriage guns and no cannon, and let's see," said the Colonel as he focused his spy glass and counted. "Yep, sixteen; she's got sixteen swivels."

John didn't want to waste a moment. He wanted to be a part of what was going to happen.

"Excuse me, sir," he said, stepping beside the colonel. "I would like to join the militia."

"We can use all hands," Colonel Foster answered, still gazing through the glass. "I noticed you have a musket; is it yours?"

"Yes, sir, and I know how to use it."

"Well, I'm not the recruiter; you'll have to see my captain." The colonel brought the glass down off his face and handed it back to its owner. Then he turned to give John his full attention. "What's your name, boy?"

"I'm John Duling," he answered, knowing the name to be a distant form of his name from the old country. It was a little insurance, just in case the British tried to trace his residence back to the Bryant family.

"Allow me to introduce myself. I am Colonel Benjamin Foster," he said, extending his hand.

"Yes, I know, sir. Your reputation in the French and Indian War precedes you."

"We will need able men, such as yourself."

They were interrupted by Morris O'Brien, an old Irish man well known in the town, and his two sons, Jeremiah and John.

"It's all settled," said Morris O'Brien. "If they threaten us, we will have to arrest them."

"I heard that Ichabod is going to try to gather up a group of townsfolk to take another vote on whether or not the liberty pole comes down and whether he can trade for lumber," said Jeremiah.

"It's too late; the first vote stands. Besides, other than Ichabod, not a soul voted to remove the pole or trade with the British. The town will not change its mind now with a warship in its harbor," said the colonel.

"Are you going to go down and meet the captain?" asked Morris.

"No," said the colonel, keeping his attention on the now-anchored ship in the harbor as the sails were unfurled by the crew. "We will let him come ashore on his own and see what he has to say for himself."

"He'll come to the tavern," said Morris. "Let's go inside and have a smoke and an ale while we wait this out."

"Come along with us, John Duling," said Jeremiah. "I'll buy you a can."

"First, I need to officially sign up for the militia."

🡑🡑🡑

When John returned to the tavern, he found Morris O'Brien and his sons sitting near the colonel in the corner of the smoky tavern.

"From your accent, boy, it sounds like you haven't been too long separated from your homeland." Morris tossed a coin on the table as the bartender set tin cans of ale to the table. "What part of Ireland are you from?"

"Our clan is from up in Limerick," answered John.

"Aye, we are from Cork," said Morris. "Can't say as I ever meet a Duling. I had a friend who knew one, but I never caught the bloke's first name. Where are you about?"

"I have been a hand with the Bryant family for five years now. They have been awful good to me and raised me like a son." As John spoke, the thought crossed his mind that he shouldn't be so open and trusting with a group of men he'd only just met.

"If we lose this fight, do you think the British will hunt us down?"

"In order to stop us, they are going to have to kill us all," said the Colonel. "Including everyone from up and down the coast of America." He took a long puff on his pipe and added to the smoke in the room in an exhale. No one spoke as they pondered his words and lifted their tins to drink. The tavern had an eerie silence as all focused on the tensions of the British presence in the harbor.

Chapter 4

The Defiant Pup

A young British naval officer in full regalia entered the tavern.

"Which man among you is Colonel Foster?" he asked. The Colonel stood up, his silver-grey hair nearly touching the ceiling.

I am," he answered in his deep, mature voice.

"You may address me as 'Captain,' if you please," he said.

"I see by your rank that you are only a midshipman. It seems Admiral Graves has misjudged us and sent a pup to enforce his illegal decree to confiscate pickets and planks."

The room fell silent. The young captain gritted his teeth, and his face turned red.

"Midshipman or not," he retorted in a calm and strict tone. "I am Lieutenant James Moore, and captain of a British warship with forty crew and a full complement of Marines. They all answer to me. You can try to belittle me in front of your townsmen, but I am who I am. You will find out just who I am if that liberty pole is not removed by Monday morning. The Margaretta will fire a cannon volley on your tavern."

"Good luck firing a cannon when all you have are swivel guns," said Jeremiah O'Brien. The British officer was growing red with anger.

"Mark my words, good sir. My fiancée is Admiral Graves' niece, and she has quarters aboard my ship. You trifle with me, and you will have the entire British Navy down your neck. I expect to take church service tomorrow with the likes of many of you. I suggest you all pray this town comes to its senses. The sooner you fall in line and settle up business allowing Mister Jones to trade his lumber, the sooner I will be out of your hair and back on patrol in Boston Harbor. As for now . . . I bid you good day." Captain Moore tipped his hat and headed out the doorway as the tavern erupted in talk.

"I don't think he is bluffing; do you, Colonel?" asked John, the younger O'Brien brother.

"We'll see how far this goes," said the colonel.

Later that evening, John was still in the tavern with the O'Brien brothers when they were summoned by the militia. They were to meet in a barn just outside of town. And the meeting was to be secret.

"Now, gather round and shut the door," said the colonel when they had gathered. "Since Moore has threatened us, we now have cause to arrest both him and Ichabod Jones, who is still determined to trade his goods to the British. We'll do it after the church service tomorrow." He went on to explain how the men who regularly went to church should go. They were to hide their weapons and not make a scene. The colonel planned to bring the rest of the militia and surround the church. When the service ended, they would arrest Moore and Jones.

"Don't breathe a word about our plan to anyone. If they get wind of it, some of our folks will die. We need to arrest them without a shot being fired."

"Captain Moore is betting that church will calm our spirits, and the women of the town will talk sense to us," said Jeremiah O'Brien.

"What they don't know," said a young man of about seventeen years, "is that, as we speak, the women of this town are melting lead weights and pewter teapots into musket balls."

"I'll need a place to stay the night," said John.

"The O'Briens will put you up," said the colonel. "Isn't that right, Morris? You have a spot for him, don't you?"

"We'll find him a spot."

"I'll head south tonight and round up some of my men, and I'll be back before church lets out."

↟↟↟

John awoke with a startle to the sound of church bells. He had a splitting headache. The last thing he remembered was singing Irish songs with the O'Briens. His whole body shook when the visions of yesterday's plans to arrest the midshipman came to light. John struggled to his feet. Glancing around, realizing he must be in the storeroom. His first thought was of his musket.

Just then, the door burst open. "You going to sleep all day?" called out Jeremiah, with his brother John standing behind him, both with big grins.

"We wondered what happened to you," said the younger brother. "You just disappeared."

"Where's my musket?" said John.

"We have it at the house for safekeeping. Here, we brought you a Blunderbuss and a biscuit to munch on," said Jeremiah, handing him a pistol with a six-inch barrel. "Ever used one?"

"Never," replied John, taking a bite of the biscuit to calm his stomach.

"It's loaded; just pull the hammer back, and don't let anyone see it. Come on, we're gonna be late for church." John put the pistol in his deep pocket to conceal it and ran his fingers through his hair to make himself presentable.

"Are we late?" asked John. They could hear singing as they walked up the steps of the church. Peering inside at the crowd, he saw mostly men and a few women. The room was stuffy, and the pastor's black servant struggled to open the windows to let air in.

"What time is it?" asked John, whispering to Morris as they stood by the door.

"Quarter past ten," whispered Morris over the singing as they found places to sit in the back. Jeremiah marched up to the front and took a spot on a bench right behind the British captain.

The service seemed to go on for hours. Despite everyone's efforts to appear calm, there was a palpable tension in the room. Time inched along as they waited for the militia to make their move. John felt the pistol in his pocket and tried to stay alert. He watched the crowd, especially Captain Moore and Ichabod Jones.

John spotted the militia sneaking through the woods several hundred yards off, toting muskets, and he tried not to look when they began crossing the wooden bridge across the creek.

Just then, the clergy man's servant let out a yell as he spotted the militia. The congregation went into chaos as men began to leap into action.

"Dastardly!" shouted Moore, jumping up and drawing his sword. He looked toward the doorway, but men had it blocked. Jeremiah drew his pistol, and Moore turned quickly and leaped out the open window, followed by Ichabod Jones close behind.

Jeremiah looked back at the door, thinking twice about the ten-foot leap. "I'll shoot," he yelled. "Stop, or by God, I will shoot."

"You couldn't hit the broad side of a barn with that thing," yelled Moore as he ran toward the bay and his waiting skiff. Jones separated from him and headed for the woods.

"We can catch him!" yelled John making the leap as Jeremiah hit the ground beside him. The two men ran to catch Moore, but he made it to his boat and manned the oars. Jeremiah came to the edge of the beach, and John ran on his coattails, pulling the pistol out of his pocket.

"Let him have it!" shouted John.

"He's right; these little short barrels are for point blank. I doubt if I could even hit his boat." The two teens stood helplessly as they watched him get away to his ship.

"What now?" asked John, as they were joined by a crowd of others.

"We'll go after Moore in ships," said the colonel as he approached with his other men. "Prepare for a battle at first light tomorrow."

⇡⇡⇡

All day and into the evening, men kept their eyes peeled for any trace of Ichabod Jones. They worked diligently to get the ships ready to face the Margaretta by outfitting them with heavy planks, all the while wishing they had some heavy guns. It would take several days before the swivel guns from the Halifax arrived, but by that time, the Margaretta would be long gone.

As John worked and prepared for this first real taste of action, he pictured Lizzie's face as he had last seen her. At almost fifteen, she was beautiful with her long, dark hair and small, upturned nose. He knew she would only grow more beautiful. He wondered if he should have said more or made any sort of promise. While they had never talked about it, over the years it seemed apparent that everyone assumed he and Lizzie would marry someday. He no longer saw her as a sister; he had never really seen her that way. But he wished he knew where she stood.

"I will see you at dawn, then?" Colonel Foster asked Jeremiah O'Brien, who had taken the lead on the ship projects. "Do you know who will be going with you?"

"Not yet," Jeremiah replied. "There are too many volunteers to take everyone. Some men take courage out of peer pressure, and still others possess it like a true virtue. I will separate them out when they arrive. It's the young boys who will lie about their age, so desperate to be men. But they are just not yet ready for a fight such as this one."

"You'll have to set an age limit of eighteen. Otherwise, you'll end up with a bunch of children going out to face hardened British sailors. We will need every musket we can muster."

"We have a fair number of muskets," said Foster, "but it's the powder that is scarce. One of my men left behind his powder horn in Pleasant River. When his wife realized it, she travelled alone in the night twenty miles to bring it to him this morning."

"Now that's devotion—devotion to her husband and devotion to our cause for liberty," said Jeremiah. "If only we had men with that kind of heart."

"We'll find out in the morning who shows up at dawn," said Foster. "If I don't see you, good sailing and good hunting."

When John arrived at the meeting point well before daylight, men had already begun to congregate. Morris and his sons were there. As they stood in the darkness, men started pouring in like rain.

"Attention, everyone," said Jeremiah loudly as the crowd quieted. "I see some faces here that look very young. I won't take anyone under eighteen, and I won't take anyone without a musket, pitchfork, sword, or scythe. Some of us will die today. Who knows, but we could all die today. If you are still a mind to volunteer, then follow me." Jeremiah walked down the path, and John followed along with the crowd to the edge of a creek. "Wait here," said Jeremiah as he leaped the near six-foot span, landing safely and dry on the other side. "This be the contest: any a man here whose foot splashes in the creek will stay behind. Fair enough?"

"Fair enough," agreed John, making the leap to dry ground and turning to face the crowd of men, near sixty in number. One by one, they followed, and the younger boys were quickly singled out as their leaps fell short. Morris O'Brien stood at the edge, getting ready for his jump.

"Father, you are sixty and the jump is too far," said Jeremiah.

34

John O'Brien, who was still on the other side of the creek, laid a hand on his father's shoulder. "We don't want you to try. We have talked it over. You would be a distraction for our wholehearted fight. We would be more concerned for you than for our own safety." Morris O'Brien conceded. Many men stayed back, but even more made the jump.

"Catch my musket, Duling," said John O'Brien, the last man to jump, He tossed the weapon across to John's waiting hand, then made the leap to dry ground, missing the water's edge by a near inch.

"That's it, then," said Jeremiah. "You men with dry feet, get aboard; let's get 'em."

As they clambered aboard the Unity, fifty in number, a man yelled out, "Who is in command?"

"It's Jeremiah, without a doubt," yelled another.

"Hear, hear, are we all in agreement, then?" shouted John O'Brien as the crowd of men cheered their approval. "Lead us to victory."

⁂

"Looks like we are all alone in the fight."

The other ships, led by Colonel Foster, had gotten stuck in the low tide and were unable to join Jeremiah and his men.

"We're too heavy," yelled Jeremiah. "If the ship was full of cargo, we would be tossing it overboard. I would toss out the planks, but we'll need them for cover; otherwise, they will annihilate us. If there is any man here who is not prepared to die today, you may take your leave without shame. The Unity needs to shed about fifteen hundred pounds, that's about ten of you."

The men stood grim faced, glancing among the crowd to see if anyone might raise a hand. "Come on, men," pleaded Jeremiah. "Don't make me choose. We'll never catch 'em with all of us on board." Five hands went up, then two more. "Make the skiff ready; I need three more." The skiff was lowered over, and three more, making an even ten, got in the boat and began rowing for shore.

"Okay, men," shouted Jeremiah. "I know I said we might die today, but the only one who will die today is Captain Moore . . . aye!" As they rounded the point, they spotted the Margaretta well off ahead about a mile with her sails furled and masts bare. A cheer went up from the men as they looked for courage.

Chapter 5

The First Shot

We've caught her by surprise," said Jeremiah. "I don't think they expected a chase."

Fair winds and good sails gave the Unity flight, as she cut through the white caps like a knife. No one said a word as Jeremiah watched the sails to get the most out of the wind, closing half the distance in a matter of minutes.

"She's going to make a run!" They watched as the crew raised the sails on the Margaretta as the wind filled them, and they began to move out in open waters just off Round Island.

"We're closing fast," said a soldier to John. "You better keep your head down when we come alongside."

"John O'Brien is boasting he will be first to board," said another.

"Men say lots of things when they aren't under fire," said John. Jeremiah pushed their ship for maximum speed as the little boat crashed in the open sea and the spray soaked her decks. John put his coat over the flash pan on the musket to keep his powder dry. Men were wet, but their spirits could not be dampened. John watched the solemn yet determined faces of his comrades.

Coming within shouting distance of the British ship, Jeremiah let out a yell, "Strike to The Sons of Liberty!"

"That's a call for surrender," said John O'Brien.

"This is treason!" screamed Moore from the Margaretta. "Standoff, or we will let you have it."

"Fire!" shouted Jeremiah. John leveled his musket and let out a shot that preceded the other ten muskets that fired in unison, pelting the Margaretta. John quickly reloaded his rifle with powder and ball, ramming the rod down hard.

Captain Moore stuck his head above cover, shouting back, "We will thrash you like a fly . . . Fire!"

John ducked as the swivel guns from the Margaretta came with a vengeance, and the lead splattered and splintered the planking. Jeremiah said not another word but turned the bow of the Unity into the Margaretta, her nose colliding with the ship. John O'Brien made a great leap off the bow, landing on the deck of the enemy. Men behind him were ready, but the two boats separated, making it impossible to follow. Marines leveled their muskets, and four shots rang out, missing him clean as he splashed overboard. He swam back to the Unity, where the men helped him back aboard.

"Give her another run," shouted John O'Brien as he caught his breath and wiped the salt out of his eyes. As their ship came close again, a militia soldier fired his musket, hitting a marine handling a swivel gun. The other British sailors on deck took cover.

"Fire!" shouted Moore again. A swivel gun blasted from the deck of the Margaretta, and the Sons of Liberty took cover behind their make-shift bulwarks. John Dowling put his head down as the blast splintered the planks just where he crouched.

John O'Brien ran to the bow, and young John followed close behind as they all leaped aboard and began engaging the British crew hand to hand. Shots rang out, and men yelled in confusion. John leveled his musket at a Brit and pulled the trigger, belching fire and smoke out the barrel. A Brit came at him with a sword, but another militia soldier ran him through with his pitchfork. Just ahead, standing on the bridge, John spotted Captain Moore, his sword drawn in defiance. Another shot rang out, and the captain clenched his chest as he fell to the deck. British soldiers were falling left and right.

A musket blast caught the militia soldier standing next to John, and he fell stone dead at John's feet. John looked in horror at the carnage around him. For a moment, a memory flooded his mind: Lizzie sitting beside the bay on a summer's afternoon. John snapped to attention. He knew what he was fighting for. Men were grunting and shouting, scythes were slashing, pitchforks lunging and muskets belching. Men were sprawled on the decks, some in fist fights, others struggling with knives drawn, others lying dead, and the wounded groaning.

"We surrender!" shouted the British second officer from the bridge.

"Throw down your weapons!" shouted Jeremiah, and everything stopped. Jeremiah walked briskly to the bridge while others followed. Captain Moore still lay on the deck, alive, holding his chest with bloody fingers. He clenched his sword by the blade and handed the grip to Jeremiah.

"The day is yours," said Moore struggling to breathe and wincing in pain.

"We'll need to get him to a doctor, quick like," said Midshipman Stillingfleet, the second in command.

"Don't you have a surgeon on board?" asked Jeremiah.

"He's fallen ill and lays now half dead below decks."

"Take care of your wounded and sort through your dead. We own your ship," said Jeremiah. "Lower the King's colors and replace it with the stripes of the colonies."

"We only have the one that's flying on the Unity," said John O'Brien.

"Then take down that foul Union Jack."

The rebels collected the muskets and swords and forced the British to huddle in a group near the bow. The two ships took to sail and headed back for Machias.

⇞⇞⇞

All went silent, and not a word came from the crowd as the town folks waited for any sign of what was happening out on the water. The June sun beat down, and a breeze blew its breath eerily across the bay. Time appeared to stand still as the villagers continued to look on with desperation. Finally, out of nowhere, from around the far point, both ships—with sails full flapping in the wind—came back toward the harbor, and the crowd cheered.

"We are victorious!" shouted Morris O'Brien. "Look, the Margaretta is absent the King's colors."

The ships moved into the harbor and dropped anchor. The crew lowered the skiffs, and faces were sober as the wounded came ashore.

"There's my boys!" shouted Morris O'Brien. "Jeremiah and John!"

The crowd gathered around to welcome the Margaretta's boats. Colonel Foster was barking out orders for the wounded to be taken to the schoolhouse, where there were women volunteers waiting. Folks whispered while they carried the British captain down the plank, his fiancée following behind in tears.

"Congratulations, Jeremiah," said Colonel Foster with a handshake. "We captured Jones and his nephew hiding in the woods."

"We missed you in the fight," Jeremiah answered.

"My ships were aground, and they are just now afloat. How is Captain Moore?"

"He took a ball to the chest; his chances of survival are slim to none."

"How many did we lose?" asked the Colonel.

"John McNeill fell dead outright, and James Coolbroth as well," said Jeremiah.

"Are there any British prisoners? What is happening with the ship?"

"Three others were gravely wounded. John Berry took a musket ball in the mouth, and it exited behind his ear. If he survives, it will be a miracle. Isaac Taft and James Cole were hit as well, but they should recover.

"In addition to Moore hanging on by a thread, four other British sailors died. I'm sad to report that it appears a man by the name of Robert Avery, a loyal colonist from Norwich, perished in the fight. He was taken captive after the British rats confiscated his main boom and gaff. Avery was shot dead, mistaken for a Brit."

The Colonel, Jeremiah, and the wounded moved away from the crowd, who were now gathering around the soldiers, patting them on their backs and cheering their victory.

⚑ ⚑ ⚑

"John . . . JOHN!" yelled a familiar voice. John Dowling spun around to see little Peggy running through the crowd, her sister Lizzie at her heels.

"How did you get here?" asked John incredulously. The joy on Peggy's face brought so much joy to his heart.

"Father brought us," said Lizzie. "We convinced him to watch the battle from Holmes Bay."

"We watched the victory off Round Island, and then he brought us to town to join in the celebration," chortled Peggy.

"Where is he?"

"He's taking care of the boat, and he told us to come look for you!" Peggy looked away shyly. "I was, we were, nervous that you died in the fight."

"I'm not going to die in battle. I already told you that."

"Here father comes now," said Lizzie, smiling at John.

"Did you get in the fight, or did you stay onshore, son?"

"No, sir, I was in the heat of the battle. I asked them not to list me among the crew, just for our family's protection."

John, Samuel, and the girls turned to join the crowd in celebration, heading toward the tavern. Lizzie seemed more beautiful than ever to

John and he found himself awkward as they walked together. What had always been so natural, now seemed foreign. He chuckled to himself. He had just fought a battle, but he could hardly get the courage to talk to the girl he had loved almost all his life. Luckily, Peggy was there with her infectious laughter, and he made himself stay in the moment and celebrate the victory.

⚐⚐⚐

As they entered the crowd, Samuel saw a good friend, David Gardner, and rushed off to meet him. To John's surprise, Lizzie also saw someone she knew in the crowd. He watched her face light up as a young man approached.

"That's Thomas Harvey," Peggy whispered in his ear.

"Who?" ask John, recognizing him as one of the men in Colonel Foster's militia group.

"Thomas Harvey. We met him last year when we came to town to do shopping. I have a suspicion he has been exchanging letters with Lizzie."

John's eye's widened. Lizzie, his Lizzie, the one whom he had thought of just hours ago in the heat of battle, was smiling widely at the figure that walked toward them.

"I'm Thomas; you must be John." The young man, John's age, shook John's hand. He tipped his hat to the girls. "Peggy, Lizzie."

"Good to meet you. I'm afraid we are in a hurry; we must rejoin their father." John was stiff, rising up to his full height.

"Oh, nonsense. Father is talking to David Gardner and will probably chat for hours. You two go ahead; I will join you after," responded Lizzie, not taking her eyes off Thomas.

"I'm sorry, I should have told you my suspicions," said Peggy quietly, but John hardly heard her.

⚐⚐⚐

Samuel and David Gardner, the owner of the local lumber mill, were in mid-conversation when Peggy and John joined them. Gardner was shaking his head.

"War comes from the lust of the flesh and coveting your neighbor."

"Where do you stand on the revolution?" asked Samuel.

"I'm a Quaker. The Gardner family comes from a long line of Quakers. We go back to Thomas Gardner, who landed in Plymouth over a hundred and fifty years ago and settled in Nantucket. He was the first Governor of Massachusetts. I come from a long history of pacifists, and for me to jump into a war would be like spitting on the graves of my forefathers."

"My family has been fighting the Brits for generations," said John, joining the conversation. "For me to stay idle when guns are blazing would be like spitting on the whole Irish nation." David crossed his arms and made a frown.

"How about you, Samuel?" asked David. "Your family goes back hundreds of years to the court of King Henry VIII. Surely you won't fight our cousins, will you?"

"I had to do some soul searching myself just today. I am an American, David. There are plenty of settlers here in these colonies who will never fight, but as for me and my household, we will stand with the Sons of Liberty."

"And I am afraid then that you and your friends will all die trying. Revolutions never amount to a hill of beans when the government is as powerful as England." David shook his head. "I promise I will take your children to visit your grave, dear Samuel." John looked down at Peggy, noting her eyes were now distressed and full of tears.

"And they will know that I didn't die a coward," said Samuel, also noticing his daughter's angst and putting his arms around her.

"I hope you are not calling me a coward."

"It's not cowardice to live the principles of your faith. So in that, I can respect you. Stand up for what you believe and show respect for those who believe that God is creating a nation. A place where birthright doesn't matter, and any man or woman—no matter what their station in life—can become whatever God intends for them. I hear they are working on a document that will declare that all men are created equal. If they do that, it will put an end to slavery."

On this, David agreed with Samuel. They continued talking for a few minutes before Samuel turned to John. "What are your plans now that you've joined the militia and got a taste for battle?"

"I am not sure, sir. I had thought about rejoining you on the farm but . . ." He looked over Samuel's shoulder, where Lizzie and Thomas were deep in conversation. "I think it is best to stay in town, in case the British return, although I am not sure what I will do."

"Well there, you are in luck, my boy," said David, slapping him on the shoulder. "I've been looking for a strong hand to help me at the mill."

"Well, that is settled then," said Samuel. "John, we shall all miss you on the farm—I know Peggy here will, in particular—but good luck on your new life in town."

Chapter 6

The Battle to Come

In the autumn after the battle with Moore and his ship, John faced the British again in a fight for Fort Cumberland in Nova Scotia. They'd almost won back the colony of Nova Scotia, but for the HMS Vulture's arrival at the head of the Bay of Fundy with a full contingent of British Royal Marines aboard to reinforce the poorly defended outpost.

John returned home, defeated and near skin and bones after trudging a hundred and twenty-five miles back in the snow. Instead of returning to the lumber mill where he had previously been working, John spent the winter recovering at the Bryants', with Peggy nursing him back to health. It was hard to leave her warm smile and tender care in the spring to return to David Gardner's lumber mill. But, if John was being honest, being back around Lizzie, knowing her heart belonged to another, was almost more than he could bear.

"They say the British are coming full force on us this time," said David Gardner as he and John stood on the shores of Gardner Lake at David's lumber mill. "After last winter, do you think you will keep fighting?"

"I still believe in the cause, David, and most of all, I believe in General Washington." John had to admit, however, that after two fierce battles, this fight for freedom was now taking its toll.

"I still don't know why you have such a fighting spirit," said David, shaking his head.

"When I heard what they did to Colonel Jonathan Eddy's wife, arresting her after she escaped to the woods with her children and torching their home up in Hailifax . . . these villains have to be stopped. But more than all that, I believe in our townsfolk here, and our families." As he spoke, John grew passionate for the cause.

"It's time to give up this silly notion of liberty. The British will bring a thousand men this time. There will be no stopping them. They will torch this whole place to the ground, including my sawmill. And they will publicly lynch every man who survives."

"We won't let it happen, David. If they come, they will be sorry they stuck their nose in here."

"You will end up dead, just like the men who fought at Bunker Hill."

"That was a great victory for America."

"The colonists surrendered in that battle. I call that a defeat." David furrowed his brow and pursed his lips.

"We were outnumbered two to one, and we cut down a thousand Redcoats. Our boys wouldn't have quit except for they ran out of powder and musket balls."

"And we lost one of our greatest American leaders in General Joseph Warren. I don't exactly call that a victory."

"The people of Boston still say today that if they had another hill like that one, they would sell it for the exact same price."

"We'll see the price we pay when the British show up here. It's hard for me to see a young man like you go into battle. So young . . . and unmarried." David paused and looked out over the lake. "I had always thought you would have married Samuel's eldest, Lizzie." John took a deep breath to erase the hurt of hearing her name, and recalled her sweet smile.

"Me too . . . but now that damnable Thomas Harvey has her eye."

"Any luck you will live, and Harvey will die when the British show up."

"I don't wish any of us will die, least of all someone that Lizzie cares for. Yes, I do love her, but most of all, I wish her happiness. I just wish she could be happy with me."

"God be with you, my friend." David took John's hand in a firm grip. "I wish you well."

⥉⥉⥉

When John arrived in town, men were already gathering at the Burnham Tavern, kicking gravel together and talking politics, as always. He spotted Samuel.

"John," shouted Samuel as he broke away from the group and stretched out his hand, "I knew you would be here before too long. How're things on Gardner's Lake?"

"I'm trying to convince David to join us."

"That will never happen," chuckled Samuel. "C'mon, let me introduce you to Thomas Harvey, my future son-in-law."

"Good to see you again, John," said Thomas Harvey, extending his hand.

"How is our Lizzie?" asked John, trying to keep a stiff upper lip.

"We are engaged to be married next year. Samuel here will be my father soon, which means you will be like a brother to me."

"Too bad; I beat you to the role of a son about six years ago now. So, you are going to join the fight, are you?"

"Sort of got pushed into it by my fiancée," he said with a big grin. John knew that Lizzie would never marry a man who wouldn't fight when all the other young men were stepping up to the call. Even if she had to suffer the loss of a future husband, she would not marry a coward. John chuckled to himself, knowing his conversations with Lizzie had likely been the cause of Harvey's enlistment.

"That's good; we need more men like you who have something to fight for," spouted one of the men in the group.

"We all have something to fight for," said Samuel. "There really is no other choice but to give it our all."

"That's a good-looking sword you have there, John," said another man. John looked down at the saber hanging from his belt and placed his hand on it.

"It belonged to my mucker. He gave it to me just before he took his last breath at Fort Cumberland."

"I'm not an Irishman, there John. What's a 'mucker'?"

"Just a term for mate or friend . . . sorry." John's eyes welled up with the vision of his friend with a musket ball in his neck, and he shuddered at the memory. "I tell you, it will always be among my most treasured possessions, and if I should die in this battle, let it be known I want this sword buried with me. And this musket here, if I should die without any descendants, I will pass my father's musket to my little sister Peggy. She'll know how to use it."

"Hey, there's Colonel Foster now," motioned Samuel as the group turned to see him approaching, followed by another officer.

"Top of the day to you," bid the Colonel as he approached the men. "There will be no more talk of death or dying here. No one ever won a battle for dying for the cause. We will fight, but we will win, and we will live." Colonel Foster hesitated as he made a smile of recognition.

"John Dowling, as I live and breathe, you are a sight for sore eyes. I was glad to hear you survived Fort Cumberland."

"I made it back, sir," said John. "Some of our boys were not so lucky."

"I'm glad that good men such as you survived."

"What's our next move, sir?" asked John.

"We're just in a waiting game and digging in. According to intelligence, the Redcoats have already departed Halifax with four ships, and they intend to annihilate us and our supplies. When they come, we will be ready for them. All the stores have been moved to safety."

"Where are all the women and children?" asked John, looking up and down the empty street.

"The old folks, women, and the children have all been removed to a safe camp well out of town. All we have to do now is wait for the dirty rats to arrive."

⇞ ⇞ ⇞

The following Wednesday, on August 13th, British Commodore Sir George Collier arrived in the frigate HMS Rainbow with forty-four guns, followed by three other ships: the brig HMS Blonde, the frigate HMS Mermaid, and the sloop HMS Hope. Collier came with three hundred men, including marines and sailors.

When the militia lookouts saw the ships, they sent a runner to warn the fifty-five men who had enlisted and prepared for battle. They had successfully negotiated the help from the Maliseet and Passamaquoddy tribes to join them in the fight. The battle was about to begin.

"Colonel Foster, sir," said John, addressing his commander as they sat watching the river mouth. "I think you should be in command of this operation."

"A lot of our boys think the same way. But Colonel Eddy has a regular commission issued by General Washington. I'm just militia."

"I fought for him at Cumberland, and you are twice the leader."

"Well, thank you for the compliment. The militia isn't ready or able to defend this town without the regular army troops brought by Colonel Eddy. Neither of us would be able to go it alone. We are like hand and glove."

"He may be leading formally, but you are leading in spirit."

The Colonel pursed his lips, not saying a word.

"I suppose history will revere him for this victory," continued John, shaking his head.

"That's not my concern, John. My only concern is that we win today, sting 'em hard, and send them back to Halifax with their tails between their legs.

"Here they come, boys," shouted Colonel Foster as he spotted two ships rounding the point some six hundred yards downriver from town.

"They will never get through our barricade."

The men watched the British sailors attempt to cut the log boom. Foster looked on intently, holding the spyglass to his eye. Militia musket fire broke out from the shore, and the British returned it from their heavy swivel guns mounted on the rails.

"Here, John, take a look." Colonel Foster handed John the spyglass.

"I can see one of the Passamaquoddy chiefs crawling through the mud, sir."

"If it's the one I'm thinking of, he's a hell of a shot. He'll take out that British officer if the damn fool don't get down."

Just then, a single shot rang out, and the Brit ducked as the bullet missed him clean. John watched intently as the chief reloaded from the cover of the dense weeds, and again, a puff of smoke rose about the grass as the musket belched a second shot. The British officer never flinched, but then his knees buckled and he fell headfirst overboard with a splash.

"It looks like our militias just might hold 'em. Here, John, I'll take my glass now." The fire subsided as the Hope drifted away from shore to a safe distance where the muskets from the shores were ineffective. The Hope let loose cannon fire in response to losing one of its lieutenants, and the militia took cover.

"This is going to be a long day and an even longer night, gents," said Colonel Foster. "Keep watch, but I don't expect them to make an assault until daybreak tomorrow."

↟↟↟

As the early morning light began to brighten the sky, the colonists took their defensive positions. John stayed close to Colonel Foster.

"As near as I can tell, there are about two, maybe three-hundred of them ashore right now," he said to the men around him. "Did we get some more reinforcements overnight?"

"Just a handful, sir."

"They'll go the storehouse and the tide mill," said another militia soldier. "They'll torch the homes and barns and guardhouse next."

"They will continue looting and burning as they go. We won't be able to do anything about it. I want every man hunkered behind these bulwarks until the Brits make their charge."

"Are we going to let them burn the whole town before we attack?" asked John.

"We are going to wait for the fight to come to us," said Colonel Foster.

Chapter 7

The Battle

Hold your fire!" called out Colonel Foster, holding his saber high and hunkering down with the rest of his men." Let them advance on us; we will annihilate them."

John was crouched behind a barricade with Samuel to his left and Thomas behind him.

"Every man there knows this is a fight to the death, Samuel," said John.

"We have no choice, son. The British are well known for their executions for treason without a trial. They will hold us all responsible for killing Captain Moore, and the siege on Cumberland. Today we will be victorious, or we will lose everything."

Just then, John turned as he felt a man come to his side and push his shoulder against his. "David!" whispered John, trying not to make a noise in his excitement and give away their position. "Have we got an extra musket, Colonel?"

"Every weapon has a trigger man, John," said Colonel Foster. "Give him a pitchfork."

"David, what are you doing here?" John looked back quickly to watch the Redcoats advancing on their position. The Patriots all had their muskets loaded and at the ready.

"If you are going to be here, you need to be armed."

"I don't intend to fight, but I thought I could at least come and help with the wounded."

"If there is going to be any wounded here among us today, they will be wearing a red coat," said John. "But I wouldn't advise going down to help them."

"I also came to tell you that I will be praying for you, John."

"You better get back and keep your head down, and for heaven's sake, stay out of the line of fire."

David patted John on the shoulder, then paused for a minute, keeping his hand there, and John knew he was being prayed over. "Shoot straight with your father's musket."

John turned to see David run back up the hill, then turned his attention back to the British Marines. More of the enemy troops came off the barges and stepped foot on Machias soil.

"Hold your fire; they are just out of range," said Colonel Foster.

"Fix bayonets!" shouted the British officer. The men paused for a minute to work on their rifle barrels, and the officer shouted again, "Forward, march!" as a sea of red columns began to move up the hill.

"They don't know we're here, men," said Colonel Foster, getting the attention of his silent ranks. He pointed at two of his soldiers. "I need you at the ready to fire when they are at fifty yards. The rest of you, hold your fire because they will fire back when fired on. Keep your heads down and wait for my command, and when they rush us with bayonets, we will let them have it. Remember what I told you: just pick out one man, and don't shoot at the group. Aim center mass at the white 'X' across his chest like you are shooting at a target."

John reached down to make sure he could feel his sword hanging off his belt, as his hands were still trembling.

Courage is not a lack of fear, he thought. He could hear the sound of their feet stepping in unison, advancing forward ever closer as John peered through the crack between the boards. *Freedom and liberty are worth fighting for, and worth dying for.*

John wondered where his life might end up if he survived the day. He glanced down the line and saw his adopted father, Samuel Bryant, with his face pressed against the barricade, ready for the command to fire.

Oh Lord, said John silently, *You know I've never been much of a praying man. But if You are listening, be with us in these next minutes. Help us to be victorious.* John saw Lizzie's face in his mind, and his heart ached for her.

At Colonel Foster's silent command, the two designated soldiers peered over the barricade and two loud cracks rang out with bellows of smoke.

Almost in unison, the response was deafening. A full barrage of gunfire blasted the bulwarks with lead, and they ducked back to safety. The British columns continued advancing, still at a rapid pace, their bayonets glistening in the morning sunshine. "Steady, men, steady . . . hold your fire until I give the command," ordered Colonel Foster. "First line, just a few more steps . . . NOW, FIRE!"

The first line of forty men jumped to their feet, leveling out their muskets and letting the British soldiers have it. John picked a man out in front with a round face and paunch belly, and squeezed off the shot like he had a hundred times before when shooting a deer in the woods. The musket bucked when the ball cleared the barrel, and, exactly where he'd aimed, the man dropped his musket and grabbed his chest. His knees buckled, and he rolled over on the hillside. All along the British line, the Redcoats fell, too numerous to count. Thomas Harvey who stood behind John, stepped up to the front, along with the second volley of rebels. As Foster gave the command to fire, their ranks gave another deadly punch.

John's hands were trembling while he poured the black powder down the hot muzzle of his musket, making ready for a second shot. In his mind were visions of everything about his life up until this moment. He remembered his family back home in Ireland, or lack thereof. Captain Dunlang, who had brought him to America. The Bryant family, who had taken him in. Mother Elizabeth, who had treated him like a son. As he watched Thomas in front of him, he thought of Lizzie, to be married soon, if Thomas lived through the day. And, he thought of sixteen-year-old Peggy, who had always loved him. If he got injured in this battle, he knew Peggy would be there to nurse him back to health.

John put a cloth wad over the end of the barrel and placed a lead ball on top of it. He pulled the ramrod from the end of the rifle and started the ball, rammed it home tightly until it would push no more, then put the rod back in its place. The British soldiers had this down to a science with their paper loads all packaged in a pouch. He could see them tearing open the paper package with their teeth and putting a little powder in the pan, then placing the rest of the makings down the barrel and ramming it with the rod. They were so proficient, they could fire four shots a minute.

The militia, on the other hand, were farmers, merchants, and fishermen, all loading with powder from a cow's horn. Only a handful of them had bayonets on their muskets. Many had brought pitchforks from the farm for just such an occasion.

"CHARGE!" yelled Colonel Eddy from the other end of the line.

The British lines broke, and they began to run for their barges. John turned and leaped over the barricade, his left hand on the top of the planking and holding his musket in his right. His feet hit the dirt, and he stumbled to stay upright. John spotted a British soldier, just bringing his rifle up on target, crouched only thirty yards away. John could see he was looking straight down the man's barrel, and in a flash of light followed by a plume of smoke, the ball came at him. With no time to duck, but like the snap of a finger, the ball passed by his ear. At the same time, John brought his rifle to his shoulder and, with a strange calmness, steadied his gun, and pulled the trigger as the man started to turn to make his retreat. John's ball left the barrel and struck the man in the side, and he rolled over lifeless.

Patriots were charging with bayonetted muskets, retrieved from dead British soldiers. John drew his saber and went on the attack. The barges were now filling with Marines, who were quickly loading their weapons.

This is suicide, chasing soldiers with a saber and an empty musket.

John glanced back to see who might have followed him and saw that both Samuel and Thomas Harvey were at his heels.

"Are you loaded?" he shouted wildly. Just then, musket fire erupted, and a ball whizzed by John's chest, striking Thomas in the leg, Thomas dropped his musket, clutching the wound with both hands.

"Take cover behind that rock," shouted John as a British soldier came running at Thomas with a bayoneted musket. John deftly stepped between them and ran the man through with his saber. The Brit groaned and rolled over as John retrieved the bloody blade from the man's stomach. Grabbing Thomas by the shoulders, John began dragging him off the field.

"How bad are you hit, boy?" asked Samuel. Thomas took his hands off his blood-soaked trousers to reveal a tear in the front and an exit on the back. "Looks like just a flesh wound," said Samuel with relief, "a couple of shots of rum, and you will be just fine."

John could see Thomas's loaded musket laying in the grass about twenty yards away and considered leaving the safety of the rock to retrieve it. "Take a shot at the barge," urged John as Samuel leaned over the rock, aiming his musket at the retreating men. John made ready and put his barrel back in the fight, then took aim at a Redcoat. He squeezed the trigger until the flintlock came down on the flash pan, sending his speeding ball with a loud blast that went wide and missed the target.

"Damn," muttered John at the same time Samuel's rifle belched fire. He watched as the British Marine splashed over the side into the Machias River, floating face down.

"I've got to get your musket," said John knowing just how dangerous the mission was to retrieve it.

"Leave it," shouted Thomas.

"Yes, leave it," said Samuel. "The fight is over; they are pulling away."

⇡⇡⇡

John had no idea how much time had passed when the return fire finally stopped and he could take inventory of himself and his surroundings. Thomas' voice broke through his chaotic thoughts.

"We must have killed a hundred of them."

John looked back up the hillside. On the battlefield lay Redcoats strewn from one end to the other. As the barge separated from shore and made its way back to the ship, the colonists began to shout in victory.

"Are you hit, Thomas?" asked David Gardner, running up beside them.

"It's my leg, but not serious." David pulled a knife from his belt to cut the fabric away from Thomas' wound.

"Easy there, David. I don't know about you, but these are only one of two pairs of trousers I have to my name."

"We will get you a new pair, but I need to get this away from the wound and get a cotton wrap on it. You'll be just fine."

"C'mon, let's get you up the hill," said Samuel. John ran out into the field and grabbed Thomas' musket, and then the men walked up the river bank toward town. Other men were picking up British muskets and retrieving ammunition from dead British soldiers.

"We showed 'em, didn't we?" said Thomas.

"We are probably related to half of them," said Samuel flatly as he stepped over a dead Redcoat and picked up the bloodstained musket. "This one is yours, John. I saw this man fall after your shot."

"His ball went just wide. That would have been me lying there with my head blown clean off. I only need one musket. You keep it; I have my father's musket."

"I think I would fear that bayonet more than the musket ball," said David.

"I try not to think about it much," said John. "I stay focused on other things."

"Yeah . . . like the face of my fiancée, I suppose," said Thomas in a pained voice.

"That thought has been put to rest by Lizzie," said John indignantly.

"Look, John, I owe you my life now. If you are still in love with Lizzie, then I will break off my engagement, and you can have her."

"You would do that?"

"I would be dead right now if you hadn't killed the Englishman. So, the answer is yes. She is your wife, if she will have you. You know you still have feelings for her."

John was silent for a moment as he continued to help Thomas up the hill, careful that no weight was put on his bad leg.

"I can't deny it. I've had feelings for her for some time now. We grew up together, but all that is over now. Saving your life should be worth something, but not that."

After all these years, John could not believe what he had just said, what he had just given up. But he knew, and had known for some time, that Lizzie was not his. She had not chosen him. As he looked down at his companion, who had weeks if not months of healing ahead of him, John couldn't help but think of whose smiling face and red hair he would want watching over him as he recovered.

"I want her to have a happy life, and if that means her marrying you, that's what I want."

⚜ ⚜ ⚜

Men began to gather on the hill with Colonel Foster, who took an assessment of the battle.

"How many men did we lose?"

"I only know of one dead, Joshua Case. He took a ball to the head and one other wounded, sir."

"Who is our wounded?"

"Private Daniel Weatherton, sir. He took a ball in his chest."

"We have one wounded here," said Samuel, "shot in the leg."

"Is it serious?" asked the Captain.

"No, not serious," said Thomas standing with his arm around John.

"We don't count scratches on the battlefield," said Colonel Eddy, approaching. The senior officer was making the rounds, taking inventory of the lost and wounded. "Looks like we killed near forty or maybe fifty men outright and wounded maybe fifty more. But if I know Collier, he will discount his losses and under-report it. He won't count any of his foreign fighters, only British citizens. He won't count any of the Nova Scotians, Germans, or any of the pressed men he forced to fight with them. He doesn't like losing, and he will turn this defeat today into a British victory."

"Any of his wounded who die tomorrow or next week, he will only count as wounded. But we will know how many are dead here in this field because we have to bury them, and none of us will ever forget. But mark my words men, he will count today as a victory, just as sure as hell."

Chapter 8

The Wedding

The following year, Thomas Harvey married Lizzie Bryant. It was a warm afternoon and the family had planned a grand affair. The field was covered with white flowers and Lizzie looked like a fairy with sprigs of Queen Anne's lace in her dark hair.

John spotted David Gardner in the crowd, and he made his way to the empty seat next to him on a wooden bench. Now eighteen, Lizzie appeared more beautiful than ever. As she walked down the aisle of the small church, John's heart ached, filled with regret that he had not taken Thomas up on his offer that day on the battlefield.

"Look," whispered John to David Gardner. "Harvey is still walking with a limp, trying to show off his war wound." *I suppose he'll receive a hundred acres for it too,* thought John.

"Are you staying for the picnic?" whispered David.

"Aren't you?" said John.

"I'm expecting those logs to arrive today from the upper lake."

John, who had come to the wedding with David, tried to decide if he should stay and celebrate or leave with his friend. While he considered the Bryants his family, this event was the first time he'd ever felt awkward around them. For so long, everyone had assumed it would be him standing at the altar. Instead, he was sitting in the back with the guests.

John glanced at Mother Elizabeth, who had a perpetual smile on her face. He was glad she was happy for her daughter, and he knew Lizzie enough to know her smile was genuine. Who was he to be bitter when there was so much love to celebrate? But still, he could not help wishing it were he who would be becoming a more permanent member of this family that meant everything to him.

He spotted Peggy, standing beside her sister. She was taller now and her hair shone like fire in the sunlight. He tried to catch her eye, but she never once looked in his direction. She had finally grown into her ears and he found himself thinking, to his surprise, how beautiful she was. Her birthday would be next month and she would be seventeen.

"How are you, good sister?" asked John as he approached Peggy at the picnic. Peggy pursed her lips and turned aside.

"Have I done something?" he asked as she walked away.

"I'm leaving now," said David, coming up behind him, observing the exchange. "Maybe you better come back early with me. There's obviously nothing here for you."

By the following spring, John had slipped into boredom. He was working for David at the sawmill and was still an active soldier in the militia. While John worked hard, David knew the younger man wasn't meant to work at the mill forever.

"Why don't you go back to farming, John?"

"I have a job; I'm defending this town."

"The fight is long gone from here. They've moved on far south to Savannah. Besides, they got their hind ends kicked last time, and they won't return for another one like that."

"Don't be so sure. They can come back here at any time, and we have to be ready."

But John followed the news and was pretty sure the Redcoats would not be returning. Without the constant threat of the British, who were now focusing all their attention on the fight with General Washington, he felt empty living in town. He longed to go back to the Byrants' and work with Samuel on the farm, but he felt that everything had changed since Lizzie's wedding. He was happy for Lizzie and knew that yes, he would miss her at the farm. But what he really could not get out of his heart was Peggy's animosity toward him. Was she angry? He could not bring himself to visit or even write for fear he had lost his best friend. And, for the life of him, he could not stop picturing her at the wedding, sunlight in her red hair.

⚑⚑⚑

One cloudy spring afternoon as John was delivering lumber to the town, he spotted Samuel Bryant accompanied by little John and Peggy.

"Samuel!" shouted John, running toward him to give him a bear hug. "What brings you to town?"

Peggy stood back, not wanting to make eye contact, and little John beamed with excitement, in awe being in the presence of a revolutionary soldier. "How is our married couple?"

"They are doing just fine."

"Any children yet?" asked John.

"Not as of yet. Have you heard any news?"

"I received word that plans are brewing in Canada and the British are planning to bring tribesmen against us. Colonel Foster is calling for recruits to brace for the fight and meet them before they arrive. But I don't think the Indians will attack; they are friends of the French," said John.

"Who knows what lies they tell them. The Brits are desperate, and they will stoop to anything, including lies to our allies."

"It's a shame we have to fight 'em. If we could only talk, I know they would come over to us," said John. "If there was a fight, I have a few native friends. I don't have the stomach for that kind of fight."

"Pa said you were a grand fighter on the battlefield, John," said Little John, with stars in his eyes.

"You will be a soldier before you know it, boy."

"Pa said I'm more ready than any boy my age," he beamed with a grin. John was passing conversation; the one he really wanted to see was Peggy.

"And what have you been up to, my dear sister?" asked John, looking into Peggy's eyes, trying to read her mood. "The young men must be trying to break down your door," he laughed, secretly hoping she didn't have a suitor calling.

"That's the Colonel there," said Samuel, "I am going to see what news he has, excuse me." He turned down the street with little John at his heels.

"Are you still angry with me?" asked John remembering back to her sister's wedding.

"Angry?" Peggy looked uncertain for a moment, clearly unsure if she should be honest with him or not. "Oh, John, I was never angry with you. I know you will always have feelings for Lizzie and that you wanted to marry her and . . . I just didn't want to get hurt again. And then you left without even saying goodbye—why?"

"I couldn't take you being angry with me."

"But you never wrote. Have you forgotten about me?"

"Forgotten?" John almost laughed. "Peggy, I could never. When I saw you at the wedding, I thought maybe . . ."

"Maybe what, John?"

"Maybe you and me," he said with a lump in his throat, struck by the beautiful woman she had become.

"I refuse to play second fiddle to anyone. Are you still in love with my sister?

"You know what happened between me and Thomas the day I saved his life?"

"No," she answered, looking him square in the eye. John hesitated, knowing if she didn't know, then her sister didn't know either. *Words between men on a battlefield are better off staying on the battlefield.*

"I can tell you that, truly, I do not love your sister anymore. How about I prove it to you? How about I come to call on you?" She turned beet red, trying to hold back a smile.

"You know I always knew we would marry, John," she said slyly. "I need to catch up with Papa. You want to marry me . . . you better ask him," she said, turning to run down the road.

"Hey!" he said, giving her pause. "You use to give me a hug when you were little."

"That was then, and this is now," she said, putting her hands on her hips. "There are plenty of women around these parts who would stand in line to hug you. If you want to come calling on me, you gotta ask Papa his permission first!" With that, she turned and marched down the street toward her father. John followed her from a safe distance, spotting Samuel talking with the Colonel. The two men shook hands, and Samuel turned and walked toward John standing in the street.

"I'm going to be a soldier," said Little John as John approached.

"John, are you here to reenlist?" asked the Colonel.

"No, sir, I've done my time. You'll find me at Gardner's mill if you need me." Turning to Samuel, John asked, "Can I speak to you before you leave town?"

"What is it?" said Samuel with a wrinkled brow. Standing near enough to hear, Peggy turned away, trying to seem uninterested.

"I'd like to come calling, if I have your consent." Samuel smiled.

"You're welcome to come home any time, son."

The following week, John set out overland to visit Peggy. He carried his musket on the twelve-mile walk, which took a piece of his day. A crow could fly it straight, but a man walking had to follow a winding trail through the woods.

When he arrived at the Bryant property overlooking Little Machias Bay, Mother Elizabeth, now fifty years old, saw him coming and ran to greet him. "Oh, John, did you come to call on Peggy?"

"I did, dear Momma. You are lookin' might healthy; you must be eatin' awful good."

"Oh John, I'm with child. I'm not getting fat just on my own," she laughed, but then turned serious. "I know you've heard Lizzie is still without a child. It's been hard for her, this," she put a hand on her belly. "But, enough of that; I know Peggy has been so looking forward to you coming."

Just then, Samuel appeared in the doorway behind her.

"Look what the cat drug in!" he called out merrily, standing on the porch with a big grin across his suntanned face.

"So good to see you, sir." John tried to hide the waver in his voice and his shaking knees. He stood frozen in the moment, not knowing what to say next. Mother Elizabeth leaned forward and whispered under her breath in John's ear. "Ask him to take a walk with you."

"Would you take a walk with me, sir?" Samuel stepped off the porch as the two men headed off toward the waterfront. "What's on your mind, son. I suppose this would have something to do with coming home."

"Ah . . . not exactly, sir." John took a deep breath and a gulp mustering his words. "It's no secret that I have had my eye on your daughter."

"Yes . . . yes, Harvey told me the whole thing. But all that is behind us now since Lizzie married . . . isn't it?"

"Well, yes . . . I mean, no." John fumbled to find the words to explain his way out of this one.

"Just what in the hell are you trying to tell me, son?" Samuel stopped in his tracks and put his hand to his chin.

"It's Peggy, sir."

"It's what about Peggy?" he demanded.

"She has caught my eye."

"You do have a thing when it comes to my girls, don't you, John?"

"I've been working hard in the woods, saving up. The government granted me a hundred acres on Gardner Lake. I think it is time to look for a wife." John held his breath while the two men continued strolling along the waterfront.

"Do you have a house? She won't marry a man without a place to live."

John nodded eagerly in the affirmative.

"But what of the cause; we are still in the middle of a revolution?"

"It appears things have calmed down for us along our coast for now, but should the scoundrels return, I'll stand with the regulars. I'd love to fight 'em again, heck, we'd all cheer if their ships came back. But to my heavy heart, all we can do here is to stand tall in case they do and pray for our boys who are in the fight along with General Washington."

"And that, my boy, is the kind of man I am looking forward to having for a son-in-law."

Samuel grinned and took John's hand in a firm grip. "I was hoping you would say, yes, Papa."

"Peggy is yours if she has a mind for it."

"She'll have me; she's been pestering me since she was a kid." John looked back toward the house, perched on the hill. Both Mother Elizabeth and Peggy were in the yard hanging laundry on the line. Peggy appeared to be busy, but John knew she had more interest in what she could see across the glade.

"Shall we break the news, John?"

"It's that or go fishing," John laughed.

"I'd rather go fishing, but I suppose we would both be hung out to dry."

As the men approached the house, all the memories of little Margaret came flooding in like a swift high tide. John remembered the little girl who came running down to meet him in the rowboat. He remembered all the times they swam in the bay, when she threw mud on him out on the flats, walking at low tide and picking up lobster for dinner.

The two women stopped their chores and watched as the men approached. Peggy tried to read John's face for a clue; as they came near, she wrinkled her turned-up nose.

"What have you two been discussing so seriously?" asked Mother Elizabeth, as if she didn't know.

"Just talkin' about fishin'," said Samuel. "You better ask my daughter first before we go any further," he whispered. John glanced back at him, and Samuel gave him a gentle nudge.

"Peggy." John paused as if the weight of the world was on his shoulders. "I came all this way to ask your father . . . I mean, I wanted to ask you . . . to find out if you'd want to spend your life with mine."

"Yes, John, yes!" exclaimed Peggy, eyes shining.

John caught her up and swung her around, and she kissed him hard on the lips. "John, I always knew this day would come. I loved you the first time we met. I always worried you would marry somebody else. Today you made my dreams come to life."

John set her feet back on the ground and brushed her hair out of her face.

"It is funny, but I always knew it too."

Epilogue—John and Peggy Dowling

John Dowling and Margaret (Peggy) Bryant were married in Machias by Stephen Jones, Esquire, on the 8th of June, 1780. They raised their family of six children on the hundred acres on Gardner Lake that John received from the government for serving in the Revolution. Their six children were named John, James, Daniel, Anna, Sarah ("Sally"), and Silas Turner.

John Dowling II married Deborah Libby and lived to be sixty-two. Apparently John Dowling II and Deborah were more than friends for many years, but according to records did not marry until the day their first son, John III, was born. He lived only thirteen days, and so their first living son became Warren Loring Dowling.

Silas Turner Dowling married Deborah's sister, Olive. The Libby sisters were descended from the Libby and the Larrabee families, who were among the original settlers in Machias. Their Uncle Josiah said he fired the first shot in the battle for the Margaretta, and some say he is the one who killed Captain Moore.

Together John and Peggy had thirty-five grandchildren. There is no official record of the death or grave marker for John Dowling the immigrant and revolutionary. According to the records, Peggy married Moses Wheaton and moved to Plantation No. 12 in Washington County, Maine on August 13, 1816. Therefore, John Dowling apparently died sometime before that, around the age of sixty.

Gardner Lake is named after David Gardner, who owned a mill with Ichabod Jones, the British sympathizer and villain of the Revolution story in Machias. David Gardner lived to be ninety-nine years old and was elected representative for the town of Machias at the first session of the General Court in the Commonwealth of Massachusetts in 1787. It is said that the people of Machias were indebted to John Dowling for his service in the fight for freedom, and named a point on Gardner Lake in his honor.

Part II—Warren and Louisa Dowling

Significant Names and Dates

John Dowling II
Born: March 11, 1785, Whiting, Washington County, Maine
Died: November 5, 1847 (age 62)

Deborah Libby Dowling
Born: c.1793, Machiasport, Washington County, Maine
Died: June 1852 (age 59)

Warren Loring Dowling
Born: May 20, 1827, Whiting, Washington County, Maine
Died: May 11, 1891 (age 64), Whiting,
Washington County, Maine

Louisa Keyes Crosby Dowling
Born: March 10, 1834, Whiting, Washington County, Maine
Died: September 25, 1884 (age 50), Whiting, Washington
County, Maine

Part II

WARREN LORING DOWLING
1827–1891

LOUISA KEYES CROSBY DOWLING
1834–1884

Chapter 1

The Visit

I'm so glad you came to visit, Warren," said Peggy. "I can't tell you what it means to see my grandson in my old age." Peggy, who had recently turned ninety-three, was sitting on her rocking chair by the fire, a quilt spread over her legs. She wore her long, white hair pulled back in a bun, keeping it out of her wrinkled face.

Warren had spent the morning listening to his Grandma Peggy tell stories about Grandpa John in the war. As she talked, he stared at the musket hanging over the mantel, the same one John Dowling had brought from Ireland and used against the British all those years ago. His favorite stories were about his mother's uncle, Josiah, who'd fought with Grandpa John for the Margaretta. According to history, Josiah had fired the first shot against the British. Warren loved being a part of a legacy that had helped form this country.

"There is the musket!" Warren got out of his chair and stepped up to the rock fireplace where the long, wooden Brown Bess hung over the mantel. He thought of all the stories it could tell. The wood had chips in the stock, and the barrel had small signs of rust from the years hanging unattended. Warren thought about how, one day, he would love to get it back into working condition. The reality of it still being in his grandmother's possession seemed a surprise.

"You know," mused Peggy, "after all those years, I think the British finally did kill your grandfather."

Warren cocked his head toward his grandmother at the comment. "What do you mean?"

"The old man got so wrapped up with the war after 1812, and the fight with that Shawnee Chief Tecumseh. John threatened many times to take his musket off the wall and join them, but he wasn't in no shape, and he knew it. I told him if he didn't stop fretting about it, he was going to send himself to the grave. He always had a bad heart. But, men . . . who can stop 'em?" Peggy tightened her lip and shook her head. "Then, one morning after ranting the night before about the British burning the capitol, and the president's mansion, he just never woke up."

She shook her head and pulled the quilt further up her lap. "I've outlived two husbands, and that musket has hung there on the mantel through it all."

Warren sat back down next to his grandmother, reaching out to take her old hands in his. They sat in silence for a few moments, watching the fire. In the years since his parents had died, Warren had grown closer to his grandmother and treasured these times he could sit and hear about his family.

"You are very special to me, Warren," said Peggy, interrupting his thoughts. "Your mother, Deborah, was quite the woman. She was like a daughter to me, being married to my oldest son. I do miss her so . . . I miss them both." Warren shifted uncomfortably in his chair, not wanting to bring up his loss or think about going back to his empty farm in a few hours.

Reading his thoughts, she squeezed his hands. "You know what time it is, Warren? It's time you found a woman," she said slyly. Her old age did not take away any of the glints from her eyes. "How come you haven't married?"

"Grandma," Warren grinned. He had known this topic was going to come up sooner or later. "I've been so busy working the ground father left me, I just haven't had the time, I guess."

"There's a girl up in Lubec. She was married to Daniel Crosby. You remember when Daniel died in that logging accident up in Marion?" Warren nodded his head, recalling the incident when he was just a boy. "What's her name, now," she mused, putting her wrinkled finger to her lip. "Hannah, that's it. She's married to a fisherman. Let's see, I think it's Ramsdell. Anyway, she has a daughter. I remember her well— Louisa, if I'm not mistaken. If she is not married, you should go pay her a visit."

Warren knew Louisa well; they had grown up near each other before her father died, and she moved to Lubec. But he hadn't seen her since she was ten years old. He smiled, thinking it strange that he had often thought about the same girl and wondered if his grandma just might be right. She usually was.

"I'm getting tired now, so I think it's time for me to have a nap," yawned Peggy. Warren stood and tended the fire. He had meant to ask Grandma Peggy about the musket. Surely the old war implement would go to one of the other men of the family, but, ever since boyhood, Warren had sat at his grandmother's feet and dreamed of someday hanging Grandpa John's musket over his own fireplace. He used to romance the idea of fighting with it in another noble battle for the country he loved. He straightened up from the fireplace, rising face to face with the musket, but when he turned around, Peggy was already dozing in her chair.

He piled some more wood beside the fireplace and put on his oversized coat. While he was lacing up his boots, Peggy stirred.

"Warren, go visit, Louisa. Don't waste a minute of your life. It goes by too quick. In this life, you will have trouble, heartache, and trials. Just remember this. If you stand on your faith in God, you will never be shaken."

Warren leaned over and gave her a hug and headed for the door, looking back to see her face and wondering if it would be the last time he would lay eyes on her. She caught his gaze and smiled back. He gave the musket one more look, wondering if someday it might be his, then walked out the door.

The following week, Warren could not get Louisa out of his mind. He loved working his farm, and, most days, the company of the open sky and birds overhead was all he needed. Every once in a while, he took a trip to visit family or sit with Grandma Peggy, but he always returned to the land, eager to get back to work and feel the breeze against his skin. But this time was different. Grandma Peggy had planted a seed, and his every thought seemed to water it.

At the end of the week, there was nothing for it but to send a letter. What to say to a girl he hadn't seen in almost ten years? He remembered the last time he saw her, sitting in the back of the wagon as her family drove away from Gardner Lake for the last time. She was ten years old, suntanned and tenacious. Her legs dangled over the wagon as she shouted, "Don't forget your promise to me, Warren Dowling. Don't forget me." He hadn't forgotten.

He remembered how, when she received the news of her father's passing and her family's imminent move away from Gardner Lake to the town of Lubec, Louisa had been distraught. She ran down to the lake and wasn't seen for hours. Warren found her, at sunset, sitting on a log overlooking the water, tears streaming down her face.

"I don't want to leave the lake, Warren," she had said, seeming far older than ten. She loved that land more than any of them. She spent every spare moment outside, often joining Warren in his chores or adventures around the lake. Looking up into his eyes, she asked him to make a promise.

"Promise me, Warren. Promise me that when we are older, you will come find me and bring me back here as your wife."

Warren had laughed at the thought but made the promise. She was grieving, leaving the place she had grown up, leaving her friends. And he could never refuse her sweet face, even at ten. He had promised her.

But now, as he sat on the same log, he worried. Would she even remember him? Remember the promise? Remember their days of youthful laughing around the lake? He rewrote the letter repeatedly and finally settled on simply asking her if he could come to visit. He hoped her response would give him an indication of how she felt.

After posting the letter, he buried himself in his work. He tried not to hope and watch for the postman. But now, he had more to think about than just his fields. What if she wanted him to visit? What if she remembered her childhood promise? What if she didn't? What if she was already taken? What if, what if . . . she wanted to be his wife?

One week went by. Then two. Warren couldn't take it anymore. If she could not even be bothered to respond to his letter, he would go up to Lubec and find out why.

When Warren reached the road to Lubec, he could hear the sound of horse hooves pounding in the distance, heralding the impending arrival of a speeding carriage. Then he spotted the morning stage come rumbling around the corner, leaving a cloud of dust behind it. As it approached, Warren greeted the driver of the bright red coach, tipping his hat as he heaved back on the reigns, bringing the horses to an abrupt halt. The two chestnut horses were young and strong, and they panted to catch their breath. A few heads in the back of the carriage poked out to see why they had stopped. A male passenger with spectacles and a brown derby made a frown, showing his distaste for the delay.

"That'll be two bits," said the driver, his wide-brimmed hat pulled down hard on his head to keep it from blowing off. Warren could only get a glimpse of greying whiskers and a red face.

"Oh, no, sir, I am planning to walk."

"Then why in the hell did you hail me? I've got a schedule to keep."

"I was just being neighborly."

The driver huffed. Warren marveled. Every time he left his small community at Gardner Lake, where he had lived and worked the land his whole life, he was astonished at how rude and fast-paced life was becoming elsewhere.

"Suit yourself; you have a long walk ahead of you." The driver slapped the horses with the reigns. Then, like a shot fired from a musket, the stage went rumbling out of sight in a cloud of dust. Warren thought, *Maybe someday I'll have money enough extra to hitch a ride like that.* But if he was going to have a wife, he would have to save every penny.

About an hour had passed when the sound of another wagon heading in his direction echoed in the trees. Warren recognized the driver as his father's little brother, Uncle Silas Turner Dowling. Silas had a round face and a wide handlebar mustache, and he wore a felt-brimmed hat one size too small that sat on his head like a little mushroom on a big stump.

"Warren! Where are you going, lad?"

"I'm heading up to Lubec."

"What's in Lubec?"

"Going to call on a girl." Warren smiled with a sheepish grin.

"It's about time you found a wife. Climb aboard, son." Warren tossed his sack on the wagon and jumped up next to his uncle, who slapped the horse with reigns. "You are going on twenty-seven now, aren't you?"

"That's pretty good, Uncle; how did you 'member that?"

"Because you are the same age I was when you were born. It seems like yesterday. In fact, isn't your birthday coming up?"

Warren had been so obsessed about this letter to Louisa, he had forgotten his upcoming birthday.

"Oh, you're right, Uncle. What is the date today, anyways?"

"Today is the nineteenth of May."

"Then, I guess tomorrow is my twenty-seventh birthday; I didn't even think of it. So busy with planting and all."

"Well, happy birthday, son. If your parents were alive today, they would be proud of how you are managing the farm. My brother was always mighty proud of you."

Warren was touched by his uncle's kind words. "Where are you taking this load of hay?"

"There's a fisherman up there in Lubec that will trade a load of hay for smoked herring. Those would be a pretty good treat. How come you didn't ride the stage, boy?"

"I don't have that kind of money to waste when I have two perfectly good legs."

"Who are you calling on?"

"A girl by the name of Louisa Crosby. Your momma insisted I go find her."

"Crosby? That's Hannah's girl . . . yeah, Hannah married some fella up in Lubec after Daniel passed. Everybody figured you would marry one of those Gardner girls."

"I don't know if I will marry a Crosby. I haven't seen Louisa since she was ten."

"I'll bet she has fond memories of growing up on Gardner Lake. I remember all you children spending summers down by the lake. And I'm sure my dad's hundred acres on the shore will be a good draw for some pretty lady. You're lucky you got that ground; you better hang on to it. The shores of Gardener Lake are a grand prize."

Warren was silent. When his father died, the land had been passed on to him, with none going to his uncles. That was the way things worked, but Warren always felt guilty. The familiar feeling of not living up to the family name weighed upon his shoulders, and he felt small sitting next to his uncle.

They rode in silence for a while, watching the fields sway in the breeze as they passed. Uncle Silas broke the silence.

"What I remember about Hannah is what a nice person she is. I always thought that she would be in heaven thirty minutes before the devil even knew she was dead." Warren laughed along to humor his uncle. "Why, she could charm the shine off a new penny and wear it on her face, and if looks could kill . . . you'd be dead from just a glance."

"That's encouraging. Maybe some of that rubbed off on her daughter."

"Always does, son . . . yep, always does. They say the apple don't fall too far from the tree."

They would soon arrive in Lubec, and Warren would find out for himself.

Chapter 2

The Princess

Lubec was a bustling place. The town was known for its herring, caught in the ocean and smoked in over fifty smokehouses. Up until about fifteen years earlier, men were still fishing at night with lanterns and dip nets. But now, fishing weirs—layers of small dams that trapped the fish—lined the bay. The herring industry in Lubec had doubled since switching to weirs. Folks said there was no way to overfish them, but Warren didn't think that could be true. Just like the timber and the moose, someday the herring and sardines would dwindle away too.

As they pulled into the town, Warren looked off to the right and saw the bay glistening in the hot sun that shone out of the blue sky. In front of him stretched the village with its church, schoolhouse, many saloons, post office, shipyard, and what seemed like hundreds of fishing boats. At the sight of it all, Warren's heart began to race. People were on the streets, walking hither and thither. Women were dressed up all fine with dresses and bonnets. Men's attire varied: some were in finery and others in working clothes. Everyone seemed to be in a hurry. The streets were dirt, and the sidewalks were wood. The shops, all with false fronts to make them look larger than they were, seemed to stretch down several blocks as far as the eye could see. Saddled horses tied to hitching posts and teams harnessed to wagons were parked along the road. Some men were loading goods, while others were offloading, making deliveries.

"How many folks live in this place, Uncle? I ain't hardly never seen so many people in my whole life."

"You need to get out more, boy. You've been in the woods too long."

Warren took a gulp. "How will I ever find Louisa Crosby? What's the name of the man who married her mother?" Warren sat frozen on the seat, knowing he had to get off the wagon with his satchel.

"Ramsdell . . . Ichabod Ramsdell."

Silas pulled to a stop to let Warren climb off the wagon. He had errands to run and wanted to make it home before the sun set. Warren stepped on the sidewalk and tipped his hat in, offering thanks to his uncle.

"Good luck and happy birthday, son. I am glad I ran into you on the road. Maybe you'll have a pretty lady on your arm next time I see you."

"We'll see, won't we?" Warren winked. Silas slapped the horse with the reins, and the wagon went on down the street.

With a deep breath, Warren decided the post office was a good a place to start as any. At least he could find out if his letter had been delivered. If Louisa herself had picked it up, at least he would know she had received it. He would also know for sure that she had chosen not to respond. He couldn't bear to think about that.

Walking on the boardwalk, Warren kept his eye out for the post office. He passed several people, but he couldn't ask, afraid of looking stupid. Walking past a saloon, he paused for a second to look in and saw some rough-looking men talking loudly and laughing. He passed a drug store, a tack supply, and the general store. Everyone seemed to be in a hustle, and no one made eye contact. Warren thought about home, Gardner Lake, and how people there would come out of their house to see who was coming up the road. He spotted the post office and hoped he would be able to get some more information.

Just as he was about to grab the door handle, the door flew open, and a man stood in the doorway, shouting, "The damn government can't even deliver a letter!" The white-bearded man with eyeglasses marched through in a huff with a scowl on his face. Warren watched him go and then stepped into the darkness of the post office. The man behind the cage seemed shaken as Warren stepped inside, and the door shut behind him. Small boxes behind the cage lined the walls, some with envelopes poking out, but most of them empty.

"Another satisfied customer, aye?" commented Warren wryly.

"He's been waiting for something in the mail, and he wants to blame the postal department for his troubles. How am I supposed to know what happened to his letter?" The man was middle-aged, with wide lips and bowl-cut hair and mustache. "How can I help you today, lad? You can't be here looking for mail because you ain't from around here . . . are you?"

"No, I'm not from around here. I'm looking for someone, a girl."

"Sorry, but we don't deliver those." The postman roared at his humor, and Warren tried to humor him with a chuckle that quickly turned into an awkward silence.

"You got a name for her, son, or do you want me to read your mind?"

"Ah, yeah." Warren's mind went blank. The man behind the counter tapped his fingers on the wooden surface. "Maybe you could describe her to me."

"I can't describe her because I ain't seen her in ten years. She is probably all grown up now." Just then, a young man some years younger came from the back with a handful of letters and began stuffing the boxes on the wall.

"If you know her, you must know her name. Come on, spit it out."

"Not sure if she goes by Louisa Crosby or Ramsdell."

The boy stuffing boxes stopped and turned, giving the older man a knowing look. The man cleared his throat, then paused, looking at the boy. "Sorry, none of that rings a bell. Nobody in these parts with that name."

The boy, whom Warren guessed was a few years younger than himself, crossed his arms and said roughly, "Guess you are out of luck. You should head back where you came from."

Warren was taken aback by his rudeness.

"Look, I don't mind it if you don't know someone I'm looking for, but you don't need to go and be rude."

"Well, there isn't anyone around here by that name that I can recall. I just hate to see you waste your time, that's all."

Warren wrinkled his brow at the comment, knowing full well the Ramsdells had to have been living in this town for many years. He tipped his hat and made his way out the front doorway and into the street bustling with activity. People were coming and going, and Warren felt dizzy just watching them. Looking up the road, he spotted an old man sitting on a bench outside a shop and made his way to sit down next to him.

"Top of the day to you, sir. Is this spot open?"

"Ain't nobody in it. Must be yours," said the skinny man with a wrinkled face and scruffy beard. "You from around these parts?"

"Naw, I'm from Gardner Lake, near Whiting. Born and raised."

"What brings you to Lubec?"

"I'm looking for a girl."

"Every boy your age is looking for a girl if they don't have one. There are plenty of those around here, from what I can see. Probably a good place to start would be the saloon."

"No, not that kind of girl. I'm looking for a girl named Louisa Crosby."

"Nope, can't say I ever heard of her."

"Her stepfather is Ichabod Ramsdell."

"Oh sure, ol' Ike . . . he's a fisherman down on the wharf. Don't know as he's got kids or not. Met him a couple times. Kind of a quiet bloke . . . keeps to himself."

"How can I find this Ike fella?"

"You just have to go down to the wharf and ask around."

Warren was glad for the kindness and information. He stood up and thanked the old man, looking around for the direction of the wharf. He spotted a young woman walking in the opposite direction on the other side of the street. Something about her looked familiar, so he turned and headed in her direction.

She had long dark curls flowing out from under a white bonnet with a red ribbon. She wore a white, frilly, long-sleeved blouse and a red jacket cut at the waist, and a scarlet plaid skirt. Her delicate fair skin and big dark eyes gave him goosebumps. He couldn't remember ever having seen a more striking young woman. Warren slowed down as she crossed the street in front of him, stepping onto the boardwalk. She turned and gave him a glance as she headed in the post office.

Warren didn't dare go in but tried to watch nonchalantly through the window. The young woman began talking to the boy who was still stuffing boxes with letters. The conversation seemed to be heated, and the boy came around the counter and grabbed her arm. Warren could feel his blood boil, and without thinking, he jerked open the door and burst in.

"Let go of her!" Warren gritted his teeth and furrowed his brow as he stood in the doorway. "Somebody needs to teach you some manners there, boy." Warren stepped toward the girl he was sure now was Louisa. "Are you okay, Princess?"

The young lady's eyes brightened, and she turned to look at Warren. The boy let go of her arm and took a step back.

"Nobody has called me that since my daddy died nine years ago." She smiled and took a moment to take him in. "Warren, you haven't changed a bit since you were eighteen."

"I can't say the same for you." Warren gulped, and his throat felt dry.

Louisa turned to the ruddy boy with curly hair. "This conversation is over," she said sternly, "and if you ever lay a hand on me again, you will have Warren Dowling to contend with."

"So, you never heard of Louisa Crosby before, is that right?" asked Warren as Louisa put her hands on her hips, giving the boy a prolonged glare. Turning to Louisa, Warren added, "I suppose you never got my letter, did you?"

"But Louisa, you're my girl," said the boy in an indignant tone.

"No, I'm not. I've told you that a thousand times. I will never marry you, Chester, and that is final."

Chester's cheeks turned red. Like a puppy with its tail between its legs, he walked back behind the cage.

"Do you want your mail?" he asked, picking two pieces off the counter. Louisa snatched it out of his hand and turned toward Warren.

"Come on, let's get out of here; Momma is going to be surprised to see you."

"You didn't get the letter I sent, did you?"

"No . . . no letter."

"I suppose he tossed it in the trash." Chester shuffled some letters on the counter, not looking up. They left him standing alone as the door slammed shut behind them.

"That's tampering with the U.S. mail! We could have him arrested," said Louisa, gritting her teeth.

"You could never prove it," said Warren.

Louisa turned down the street, and Warren followed her, suddenly feeling awkward. "You caught me without flowers. I intended to get some and hand them to you at your door . . . If I could find your house."

"Sounds like I have ruined everything." Louisa looked up at Warren with a sweet smile that made his knees go weak.

"Oh, heavens, no. You have made my day." Warren did not even see the town; all he could see was Louisa beside him.

"I'll take you to see Momma. She's gonna be excited you came to Lubec." Louisa took his arm and pulled him down the boardwalk. They walked past a smoke house, and Warren could smell fish in the air.

"Do you like living in this place?"

"It's just a fishing town," Louisa shrugged. "You know what I miss?"

Warren waited for her answer.

"I miss Gardner Lake. I have such fond memories of that place from when I was a child. I always used to walk to your house and your parents . . . oh I'm sorry, I heard they passed on."

"Yes, father died seven years ago, in forty-seven, and mother died just three years ago. Life is strange, isn't it? One minute you are sharing meals together, and the next day they are gone. Life and death are such a strange concept. Sometimes you wonder how this all came to be." Warren looked over at her, afraid he had rambled. But there she was, beside him clinging to his every word.

"Momma said we were meant to lose the people around us because how else would we know how important the ones are that we still have?"

They were silent for a while, enjoying each other's company as they walked. They kept talking as they walked through the town. A woman had cut wildflowers in pots on the street corner, and Warren stepped up to look at them.

"How much are your flowers, ma'am?"

"They are two and a ha'penny a bunch." The woman had a full head of grey hair and kind eyes.

"I'll take two bunches. Can my lady pick them out?" Louisa looked up at Warren and batted her eyes with a smile.

"Oh, yes, sir . . . Miss, take your pick."

"I'll take the assortments of purple asters, black-eyed Susans, and daisies. They are so beautiful. Did you grow them?"

"No, ma'am; they grow wild in the field, and I pick them up fresh every morning. Here you go, sir. Beautiful flowers for a beautiful girl," said the woman as she wrapped them in paper then handed them to Louisa. Warren reached in his pocket and gave her a nickel.

"I hope they do the trick for you, sir." Louisa smiled, and her cheeks turned flush.

"Come on, Warren, I can't wait for Momma to see you." As they started down the street, Louisa took his hand in hers.

Chapter 3

Answered Prayer

Louisa and her family lived on a farm outside of town. As they walked down the dirt road, Warren was happy to be free of the buildings and people and surrounded by wide open fields again. He didn't want this time with Louisa to end.

"Do you remember the day our family left Gardner Lake?"

"Like it was yesterday."

"Do you remember what I told you just before mother and I got on that wagon?"

"I have never forgotten. You told me to come find you when you were all grown up, and you would marry me."

"Here I am. I am all grown up now, and I will be twenty next March." Warren couldn't help but smile, understanding the impact of what she was saying.

"I would have to say, of all the happiest days in my life, this one would take the cake." Louisa smiled as she held up the bundle of flowers.

"So that's what this is," Warren chuckled at the thought. "It's a cakewalk."

"Our life together—should you ask me, and I ain't saying how I would answer—won't be no cakewalk. But I promise I will always love you and respect you. I can make you a nice home and, God willing, raise children alongside you. So, what do you say, Warren Dowling?"

"That sounds good to me."

"No, Warren, you have to ask me the question."

"Just like that? What would people say? We haven't even courted. Don't I have to ask your father first?"

"Ichabod, that old fisherman, he isn't my father. My mother is going to cry tears of joy, so asking her is a waste of time."

"I didn't come prepared to ask you that in such a short time. I don't even have a ring."

"No, but you did bring a knee." Louisa stopped on the road, letting go of his hand and looking back to see if anyone was following. It was the golden hour, and the sun was turning the fields around them to gold. The light on Louisa's dark curls gave her an amber halo. Warren wanted nothing more in the world than to kneel in the dirt and ask this princess to be his queen. But he didn't want to do anything wrong to lose her.

"I ain't never done this before. Besides, you don't even know me."

"I know you, Warren." Louisa took one of the flowers out of the bunch by the stem and held it with her fingers. "A man don't change his character much beyond boyhood. I remember when your old dog died, and you let me tag along, and we buried him on the lakeshore. I watched you so tender and loving with that dog of yours as you dug a hole and laid him to rest. I saw the tears and the love and compassion. I see a man who knows how to love."

Still holding the flower, Louisa drew her attention toward it. "I see a man, a farming man who knows what it takes to grow a flower. A man who works the soil and plants the seed, gives it fertilizer and water, tends to the weeds, and then makes the harvest when it's time. Like this flower, I know you will always hold me by the stem and let me flourish. You will nurture me with love and compassion, and I will be safe in your arms. That's the kind of man I know in you, and that's the kind of man I want to marry. So, just give it a go and see how I answer."

Warren looked around to make sure nobody was watching. He put his knee in the dirt and look up at her. The butterflies were thick in his stomach as he took her hand and gazed into her beautiful brown eyes. Words didn't come easily to Warren.

"Louisa, you know me like we were brother and sister, but thank goodness there is no blood between us." Warren paused, trying to gather himself. Louisa put her finger on her chin as if she were getting impatient and had some big decision to make. "I thought I had waited too long, and you would already be married. I promise to always love you and protect you, and support you. If you should have me, I will always be faithful. So, if I should be so bold, I will propose this question. Will you marry me, Princess Louisa?"

"In a heartbeat . . . Yes, YES," she answered as she knelt down, and placed the flowers down gently down along with her handbag, then threw her arms around his neck and planted a kiss on his lips. His big mustache tickled her lip, and she giggled with joy, grabbing up her things as they stood up together.

"I guess that's it, then."

"No, there is a lot more to it than that, but this is the first step in the rest of our lives." Louisa grabbed his hand and pulled him to get him going up the street again. "C'mon, Momma's heart is gonna fail when she hears about this."

↟↟↟

"That's our house, the white one," said Louisa, pointing out a two-story house with a big front porch surrounded by a white picket fence. Louisa pulled Warren by the hand, unlatched the gate, and then let go and ran up the front steps.

"Momma, look what I got at the post office!" she shouted as she burst through the front doorway with Warren trailing behind her.

Warren walked up the front steps and stopped at the open front door, not wanting to enter the house without a proper invitation. He heard a screech and Louisa's giggles coming from the next room, and she appeared with her mother in tow.

"Warren Dowling, as I live and breathe. Why, you grew up to be a fine young man, didn't you? You look just like your father; God bless his soul. Now, what's this news about you came all the way up here to Lubec to ask my daughter to marry you, and you don't have a ring."

"Oh, ma'am, I have a ring, but I certainly didn't plan on asking her on my first visit." He wasn't sure if she was joking, so he quickly continued to reassure her. "The ring belonged to my mother, and on her deathbed, she took it off her finger and gave it to me, telling me to use it when I found a wife. It's not a big ring, but it has much more meaning and worth than any diamond."

"I can't wait to see it," said Louisa closing her eyes just to imagine.

"You must be famished," said her mother, Hannah.

"Now, don't go and spoil his dinner, Momma. How about you and me put on a special dinner just for the occasion?

"You two can go out and pick some beans, and I'll get things ready here. Jacob, Laura, and Samuel will be home from school in a bit. They can fetch the spuds from the cellar. I'll send Daniel down to the docks to find Ike and tell him to bring home a good-size halibut."

"Momma, we don't want everybody thinking Warren Dowling came to town just for the halibut," laughed Louisa, pronouncing it *hell of it*.

"You watch your tongue, missy. Besides, that joke is so old even a dinosaur wouldn't laugh. You best be finding some new material if you are going to go on vaudeville."

"If you tossed it in the yard, even the crows would come around for that one," laughed Warren.

"Now that's funny," laughed Hannah.

"Oh sure, Momma, you would laugh at anything he said."

"We still need those beans," said Hannah, tapping her toe on the hardwood floor.

⇈ ⇈

That evening at dinner, the whole family sat down together and feasted on baked halibut, roasted potatoes, and fresh-cut green beans. Warren met Louisa's siblings and Ike when they returned home. They were all surprised by the sudden engagement but made Warren feel welcome, even if they did tease him a bit.

"Here is what I want to know, Louisa," said Ike at the dinner table. "Your mother said you always knew from when you were ten years old that you would marry this young man?"

"When I was young, Momma and I went to a wedding up in Marion of her good friend Johanna. Remember that, Momma?"

"Ah, yes, I do."

"I brought a piece of that wedding cake home and put it under my pillow, and that night I dreamed about you, Warren. I saw us living on Gardner Lake with a whole gaggle of children, and that's when I knew." She looked over at Warren. "I gotta say, you had me worried. I was about to give up all hope on you after all these years of losing touch."

"But miracles, they never cease," said Hannah.

"By gosh, Momma, this was a miracle to me. Just last month, I prayed about you, Warren, and here you are. When I saw you on the street, it took me a minute 'cause you looked familiar. Then, when you came into the post office, I knew my knight in shining armor had come to rescue me. That was no coincidence; that was a divine appointment."

"Did you have some time to chat in the garden, my dear ones? Have you two decided on when you will have the wedding?"

"We are going to wait till next spring and do it up right, Momma."

"If the two of you can wait that long," said Ike, giving Warren a wink so his wife couldn't see him. Warren felt like he had known old Ichabod for years; he reminded him of a lot of his own father. After dinner, the two men retired to the front porch for a smoke while the women cleaned up the table dishes and straightened up the kitchen.

"Do you think they need any help cleaning up in there?" asked Warren, taking a cigar from Ike's hand.

"Oh heavens, no, us men would just get in the way." Ike walked ahead and took a seat in a wicker chair. "Louisa is strong willed; you are going to have your hands full with that one."

Ike took a wooden match and pulled the head across the bottom of his pant leg, and it came up with a flame; then he lit his cigar, taking a long puff. Warren gazed off across the hillside where the town sat nestled against the harbor with boat sheds, and docks littered the shore and anchored fishing boats relaxed in the quiet waters.

"I think she will do just fine." Warren leaned forward with his cigar in his mouth and shared the last of the flickering flame from the wooden match. Just then, Louisa appeared through the doorway with a bottle of whiskey and two small glasses. "Here you go, Momma said to bring these out to you." Ike took the half-empty bottle from her and set it on a round table in front of them. Louisa set the glasses next to it. She stepped back, then turned and went back into the house without a word.

"Do you indulge?" Ike gave Warren a devilish grin as he poured a shot from the bottle in a glass.

"I have been known to," said Warren as he took the glass from Ike's hand. "Although not regular."

"Like I said, you will have your hands full; she can be wild." Warren didn't mind wild. He loved that even as a child, Louisa had always spoken her mind.

"Do you have any advice for me? This is your second marriage, right?" Ike nodded and smiled.

"They will talk your ear off, but just listen. Most of the time, a woman don't want your opinion. They just want a listening ear." Warren thought he didn't mind the idea of listening to Louisa, but what did he know. He was excited to learn about this new adventure called marriage.

Warren put the glass to his lips, sipping the whiskey, and it warmed his mouth and throat as he swallowed. They sat and watched the lightning bugs in the yard. As much as Warren was enjoying sitting outside with Ike, he kept thinking about Louisa.

"How many days are you staying, boy?"

"Oh, I'll have to get going back tomorrow. I'm right in the middle of planting, and I have to get the rest of my crops in."

"I was going to take you out in the boat and see what we can catch. My day starts early, so I think I will retire," the older man said, taking his cigar and putting the ember out carefully on the table to save it for later.

"How about next time?" Warren asked eagerly. "I'll come up after I got the farm set for the growing season. Maybe I can stay for a few days?"

Ike simply nodded. "Welcome to my family, Warren. It will be a pleasure."

Chapter 4

Sharp as a Hook

The two men sat quietly, watching the fireflies dance in the yard. Warren remembered how, the previous evening, he had sat alone in his home, nervous about his trip to Lubec, hoping beyond hope that he would get to see Louisa. Now, twenty-four hours later, he had gained a fiancée and a family all in one day.

"I like you, Warren," Ike said, downing the last of his whiskey.

"Thank you, sir. It has been a pleasure." Ike stood up to retire for the evening. Warren stood up as well and shook Ike's hand, wishing him goodnight.

"There's a soft place for you to flop in the hay barn. Hannah will find you a blanket," said Ike, walking toward to door. He stopped and turned back. "You know, you can tell a lot about a man in the firmness of his handshake. Too hard, and he is challenging you. Too soft, and you can tell right off the man has no self-confidence, and he ain't worth his salt. But, a good firm grip tells you the man has something going for himself. And if he looks you square in the eye like you just did, it means he is going somewhere important, or else you best listen to what he has to say."

"I appreciate that, sir."

"And from here on out, you can call me Ike; that's what my friends call me."

"Good night, I'll see you next time I come. Sometime in late July . . . after all the crops are up."

"That sounds good to me. We'll see you then."

Warren downed the other half of the shot of whiskey then took a breath to soften the heat.

"Are you men turning in?" asked Louisa as she came out on the porch.

"No, just me," said Ike. "Besides, you too have a lot to talk about."

"Momma made you a place in the barn, Warren," she said. "Good night, Papa."

"Good night, Louisa; I like it when you call me 'Papa.' I'm so happy for you, my dear. I am sure you miss your father in these moments; I know he would be proud of you, just like I am. If you let me, it would be an honor to give you away."

"That would be nice, Papa." Ike kissed Louisa on the cheek and shut the door behind him, leaving Louisa and Warren alone on the porch.

After an evening spent laughing and talking with her family, Warren suddenly felt shy in the quiet intimacy of the moment. He had been waiting all evening to get another moment alone with the woman who was to be his wife. It all still felt surreal, and Louisa looked just as beautiful in the moonlight as she had when he proposed.

Louisa sat down in a chair opposite Warren. "Can I get you anything? Coffee or a cup of tea, maybe?"

"Oh no, I'm just fine." Warren sat back, taking a puff on his cigar. "Coffee and tea before bedtime puts toothpicks in my eyes."

"I like the smell of cigar smoke. I tried it once, and I found out right off I don't like to smoke."

Warren laughed, putting out the cigar. "I used to smoke with my father; the smell always reminds me of him," Warren sat silent a moment. "It was nice to sit here with Ike this evening. And it was nice to have dinner with all your family. This whole day has been a dream.

I've been alone for so long, Louisa." Warren stumbled over his words as his emotion took over. "And today . . . I saw you, and everything seemed right with the world."

Louisa smiled. The big man who had barged into the Post Office did seem so different in this light. His vulnerability only made her love him more.

"Well, Warren, I expected to pick up a letter at the Post Office, not run into the love of my life. So I guess it has been a pretty successful day for the both of us."

As they were talking, Louisa's three younger siblings came out to say good night. They giggled and made faces at Louisa until Hannah came out to hustle them all away. Louisa watched them go, then asked abruptly, "How many children do you think we will have?" Warren's cheek's turned red. He knew Louisa wasn't shy, but this was not the question he had expected to have so soon. And while they were alone on the porch at night. Her coy smile made his stomach tighten.

"Many as we can, as long as we can. Maybe eight or ten, I suppose." He took her hand and grew serious, "Folks say you need to have a large family to help you on the farm and to take care of you in your old age. And better to plan on more, just in case . . ."

" . . . in case of death." Louisa became quiet and thoughtful. "My mother always says to have a handful just in case you lose one or two along the way. It will soften the blow." It was a strange thought for the both of them. This is what family meant, a combination of life, love, and loss.

"I just attended a funeral on our family grave plot a couple of years ago of little Susan. Do you remember her? She was the twelve-year-old daughter of the neighbors, Mary Maker and Charles Gardner."

"Oh, how sad. Yes, I remember the Gardners, and I remember Susan when she was born. How did she die?"

"She got kicked in the stomach by their milk cow, and it musta did something to her insides; she was dead in four days. Everybody tried to keep a stiff upper lip on that one, but it was tough, especially tough on her mother."

"That's strange," said Louisa putting her fingers on her chin.

"What's strange?"

"I just realized that Mary Maker never changed her name to Gardner."

"Yea, that is strange, but you're right. She is a tough old bird and has a mind of her own, and I guess she just liked her family name."

"I suppose," said Louisa. "Do you think maybe they never really got married?"

"Now, I don't know about that, but I suppose they had to, don't you? Do you think somebody would actually do that? Have kids and not be married?"

"I can't imagine it. It just wouldn't be right."

Warren sat back to ponder the whole thing. He never had thought much about marriage beyond the fact that he wanted to find a wife. All the particulars of it now loomed enormous, overwhelming, and exciting all at once.

They sat together on the porch, watching the sky turn purple. "You and Ike seem to have hit it off," she said, lowering her voice. "You know he ain't the easiest person to get along with. He has never laid a hand on my mother, not so as I would know anyways, but I have seen those two in some pretty tough and heated arguments."

"By the time you are pushing fifty, I think you are pretty set in your ways. It would be tough to start a new marriage after you lost the first one you married for affection."

Louisa stiffened, and Warren could tell something was bothering her.

"I don't want a marriage like that, Warren. I don't want something to simply stave away the loneliness. So many people marry out of necessity. As a woman, I need someone to provide, and as a man, you need someone to take care of the house. It's practical, and it satisfies everyone's needs. I understand that. But I want love, Warren. Do you love me?"

"Now, what sort of question is that?" He knew there was truth to what she said. He also knew he was trying to avoid the question, unsure how to reply.

"Well, I suppose a woman should know what she is getting into when a man has asked to marry her; she deserves to know if the man loves her or not."

"I've only known you for about six hours so far. How about we see how it goes?"

"No, that ain't good enough. You know me; you have always known me. Heck, we grew up together. Just because we took a ten-year break don't mean nothing. I have always loved you ever since I was just a little girl. All I'm asking is that you think about it. I don't need your answer right now," she said, folding her arms across her chest.

"I don't have to think about it. When I saw you walk into the post office, I knew the instant I saw you that you were the one. A chill went up my spine, and my heart nearly jumped out of my chest when I laid eyes on you. If that's love, then give me some more of that. I think when two people get married and begin to experience life together, and they sleep in the same bed and all, that's where love starts to grow. When hardships come, and there are bumps in the road, that's when love gets tested, like putting iron in a hot fire and putting that red-hot rod on an anvil and pounding it into something useful. That's when you know you love someone. So the question is, do I love you?" Warren sat up in his chair and looked Louisa in the eyes. "I guess I do in a naïve and silly sort of a way, and in time I believe that little seed we've planted will grow into a mighty oak tree that will stand the winds and the tests of time. But for now, let's just be content with the little seedling we have started together from this day forward."

"You see, Warren, that is why I love you. Now, where in the world did you get that from? I know you didn't come up with all that yourself," she laughed.

"From my Grandmother, Peggy Dowling. She married my Grandfather, John Dowling, who fought in the Revolution. They grew up together, in a way just like we did. Grandma said she loved him the minute they met. She is the one who taught me everything I know about love and marriage."

"She must have been a smart lady."

"No, she *is* a smart lady, and she is still kicking at age ninety-four."

"I want to meet her."

"Oh, you will, she lives in Whiting with my Uncle Daniel and Aunt Olive. For my grandmother's age, she is sharp as a hook, and believe me, she will hook you with her charm."

"You have lots of family up there in Whiting, don't you?"

"Yep, my grandmother and grandfather had a big family. I don't think any of them are really happy about me getting the family property. I guess that's just how inheritance goes. The oldest son gets the lion's share. I love that land, but to be honest, what I really would love is the musket hanging over the fireplace, the same one my grandfather John brought over from England. I suppose one of my uncles would shoot me just for asking. But when I imagine my future home, with my future bride, and I can see it hanging over our fireplace while our children play."

"That's a beautiful image, Warren. That gun is your grandmother's, and she can give it to whoever she likes. So maybe someday that dream will come true. But what I know is that my dreams are coming true right now, here with you."

Chapter 5

A Gift of Honor

Warren woke as the morning sunlight poked through the cracks. He jumped up quickly, shaking the straw off the wool blanket and wrapping it under his arm. Coming out of the doorway, he saw cooking smoke coming out of the chimney, and the sweet smell of bacon drifted off the front steps. He remembered that today was his twenty-seventh birthday, but he didn't want to breathe a word of it and have them make a fuss.

Eleven-year-old Jacob Crosby saw him coming and threw open the door. "Momma said you were going to sleep all day."

"I don't know what happened; I never slept like that before."

"It's about time you got up, sleepy head," said Louisa, coming out of the kitchen wearing a white apron. Warren took another look at her and goosebumps rose on his arms. She came across the room and threw her arms around his neck. "Do you love me, Warren?"

"Yep, I do, Princess." Warren kissed her on the cheek, and Louisa squinted her eyes at him, then planted a kiss on his lips.

"Ewww!" squealed Jacob. "They are kissing!" Louisa reached out and swatted him on the bottom, and he giggled as he ran away.

"I waited for you to come visit me last night," he whispered.

"Warren Dowling, you scoundrel," Louisa waved her finger at him with a smile. "What sort of girl do you think I am? Come on, we have breakfast ready."

"We were just getting ready to come and get you," said Hannah. "The stage leaves from the hotel in an hour and a half."

"That'll be cutting it close," said Warren. "I was thinking I would walk."

"Oh heavens, that's a ten-hour day. Papa left you two bits so you could afford to ride when he heard you walked most of the way here."

"That was awful nice; he didn't have to do that."

⁂

After breakfast, Warren got his things together and bid Hannah and the children goodbye. Louisa walked with him to the end of the road.

"You better get moving, or you will miss the stage."

"I'll be back just as soon as I get everything planted, but that might not be until the middle of July before I get a chance. Weeds will be coming up quick, and you got to stay ahead of them, or else they will choke you out."

"Oh, I know what you mean. We have the same thing here. But by July, the crops have a good start, and you'll be ready for a break. Me and Momma will start making plans for a wedding. And don't forget to bring your mamma's engagement ring next time."

"Oh no, I won't forget. And tell Ike thanks for the fare."

"I love you, Warren." Louisa looked into his eyes, hoping for a response. Warren paused, then put his hands on her shoulders and faced her head on.

"Don't you worry none there, pretty princess. I love you, and I will always love you." Then he pulled her close and kissed her hard on the lips. "That one will have to last till I come back." Louisa stepped back with a smile on her face as she nodded her approval.

The journey back to Whiting and then on to Gardner Lake seemed to take twice as long on the way back. He had a lot of work ahead of him to bring the farm up to shape. A lot of work on the old house needed to be done to get it ready for a woman's presence. But more than the work ahead of him, he had a terrible time getting that beautiful young girl out of his head. Warren never knew kissing a girl would be such fun.

Over the next two months, Warren dove into his work and brought the place up ship-shape. He mended fences, replaced some broken windows on the house, and patched up the roof's leaks. The front porch had dropped about six inches on one side, and he leveled it up to make the place look more presentable. Warren had seen it done before by setting a bowl of water on the porch and then lifting it until the water became level in the bowl. Between planting and all his repairs, Warren was hardly sleeping, but he didn't notice. Ever since his trip to Lubec, he'd felt like he had been given a new lease on life. Before, it had just been him and the farm, day in and out. Now, there was hope, and Warren spent the summer working hope to the bone.

By mid-July, he was exhausted and more than ready to see Louisa again. He hadn't anticipated how much he would miss her. Before, his home had felt suitable—a place to sleep and eat after a day of work—but now it felt lonely and dark. He reminisced his evening at the Crosbys' over and over again, hoping one day his house would hold such life.

With only a few more weeks until he saw her again, Warren began working in the garden, making a space for Louisa to tend when she arrived. The garden lay right off the porch, with a good view of the road. Looking up in the late afternoon, Warren spotted someone walking down the road toward him. And, if his eyes didn't deceive him, it was a woman. He watched for a minute, curious, and then went back to scratching the weeds out of his beans. After a minute or two, he looked again and saw her turning onto the pathway to his house.

Then he recognized her, dropped his fork, and began running.

"Louisa!" he shouted to get her attention as she saw him and started running. They collided, and she threw her arms around his neck.

"Why have you come?" She pulled away, and big tears ran down her cheeks. "What's happened?"

"It's Papa," she said, trying to calm her voice. "They found his boat adrift, but there is no sign of him. Momma is in a terrible way, and the only thing I could think to do was to come and get you. I know it's silly, but I had to come."

"No, you did the right thing, I'll toss some clothes in a bag, and we will leave immediately." Warren looked down the road, realizing it was almost sunset.

"We'll have to go first thing in the morning," he said, "There won't be another stage until then." Louisa took a deep breath and nodded.

"You can stay with the Hills next door. I think that's most appropriate, don't you?" Warren wiped the tears from her cheeks with his shirt sleeve. "Have you had anything to eat?"

"No, I'm famished."

"Now, I wasn't really expecting company," Warren smiled down at her, trying to bring a smile to her face. "And I ain't much of a cook or a house cleaner for unexpected quests. But we will figure something out. Come."

He gently put his hand around her waist and led her toward the house. He couldn't believe she was here, beside him, at his home. She had come to him in trouble and found peace in his arms. He knew at that moment that he would spend the rest of his life doing everything he could to protect her.

"I got a fat hen out there that has been eating up grain and giving me no eggs in return. The old girl has been itchin' for a special occasion just to jump in a stew pot. Tonight could be her lucky night if you give the word."

"Don't make me feel guilty about killing a hen. You chop her head off, and I'll do all the rest. You bring me some spuds and anything else we can find around here to throw in, and I will make you a dinner fit for a king."

"Welcome home, my queen."

They walked through the door, and Louisa took a look around. The overstuffed brown corduroy chairs in the parlor sat close to the circular woolen braided rug that covered the pinewood floors. The grey rock fireplace, built with rock taken from Gardener Lake's shores and filled with remnants of last night's fire, stood cold. Aged, rough-cut cedar boards covered the walls, and two beautiful oil paintings of sailing ships hung on opposite sides of the fireplace. Two modern oil lanterns stood on two small tables next to the chairs. Louisa reached up to touch the lead cut crystal bowl on the fireplace mantle and ran her hand over the Scottish Highlander's porcelain figurine next to it.

Warren left her to finish her inspection in peace. Grabbing the ax lying near the front door, he went outside, letting the door slam behind him. Louisa could tell the home hadn't had a woman's touch since Warren's mother died. She made her way to the kitchen and felt the heat coming from the ornate cast iron wood cook stove. She opened the latch on the firebox, letting the door down, peering in to see if she might resurrect the flames with a few sticks of kindling. A warm feeling of joy spread over her as she imagined herself living in this home. She thought about what she would change and what it would be like to live here with Warren and their future children.

Suddenly, she felt guilty. Her stepfather was most likely dead, and her mother was grieving. She had hated the old fisherman for so long, resenting him for not being her real father and for the way he had treated her mother in the beginning. But in the past few years, things had changed. Just as she had started to like the man, God had taken him away.

Warren returned with the chicken, and together they worked to make dinner. Warren performed the outside chores, occasionally coming in to check on Louisa, which was really an excuse to kiss her. Louisa was amazed how well they worked as a team. When the soup was done, they ate together on the porch, watching the sunset.

When they had finished eating and done the washing up, there were no more chores and no more excuses.

"Well, I should probably get you up to the Hill place before it gets dark."

Louisa took Warren's hand.

"I don't think the neighbors know I am here, and if we leave first thing, I don't think anyone will even know that I came to get you." Warren's eyes widened, understanding her implication.

"We are betrothed," he said with a grin. "Wait a minute, let me get that ring, and we'll make it official." Warren disappeared through the hallway and left Louisa standing at the fireplace. Louisa tried to erase guilt's feelings at her suggestion, justifying it with the knowledge that they were already engaged.

Warren returned with the ring and slipped it onto the ring finger on her left hand. The gemstone sparkled in the flickering light from the fire in the fireplace.

"It belonged to my grandmother, Polly Patty Larrabee, given to her by my grandfather, Nathan Libby."

"I will always cherish it." Louisa couldn't take her eyes off of it as it sparkled.

"Want me to tell you about my family?"

"I would love to hear." Louisa sat down in the overstuffed chair, and Warren sat in the other. "The Libbys and the Larrabees were some of the first families to settle in Machias. There was a drought in 1762 in Scarborough where all those folks lived, so in May of 1763, sixteen of them set off to find greener pastures: the Scott brothers, Samuel and Sylvanus, Timothy, David, and George Libby, Daniel and Japhet Hill, Isiah Foster, and Isaac Larrabee. The other names are fuzzy, but their last names were Berry and Fogg."

"That's appropriate," laughed Louisa. "There is plenty of berries and fog here in Whiting. But, really, they should have left the fog at home." Warren laughed along at her sense of humor.

"Anyway, they found good salt grass here and a good stream at the head of the inlet. There was plenty of timber and fish here, so my great grandparents, the Libbys and the Larrabees, were among the first who settled here almost a hundred years ago. Josiah Libby was with my grandfather, John Dowling, when they fought in the battle for the Margaretta."

"Wars," said Louisa shaking her head. "I hope we don't have wars like that in our lifetime. By the way, why didn't your mother give this ring to your sister?"

"Harriet never really planned to marry. She was always quiet and shy, never talked much. You do remember Harriet?"

"Yes, I remember, and I remember your mother was so good with her."

"Mother knew she would never get married and gave the ring to me. I have Harriet's blessing."

"Where is she now?"

"She lives with a family and takes care of their house. After mother died, she said she had to go, because all the memories of our parents and growing up were too much of a sad reminder for her."

"I can understand that. I can't believe my mother has to live in a house where she will miss two husbands. Why is death so cruel?"

Warren took her hand, thumbing the ring on her finger.

"From when I was old enough to remember, I saw that ring on my mother's hand, and I used to admire it."

"It's an emerald, right?"

"Yes. I've seen it all my life, but it looks different on your finger."

"You better get used to it because it will be on there for as long as I live. You were lucky it fit so perfectly. Your mother and I must have exactly the same size fingers."

"You remind me a lot of my mother. I heard it said once that a man usually looks for a woman who reminds him of his mother."

"Just let me say," she said with a devilish smile. "After tonight, I don't think you will ever say that I remind you of your mother."

Chapter 6

The Wedding Gift

After breakfast, they hurried quickly to get to the main road that morning to catch the stage coming from Machias, hoping it wouldn't be full up, and they could find a seat. They waited for nearly thirty minutes in the chill of the fog until they heard the horses and the stage rounding the bend. This time Warren made a gesture that was evident to the driver he wanted a ride.

"Got any room?" asked Warren. It was the same driver he had talked to months earlier. He stopped the team, impatient.

"One seat left. Sorry, that's all the room I have."

"Mind if we pay two fares, and the lady sits on my lap?"

"Suit yourself." The driver gave Warren a smirk. "Who wouldn't mind a pretty girl like that one sitting on your lap? I dropped you off last night. And you, I remember you hailing me some months back and not taking a ride."

Warren smiled as he took the carriage door, then climbed in and found the empty seat. There were six seats; five of them were taken. The woman next to the door rolled her eyes as Warren got in first, then put his hand out to help Louisa up the step, and she sat back in his lap. The door closed, and the coach lunged forward as it began bouncing down the road filled with potholes. The older couple sitting next to them tried to carry on a private conversation.

"That young boy will never be faithful to her, you know that, Walter," said the woman.

"I know that, Rebecca, but how will we ever convince her about this Hicks boy. She is so young and naive about life," answered the man they now knew as Walter.

"We've just got to talk sense to her. You know I have heard he drinks." Rebecca tightened her lip and shook her head.

"I think they are talking about Benjamin Hicks," whispered Louisa cupping Warren's ear so her words wouldn't escape. "That's a boy I grew up with in Lubec. He is an upright fellow, and I have never known him to carouse."

"Next time he comes around, I will just have to tell him to move on."

"Your daughter loves him, Walter. It won't be that easy."

"I don't care. A father doesn't raise a child up just to throw her life away on some farmer." Louisa tightened her lip, and Warren rolled his eyes at his comment.

"Now hold on just a minute there, Mister," Louisa raised her chin and pointed her finger up to make her point. "There ain't no shame in owning land and working the soil." The woman wrinkled her brow and shot Louisa with an eye as sharp as her words.

"This is none of your affair," she said sternly. "You should keep your nose out of other people's business."

"If you would keep your discussions out of other people's faces, maybe it wouldn't be anyone's business but your own," Louisa shot back like cannon fire. "Besides, I know Benjamin Hicks, and he is not what you think."

"Does that mean he isn't a farmer?" laughed the woman.

"No, he's a farmer, all right, but he is not a philanderer like you say."

"Is that so?" said Walter, folding his arms across his chest.

"Yes, that is so. I have known him since I turned eleven. We grew up together, and he is an honorable gentleman in every way. You should feel privileged that your daughter wants to marry a man such as this."

"You could do worse than a farmer," chimed in Warren. "It so happens that I come from a long line of farmers all the way back to Ireland. It's a noble and honorable profession, making the land produce out of the sun and rain. It's the kind of life you have to make for yourself."

"And at the same time relying on God to help you all your days," said Louisa with a broken voice. "It's not as dangerous as being a logger or a fisherman, for heaven's sake. My Papa went missing up in Lubec just two days ago. They found his boat, and I hope when I get there, he'll be okay, but I don't have much hope."

"We heard a man went missing up there. That was your father, dear? We are so sorry," The woman, obviously having a change of heart, reached out and patted Louisa on the hand as Louisa wiped the tear coming down her cheek with her sleeve.

"This is the second one I have lost," said Louisa.

"The second what?" asked Walter.

"The second father. I lost my real father when I was almost ten in a logging accident."

"Death does carry a sting, doesn't it, honey?" The woman took Louisa's hand in hers and gazed at the ring on her finger. "But looks like you got joy in your life with a nice young man. How long have you two been engaged?"

"Since May." Louisa looked up with a smile.

"Such a pretty ring for a pretty little girl."

"It belonged to my grandmother," said Warren proudly. "What sort of work do you do, sir?"

"Finances, son, I'm a numbers man. Some people know fishing, farming, logging, I know numbers, and I keep all those folks in business. Without finances, they would all go broke."

"Maybe so," said Louisa. "But without the fishers and farmers, you would go hungry, and without the loggers, you would have no place to live because there would be no lumber for you to build a proper house."

"You have a point, child, doesn't she, Walter?" Her husband rolled his eyes and smiled without a word, then looked away, watching out the window. Louisa reached down her hands and found Warren's hands, then pulled them up in her lap as she sat contentedly with his arms around her as the coach bobbed and weaved down the road through the ruts. The noise filled the cab from the horse hooves pounding the ground, and the wheels whistled from time to time as if they needed oil. Dust came in the windows, and there came an occasional yell from the driver as he encouraged his team.

The stage ride from Gardner Lake to Lubec took two hours to travel the thirty miles. Before they knew it, the stage came rolling into town and pulled up in front of the hotel. Warren helped Louisa off first, and he turned to take the older women's hand to help her safely to the street.

"I hope everything turns out for you," she said, grabbing Louisa's arm.

"And I hope everything turns out for your daughter," said Louisa. "I might know her."

"Her name is Francis Stevenson."

"I might have heard the name once, but you probably live on the other side of town," said Louisa.

"Sorry to say there has been no formal introduction, dear. We are Rebecca and Walter Stevenson."

"We are Warren Dowling and Louisa Crosby," said Louisa knowing that would be her name until the wedding.

"Come on, Louisa, let's get to your house. Nice meeting you, ma'am," said Warren, tipping his hat.

Warren held Louisa's hand tightly as they walked toward her house. This time felt a world away from the last time they had walked this way together, beginning strangers and ending fiancés. Now, the weight of grief hung over them as they walked toward the bad news and suffering they were sure were coming.

Warren had seen enough death in his life. When he was just nineteen, his father had died at age sixty-two, and when he was twenty-five, his mother had passed away at age sixty-four. Louisa had lost a father and was now about to find out she'd lost another.

When they reached the house, Louisa's younger brother by three years, Daniel, greeted them. He stood in the doorway with a solemn face.

"He's gone, sister; they found him yesterday washed up on the shore south of Cutler.

"Where is Momma?"

"She is in her room, resting."

"I will go to her. Warren, find yourself some coffee." Louisa went to her mother's room on the main floor, knocked quietly on the door, and then opened it softly. Hannah looked up as she lay on her bed and tried to smile as she saw her daughter standing in the doorway.

"They found the poor man drowned," said Hannah. Louisa approached the bed as Hannah sat up, and they embraced. Louisa began to sob at the reality of never seeing him again.

"He was a good man," said Hannah. "I'll never have another man. I guess two is enough. Maybe it's me, maybe I'm cursed."

"Oh, don't say that, Momma."

"I told him not to go out in the wind. He knows better, but he was always stubborn as a mule."

"We are going to be okay."

"We'll be okay. I know that. I just worry about Jacob. Eleven years old. He was only two when his father died, and Ike was the only father he ever knew."

"I know. I was eleven when my father died. We are all going to be sad for a while. But life will go on."

"For now," said Hannah, wiping her face, "we have a husband and a father to put in the ground. Now our lives are going to change immensely without a breadwinner."

"But you just wait and see, Momma. We are going to make it. You just wait and see."

The following spring, Warren and Louisa were married in Whiting, surrounded by family and friends on Gardner Lake's shores. Fall and winter passed in grief and loneliness. As much as Louisa missed Warren, she was grateful for these months with her mother and siblings as they all adjusted to life without Ike. Louisa's younger brothers found what work they could in town, and Louisa and Hannah spent their days preparing for the wedding in the spring. Each night, Hannah embroidered while Louisa wrote to Warren. A spring wedding was just what everyone needed to lift the spirit.

It was a sunny morning, and the light reflected gold on the water. A slight chill blew off the lake, but the crowds were full of warm hearts, and the sun shone brightly on their bright future. Louisa wore the white wedding gown trimmed in lace and a veil with tiny yellow violets that her mother had worn when she married Louisa's father, Daniel. Warren wore a black suit jacket he had borrowed from his uncle and a black bow tie and white shirt. His favorite farm hat had been left back at the house, and he had trimmed his wide mustache just for the occasion.

Standing in front of Warren, Louisa could hardly contain herself. When it came time for Louisa to place a ring on Warren's finger, she used the gold band her father Daniel had worn when he married her mother. Hannah beamed with pride as she watched her oldest daughter recite the wedding vows. She had such great hope for their happiness.

"I now pronounce you man and wife," said the preacher. "When two are joined together by God, let no man put asunder. You may now kiss your bride."

Warren put his arms around his beautiful bride and planted a kiss on her lips, deep and passionate. Louisa melted in his arms. She had left this lake so long ago, and after years of patience and prayers, he had found her and brought her back.

"I promise to make you happy and to make you proud of me," she whispered.

"You are doing both of those things wonderfully right now," said Warren under his breath.

Warren looked toward the crowd with his arm around his bride, beaming with excitement.

"I would now like to introduce to you Mister and Missus Warren Dowling!"

🌲🌲🌲

After the ceremony, everyone gathered around the lake for a picnic and music. A large wooden table had been made of planks and piled with food brought in from neighboring farms. Games were set up in the grass, and some of the kids were skipping rocks across the water. Warren's Uncle Silas came forward to shake his hand. "She is every bit as pretty as her mother; good going, boy." Silas shook his hand with a firm grip.

"Every bit as beautiful as I had hoped from the day we took that wagon ride to Lubec."

"All the best to you and your new bride. Now, wait here a minute," said Silas making a fist and pumping Warren on the shoulder. "Me and your uncles have something for you." Silas turned and disappeared, setting off to grab something from his wagon.

When Silas returned, he was carrying his grandfather's musket. Warren's heart stopped, not believing what he saw.

"That's the musket!" exclaimed Warren, trying not to let his jaw hit the floor as the crowd went silent and the family and friends gathered around.

"Warren, you know my mother, your Grandmother, Peggy, would have loved to be here today. She lived a good long life. Not many folks live to see their ninety-fourth birthday. She was a wonderful woman and a wonderful grandmother. She told me how you stopped by last year and how much that made her happy. From her telling, this whole wedding was really her idea."

Warren hugged Louisa tightly as he listened to his uncle. Peggy had died just a few months earlier, and her absence was strongly felt. He wished so much she could have met Louisa; he knew they would have loved each other immediately.

"My mother told us on her death bed just last month that she wanted you to have it, you being the oldest son of our oldest brother," said Silas. Warren gazed at the prized possession he had seen many times, hanging over his grandmother's fireplace.

"The stories this thing could tell if it could talk." Warren wiped a tear from his eye, the overflow of emotions in his spirit, as he reached out to take the old Brown Bess in hand. "Every scratch has a story; every nick has a memory. This musket represents the freedom of our country that was bought and paid for in blood. I think it might be more of a symbol of freedom to me than the stars and stripes of old glory. This musket is personal because it came from Ireland, where my great-grandfather fought the British in Scotland over a hundred years ago. This musket was on the deck of the Margaretta and defended the town of Machias against certain annihilation seventy-five years ago. I feel so honored."

"We talked about it," said Silas, nodding to his brothers. "We know the kind of man you are, and we are confident this family heirloom is in good hands.

Chapter 7

Letting Go

Mother, it is so good of you to come." Warren took Hannah's hand and helped her off the stagecoach. In the two years since their wedding, Warren and Louisa had been so busy with their land, they had only seen the Crosbys for occasional holidays.

"You really don't think I would have missed the birth of my first grandchild, do you?"

Warren smiled mysteriously as he grabbed his mother-in-law's bag from the coach and offered her his arm. He helped her up onto the wagon seat, secured her bag, and settled himself on the seat beside her before picking up the reins and signaling the horses with a "Tsk, tsk."

As they set off toward the Dowlings' farm, Hannah peppered Warren with questions.

"How's our princess?" she asked him worriedly.

"She has taken this on like a mother bear. She is a tough girl on the inside. A lot tougher inside than she is on the outside."

"She always was," said Hannah.

As they rounded the bend toward the farmhouse, they saw Louisa standing on the porch, waiting, and she waved as she waddled toward them.

"You should have told her to stay indoors," scolded Hannah.

"The midwife says the best advice for a lady in her condition is to get fresh air," said Warren.

"Momma!" yelled Louisa, and Warren was glad for the interruption. He felt grateful for Hannah's help; he certainly did not know anything about delivering babies. But the thought of his mother-in-law coming to stay made him a little nervous.

"My land, girl, look at you! You are all baby!"

Louisa put her arms around her swollen belly and grinned. "No, Momma; I am all *babies*. The midwife thinks there are TWO!"

Louisa and Warren both erupted with laughter at the stunned look on Hannah's face. For once, she was speechless.

"Surprise, Momma!" chuckled Louisa, opening the door in front of her mother as she and Warren came up the steps. "Welcome to our home!"

Louisa smiled understandingly as she caught Warren's eye, knowing how he felt about Hannah's visit. But she was elated to see her. Having her mother stay with them would be a big help. Warren smiled back reassuringly, and put his hand on Louisa's belly as they all went inside.

🌲🌲🌲

The following week, Louisa went into labor and gave birth to beautiful twins. Willie Edwin was born first, and Adelaide Evelyn was born three minutes later. Louisa had a difficult time with the delivery, but the elation of two beautiful and healthy children was a prize worth the price when it was all over. "You should be proud as punch with these babies," said Hannah.

"God has blessed me, Mother," Louisa replied happily. She was laying in her own bed, propped up with pillows as she cradled a son under one arm and a daughter under the other. "Aren't they the most beautiful babies you have ever seen? Oh, I know that sounds silly, but look at them. They really are beautiful."

"They are beautiful, but that is how God intended for you to see them. You earned every hair on their heads, and they are part of you. All their life, you will have a soft place in your heart for them as they grow and mature and become adults, and have their own families. They will always be your babies just in the same way I see you, darling."

"Momma, life is so beautiful, isn't it?"

"Life can be beautiful, and it can be very harsh and unforgiving at times as well. That is why we need God's joy."

"I'm glad God gave me a wise momma like you," she said.

"I don't know about the wise part. But I am thankful He gave you to me."

"My princess," said Warren, poking his head into the room.

"You go wash up," said Hannah. "You've been out in the field working all morning! The least you can do is clean yourself up first before you go offering to handle one of these precious gems."

"I'm going, I'm going, but first, just let me get a peek at them," he said, leaning over the bedside. Louisa positioned them so he could get a better look. "Yep . . . they look like babies, all right."

Coming back into the room after washing up, Warren beamed at Louisa. Hannah gently placed Willie Edwin in his arms and grabbed Adelaide for herself, giving Louisa a break. As soon as Willie left Louisa's arms, he began to howl. Hearing her twin, Adelaide too began to cry.

"Rock him gently, like this," Hannah directed. She swayed her body, but both babies kept crying.

"Hand her back to me. Louisa reached out for her baby girl, wondering if they needed a feed.

"This is going to be harder than we thought," Warren laughed over the sound of the howls.

"Here, let's switch." As soon as Adelaide was placed in her father's arms, she went silent. Willie, similarly, quieted down as Louisa held him.

"Well, well, well, Warren, it looks like you have a daddy's girl."

Over the next year, Hannah's words would prove true. Warren had a connection with Adelaide, whom he called Addie, that made Louisa marvel. She had always known that his hard exterior melted around his daughter. While Louisa had become his queen, it seemed that little Addie had become his new princess.

Late one night in the spring of 1858, Louisa woke to the sound of coughing. The moonlight glistened through the open window just enough to make out the pathway to the children's room. As she came to the crib, reaching down, she felt Willie's head. He was warm, but not alarmingly so. Louisa left the two children sleeping in the crib together and pulled the blanket up to cover them both. As she lay back down in her own bed, she heard him cough again, then said a prayer for him not to get sick as she dozed off to sleep.

As the morning light began to break, she felt beside her and realized Warren had left the bed, up with the chickens. She heard Willie coughing again and made her way back to the children's room. This time when she felt his head, the signs of fever were obvious.

"He is getting sick, isn't he?" asked Warren, appearing at the bedroom doorway.

"He has a fever," she answered. "I am sure it is just a cold."

"How is a little one like this going to catch a cold? He hasn't even been outside. Is there anything we can do?"

"Just wait it out, I guess, and pray, of course."

"My grandmother Dowling use to say you can pass small snails between the hands of a sick person then hang them by a string on the chimney. She swore the cough would leave as the snails die."

"My grandmother said if you wrap a house spider in muslin above the mantle, when it dies, the cough will leave. She also said you can feed the sick child's hair to the family dog and hide it in a piece of bread. If the dog dies, then the baby will recover. But let's not try any of those methods just yet." Louisa smiled, but Warren could see she was worried.

"I will ask around to see if anyone might be making a trip to town and could get the doctor, just in case."

As the days progressed, both children fell ill to the cough, and their fever increased. When the doctor arrived, he had little to add in the way of a remedy. He did provide a diagnosis: whooping cough.

"You should have separated them at the first signs of the cough. Would you leave a bad apple in a barrel?" he scolded.

"How was I to know?" Louisa answered, defensive.

"There is nothing to do now but to let nature take its course. You must feed a cold and starve a fever, but this is not a common cold. My advice is, don't give the children any food for the next several days, and that should starve out the fever. Once the fever is gone, then you can start them out on food again. I will have to bid you good day now, as I have more homes to visit up the way."

"I will see you out," said Warren. As the men stepped out on the porch, the door shut behind them. Then the doctor turned stoned face to Warren.

"Warren, I was not entirely truthful to your wife back there. The children started out with whooping cough, but it has now progressed into pneumonia. If they were adults, you could adjust the humors, but it is very hard in babies so young. Bloodletting is the only cure I have seen, but risky with children because they don't have as much blood in their veins. I have seen it repeatedly with small children, but the children will not survive beyond a miracle. There is no cure for pneumonia. I want you to have the hard facts to prepare for the worst. I'm sorry to be the one to give you this news, but I thought you should know."

"Is there nothing we can do?"

"Purging the body of phlegm is what I know. Use the herb thyme and make it into tea, then put a pinch of poppy seed powder. Sweeten it with honey to make it palatable for the children. The drug in the poppy will curb the cough, and the thyme will purge the phlegm. Beyond that, there is nothing to do."

The doctor tipped his hat and walked back to where he had tied his horse in the yard and road away. Warren stood on the porch and watched the doctor ride away, feeling like he'd just been sucker-punched in the stomach. *What will I tell Louisa?* he wondered. Warren turned toward the doorway, pausing to clench his fists and grit his teeth. Before he could reach the doorknob, it began to turn from the inside. The hinges squeaked, and Louisa stood on the other side.

"Come inside; it's too cold out there to be without your sweater." Warren stepped across the threshold and into her waiting arms. "We need to prepare for the worst, darling," spoke Louisa softly. "Even though I know it's just whooping cough."

"I'm not giving up on hope yet, darling," said Warren. "I have a tea recipe from the doctor. I'll get the ingredients ready."

Warren turned away and stepped through the children's door to look on them again, hoping they would perk up. They looked so pale and still, lying next to each other on the bed.

He watched as Willie took a deep breath, opened his eyes wide, and then shut them. Warren waited for the next inhale, but it never came. Reaching out, Warren put his hand on the boy's forehead to feel his lifeless body.

"Is he gone?" asked Louisa with tears coming down her cheeks. Warren tried to speak, but no words came. All he could do was nod his head in agreement.

"No," she shrieked. "No!"

Louisa fell to her knees, sobbing uncontrollably. She made fists and started pounding the floor. "No, no . . . no!"

Warren stood over her, helpless to change the outcome. He looked back at the lifeless boy lying next to his sister.

He reached in the bed and lifted the boy, cradling him in his arms, then broke down sobbing like a child. Then he stood, willing time to turn back, to go back to the way things were before the children got sick. Back to a happier time, and erase the horror. He tried to pray, but he was too angry for coherent thought. Closing his eyes, he listened to the whimpering of his grieving wife. Opening them again, he glanced over at the bed. There sweet Adeline lay, with her eyes and her mouth open, and the reality struck that she was gone too.

Chapter 8

The Aftermath

Louisa shivered as they stood in the cold rains on that April afternoon. Friends and family gathered, all dressed in black, at the grave plot on the Dowling property overlooking Gardner Lake. Louisa bit her lip, tasting blood, while the minister read from the Scriptures. The words he spoke were like a bucket of cold water tossed in the two open graves. Hannah stood next to her daughter, sharing in the grief and horror as she gazed at the graves of her dead grandchildren.

Louisa's eyes were dull and lifeless. Along with her twins, she had lost her hopes and her dreams. Though she already had a new baby growing inside of her, she felt no peace and no joy, no hope that her life would be good again. No one said a word as they left the small cemetery.

Later that afternoon, while Warren went out to the fields to bury his sorrows in his own dirt, Louisa and her mother sat together in silence.

"Why did God do this to me, Momma?" asked Louisa, trying to stop the flow of tears that had been constant since the first of her twins had taken his last breath. "He must hate me for something I have done." She remembered back to the night she had come to get Warren when her stepfather died. She felt certain she had provoked God's anger and was now being punished for her sin.

"That's not who God is, my dear. He doesn't punish us for our sins like that. He loves us and wants the best for us. Listen to me. He did not kill your children."

"If He is a God of miracles, then He could have answered my prayers and made them well again if He wanted. I am afraid He has turned his back on me, Momma. How can Warren and I ever recover? A new baby is on the way, but even that does not bring me joy—only fear that it could happen again." Louisa paused, choosing her words. "If it happened to me again, I would stick my head in a rain barrel."

"Oh, Louisa, don't even talk like that. If you want to lay blame, then blame Satan. God wants us to look to the heavens. The Good Book says we are to keep our eyes on heavenly things and not earthly things.

"Oh, Momma, that is too tall of an order for me to measure up to. Where would I even start? I am so angry with God right now that His glory is only darkness."

"Louisa, Willie Edwin and Adelaide Evelyn are now more alive than you and me. They are giggling and chasing each other just as they did in this house. You will be united with these little ones in heaven soon enough. Until then, you must keep going. God has told me that one day a seed from us both, your great, great-grandchild will be raised up, and your story will be told, and God's blessing for all the generations will be preserved. On that day, both you and I will look down from heaven together and smile that what happened to us will be used for the Glory of God."

Louisa thought about it and touched her stomach. Momma was always saying she heard from God. Oddly, the things she said she heard usually came to pass. A spark of hope began to flicker in Louisa's heart.

She was hardly showing yet. It was hard to think of any sort of future without Willie and Addie. But, for the first time since their death, she felt grateful for the new life growing inside her. She didn't have the energy to keep going for herself—grief was too large—but this life inside her would force her to keep going.

"What about Warren? I am not sure he will ever recover from this loss. He is blaming God for it. Addie was his joy and his life. I think a piece of his heart has died with her."

The rain fell softly on the roof. Louisa imagined her husband out in the fields, angry and freezing. He needed to be alone. He hadn't talked or even cried at the funeral.

🌲🌲🌲

As the weeks passed, Warren drew inward. He worked long, hard days in the field, and when he returned home, he hardly spoke at all. Louisa sat beside him as he ate his dinner, but he barely acknowledged her and excused himself after he had eaten to go back outside to work until it was time to sleep. When they did talk, it was about everything except the children.

Weeks turned into months as the summer dragged on. The heat felt stifling and summer held none of its usual joys. It was a summer of silence. Louisa somberly prepared for the coming child as Warren seemed to ignore all signs that another child would soon enter their lives.

One evening in late summer, Louisa broke the silence.

"I'm due to have this child soon," said Louisa as they sat down together at the dinner table.

"That's something," he said, looking up from his food, trying to hold back his emotions as he scooped the cooked green peas on his spoon.

"Something wonderful for the both of us," she said.

"I suppose," said Warren, not looking up but taking another bite.

"Look, I know you are hurting, but we have to talk about them."

"I can't," he said.

"What are you afraid of?"

"Afraid?" he said with a scowl. "I am a man, and I am not afraid of anything."

"You know you are my everything: my protector, my provider, my friend, and my lover. You have been my rock in my darkest hour; I couldn't have made it without you. But we have to talk about this."

After dinner, Warren went outside as usual. But instead of leaving to go work, he sat down in one of the chairs on the porch. The sun was just beginning to set.

Louisa went into the kitchen, popped the cork on the half-empty plum wine bottle, and splashed some in Warren's favorite cup. She grabbed a cigar out of the half-empty box and grabbed a wooden match off the kitchen's fireplace mantle.

"Here you go, my dear," she said, putting the cup in front of him and handing him the cigar.

"I'll get my shawl and join you." Warren nodded, looking slightly nervous.

Louisa grabbed her shawl, hanging near the door, and hastily wrapped it around her shoulders. Then, pausing for just a moment before opening the front door, she said a prayer that God would give her the words to speak. She lifted the latch and took a breath to calm herself, then stepped outside, where Warren sat with his feet up on the rail, puffing on his smoke.

"This is a good batch of wine from last year," he said, putting the cup to his lips and taking a sip. "Hope we get plenty of plums from those trees along the lake this year. I'll put up some more."

"Can we talk about our children?" asked Louisa.

"If I had a busted leg, would you come out here thinking that if you kicked me in the knee, it would somehow feel better?"

"No, but if you had a stiff muscle, I would work the kinks out of it with my fingers. The hurt would be intense, but that would make it go away. If you had a festering cut and I put salt or whiskey on it, it would seem to burn down to the bone, but it might cause the infection to subside. Momma prayed with me, and all the talking and crying is helping me to heal."

"But you are a woman. Nobody is going to ridicule you for shedding a tear. That's just what women do. If I cried like a baby, I'd be labeled as a coward. Men are men, and we respect each other for being tough. We just have to take our emotions and stuff them away and find the pluck to deal with life. I don't want to cry in front of my wife."

"You have to cry in front of me. If you don't let this stuff out, it will be with you your whole life, and it will come back someday to haunt you. God made tears for a reason, to wash away the hurt."

"God didn't think much about me when he killed my twins, did He?"

"Warren, God didn't kill our children."

"He sure as hell did," said Warren with a frown blowing the smoke off the front porch rail. "Don't even talk to me about God. If there is a God at all, then He is a monster."

"I don't understand this either. But I know God loves us. We have to trust that He will use this tragedy as a triumph."

"I just don't see how taking two beautiful children out of the world can be an act of love."

"You have to do the hard work of healing."

"I have asked *Why, why, why* . . . but there is no answer," said Warren.

"You are asking the wrong question; we have to ask God to help us through this transition. If you can deal with the stuff you kicked to the bottom of the well and bring it to the surface, you can begin to heal. But you have to be willing to poke the place that hurts. You have to be willing to be vulnerable and even more willing to deal with the hurt it will cause you."

"Louisa, I can't deal with it," he said, wiping the tears from his cheeks. "If my father or my grandfather saw me crying, they would turn over in their graves. It would be like spitting on their gravestones."

"That's a little strong, don't you think?" she asked.

"I never knew my grandfather, but he was an old revolutionary soldier. I am sure he saw plenty of tragedy in his life, and he would have dealt with it in a manly way."

"But the way you think someone 'deals' with tragedy isn't always the way they actually deal with it. Maybe that's why your grandfather only lived to be in his mid-fifties. You know the things we stuff away have a way of growing and coming back to get us with a vengeance if we don't deal with them up front."

"How do you know all this, anyway?" asked Warren.

"Momma told me. I know I'm only twenty-two, but my Momma is forty-four, and she is a wise woman. She has lost two husbands, and she has seen a lot of death. She knows what she is talking about."

"I do love your mother; sometimes, I think of her as my own." He turned and looked her deep in the eyes, something he hadn't done in months. "I will think about this when I am in the field tomorrow."

⚘⚘⚘

In mid-August, once again, Hannah traveled to Gardener Lake as Louisa approached the time for her delivery. This time Louisa's nineteen-year-old sister, also named Hannah, and her brother, Jacob, age fifteen, traveled with her. When the twins had died, Louisa's mother had left her other children at home in Lubec, not wanting to expose them to their sister's grief. Now Hannah expected her visit to be a joyous one.

So, when she went into labor on August 18th, Louisa was surrounded by her sister and her mother. She felt glad to have the younger Hannah there to hold her hand and wipe her brow.

"I don't think I ever want to have babies," said young Hannah.

"Nannah, don't you talk like that," said her mother in a stern voice. "God will hear you and give you just what you ask for."

"Right about now, I think I want God to hear me," she whispered to Louisa, out of earshot of her mother. Louisa could not reply; she could only squeeze her hand and grit her teeth as another contraction overtook her.

"You will see, Nan," said their mother, "when this little bundle of joy comes in the world. All the contractions in the world wouldn't have been enough to curb your sister's appetite to have another one."

"Momma, can we not talk about having another child right now?" whimpered Louisa breathlessly. "Let me get through this one first."

"I know now why it's not a good idea for husbands to be in the same room during the delivery of their children," smirked Nan.

"Why is that?" asked her mother.

"Because they just might get close enough to their wife for her to get her hands around his neck." Louisa began to laugh but then stopped short when another contraction overtook her.

"It's almost time for you to push," said Hannah. "We are getting really close to having a baby."

"Where is Warren?" asked Louisa in a strained voice.

"He's on the front porch," said Hannah. "I think he is having a smoke."

"This must be just as hard on him as it is on me," said Louisa as the contraction subsided.

"That's what they would have you think," said Hannah. "But believe me, they don't have a clue. If we left childbearing up to men, the species would have gone extinct a long time ago." She readied her supplies and took up her position at the foot of the bed. "Okay, now let's get down to business," said Hannah. "Let's get this little one out of you and into the world. Can you try to push?" Louisa held her breath and puckered her face to push the baby into the world.

"There is the head!" announced Nan.

"And there's the shoulders . . . push again. He or she is coming into the world!" A split second later, Hannah was cradling the slippery infant, looking with anticipation to discover the gender.

"It's a girl!" squealed Nan. Hannah slapped the baby on the bottom, and she opened her lungs and let out a big cry.

"Nan, why don't you go break the news to Warren that he has a daughter? I'll call you when we're ready."

"Okay, Momma," said Nan happily as she scampered out of the room.

"And tell your brother I better not catch him puffing on a cigar!" Hannah called after her. In the waiting basin, she washed the baby as best she could, then wrapped her in a clean, warm swaddling cloth. "Here, Louisa, take your little bundle." And with that, she laid the precious bundle in Louisa's arms, and turned to begin cleaning up.

A short time later, Louisa looked up and saw Warren standing in the doorway.

"I will leave you two alone," said Hannah, squeezing Warren's arm as she walked out the room. Before exiting, she turned to smile broadly at them and wish them a warm congratulations.

"It looks like I have another princess," said Warren, coming over to sit next to Louisa on the bed. "This time, princess, you saved me."

"Who are you talking to? Me or her?" Louisa laughed, handing him their newborn daughter.

"Both of you," said Warren, his eyes misty. He fixed his eyes on his daughter, and whispered with emotion, "Hello, little one. You have an amazing mother, and you come from a long line of amazing men and women. We have lost some along the way, but we will tell their stories. Come, I have something to show you."

"You're going to show her the musket, aren't you?"

"How did you know?"

"I know you well, Warren Dowling. Now you tell her our story as I get some rest."

Epilogue—Warren and Louisa Dowling

Life is rich, mixed with joy and happiness along with tragedy and grief. Warren Dowling and Louisa Crosby grew up together on Gardner Lake and spent their whole lives there. They were family friends. That is how it was for so many back in those times. A horse and buggy were the primary transportation, so no one went too far from home. Most people married close to their circle.

Warren and Louisa raised their children on the property passed down by John Dowling, Sr., Revolutionary Soldier. When my wife Sue and I visited Machias in 2016, we asked several people if they knew of a Gardner Lake Cemetery. After going to several other sites in the area and looking for graves, we began heading out of town toward Whiting. We passed a sign that said, "Gardner Lake Road." Sue suggested we drive up there, so we turned around.

I laughed and said, "We could find someone walking by who says, 'Yep, it's just up the road a mile or so on your right.'" After turning north from U.S. Rural Route 1 onto Tech Camp Road, I saw a guy on his porch. I pulled in the driveway and waved to him as I got out of the car. I said, "Hey, we are looking for a Gardner Lake Cemetery, any ideas?"

"I'm not from around here, let me ask my wife. She grew up here," he answered, as he ducked inside the house. After just a few seconds, he came back on the porch. "My wife said it's just up the road about a mile on your right."

The road quickly changes to Gardner Lake Road, and sure enough, about a mile in is a small graveyard on the east side of the road. There we found all the family graves, including Dowling, Maker, Gardner, and Cates. The small headstones of the Dowling twins are located between the graves of their parents, Warren and Louisa. One could imagine the gatherings of family and friends as each one was laid to rest with sweet memories and heartbreaking tears.

Life and death are what life is about for all of us. Like a roller coaster ride, you have to hang on to stay in your seat. One never knows what is just around the corner; maybe even a small miracle.

Part III—Edwin and Lucy Dowling

SIGNIFICANT NAMES AND DATES

Warren Loring Dowling
Born: May 20, 1827, Whiting, Washington County, Maine
Died: May 11, 1891 (age 64), Whiting,
Washington County, Maine

Louisa Keyes Crosby Dowling
Born: March 10, 1834, Whiting, Washington County, Maine
Died: September 25, 1884 (age 50), Whiting,
Washington County, Maine

⚑⚑⚑

Simeon H. Cook
Born: December 28, 1846, East Machias,
Washington County, Maine
Died: April 9, 1909 (age 62), Lowell, Middlesex, Massachusetts

Ida E. Gardner Cook
Born: March 7, 1850, Whiting, Washington County, Maine
Died: June 14, 1910 (age 60), Lowell, Middlesex, Massachusetts

⚑⚑⚑

Edwin Joseph Dowling
Born: February 17, 1862, East Machias,
Washington County, Maine
Died: April 10, 1928 (age 66), Everett, Snohomish County,
Washington

Lucy Delia Cook Dowling
Born: November 27, 1872, Maine
Died: April 6, 1910 (age 37), Everett, Snohomish County,
Washington

Part III

Edwin Joseph Dowling
1862–1928

Lucy Delia Cook Dowling
1872–1910

Chapter 1

A Cold Sweat

Edwin Dowling tried to ignore the pit in his stomach as the steamer approached Boston Harbor. The sun was just beginning to rise from the east, and there was a low fog over the city. As he stood on the deck, holding the rail, the cold morning wind blew in his face. Edwin could feel his mustache flying like a flag. He pulled his hat down hard on his head to stop it from blowing away.

This was Edwin's first time in a big city. Although he knew he would just be passing through Boston on his way to Lowell, he could already feel in his bones his dislike for his surroundings. The tall smoke stacks blew black, billowing clouds of air, and he could already see crowds of people lining the shore. All Edwin wanted to do was get off this ship, make his way through the crowded city as swiftly as possible, and get on the train toward Lucy. At the thought of her, his heart lurched. Only one thing in the world could drag him away from his beloved horses, and that was the thought of meeting Lucy.

An hour later, Edwin disembarked and found himself in the middle of Boston's hustle and bustle. Everyone seemed to be in a hurry, and nobody looked anyone in the eye. As he started down the street, he saw horses pulling carts of all sizes and shapes, some loaded with goods, others empty. The towering brick buildings were too numerous to count, and he wondered who had laid the cobblestones so neatly in the street. It was so very different from the muddiness of the rainy season in Machias. Edwin realized how sheltered he had been, growing up on Gardener Lake, raised by his father Warren and his dear mother Louisa who died when Edwin was twenty-two.

After walking three city blocks, he was relieved to spot the train station. The grand entrance, with its massive sandstone columns, stood seventy feet tall. Edwin broke out in a cold sweat, looking at the crowds and the line in front of the ticket counter.

After standing in line for thirty minutes, Edwin finally purchased a ticket and made his way to his rail car. Settling into his seat and taking a deep breath, he thought of the girl he was pursuing: Lucy. For a fleeting moment, he hoped all the effort and all the hassle would be worth it.

The train began to move through the city, passing block after block. Edwin could not keep his eyes off the horses, comparing one to another and trying to pick out the most beautiful ones. Then, suddenly, the city dropped away, and the train sped up into the Massachusetts countryside. He continued to watch out for horses, dreaming of moving out West one day, where the land was still untamed and vast. But in his dream of going West, he was never alone; there was always someone at his side. Perhaps, Lucy would one day be that someone.

Edwin's knees were weak. He had rehearsed this moment over and over in his mind. He walked up Moody Street in Lowell, Massachusetts looking for number 20. Then he spotted the house. He stood there, paralyzed at the thought of climbing the thirty steps to the front door.

His feet weighed a hundred pounds each as he put one foot in front of the other. He gulped to help the pit in his stomach go away, then made a fist and rapped the front door.

A middle-aged woman wearing a neatly pressed calico dress and apron answered the door.

"The name is Joseph Edwin Dowling, and I've come to call on Lucy Cook," Edwin said, holding out his hand.

"Mother said in her letter you would be calling, but I didn't expect you so soon. Please come inside. Lucy will be home in a while. She's an operator at the cotton mill and won't get home till supper time. Come inside, come inside. I'm Ida."

"I met your mother, and she insisted I come. I was visiting my mother's grave at the family plots. She is a forceful woman, that Mary Maker."

Ida rolled her eyes as she walked inside and directed him to a kitchen table where a young girl sat peeling potatoes for dinner.

"This is little Ida; she's ten," said Ida, as she poured him a cup of coffee.

"My sister's name is Ida," said Edwin.

"Of course, she is," said Lucy's mother. "She is named after me, you know. I attended your parents' wedding when I was just five years old."

"It's a form of a name from old Ireland," said Edwin to little Ida. "It means to have a thirst for goodness or knowledge."

"Wow, I never heard that before," said the little Ida. "Do you want some butter on your bread?"

"Yes, please."

"Well, I don't know how much Irish I have in me," said Lucy's mother. "We Gardners all go back to England. A man in my ancestry by the name of Sir William Gardner is credited with killing King Richard III. It happened at the Battle of Bosworth during the War of the Roses. William was a commoner, and he knocked the king off his horse with a poleaxe and took his crown. They say King Henry Tudor knighted him on the battlefield. He went from a nobody to a prominent member of the house of Tudor. He even married Jasper

Tudor's * daughter. I think there were plenty of them Gardners who were loyal to the crown during the American Revolution. I have a bunch of relatives up in Gardner Lake. It's named after my great-grandfather, David Gardner. He and your great-grandfather, John, were terrific friends."

Edwin noticed that Ida didn't have any trouble taking control of a conversation; she went on for several minutes about their shared family history. But Edwin didn't mind. Ida was full of interesting genealogical tidbits. But when she shifted to the Revolutionary War era, he was particularly engaged.

"Oh, don't get me started on the Revolution! I could talk about it for ages! We had my great-grandfather's musket hanging over the mantle in our house all my childhood. My father handed it down to my brother Jake before he headed West." Edwin paused as he thought about that moment with a pang of foreboding, knowing how irresponsible Jake tended to be with things of that nature.

"Then you and my husband will get along just fine. He loves to talk about the Revolution."

Edwin took a large sip of coffee and they began to talk about his life in Gardner Lake.

"Oh, how I miss Gardner Lake. How is my mother? I mean, I receive letters, of course, but I haven't actually seen her in years."

"Seems to have a lot of spunk for her age," laughed Edwin. Ida chuckled and then turned to her youngest daughter.

"Run along now, Ida. Don't you have some studies?"

"Yes, Mama."

"Now tell me, Edwin," Ida said, pausing as she listened to her daughter's footsteps going up to her bedroom. "What are your intentions with my oldest daughter?"

---

*Jasper Tudor was the uncle of King Henry VII. William Gardner's son became a Bishop in the Catholic Church and was the Chaplain for Queen Elizabeth in the 1500s.

"I'm not sure of my intentions yet, Mrs. Gardener. I haven't seen her since your family left Gardner Lake when she was just a little girl. I came on account of your mother's insistence. I would like to meet Lucy and get to know her."

"I understand, but then tell me what your hopes and dreams are, lad."

"I've thought about going to Oregon and making a life there."

"Now, why would you dream of going so far away?" said Ida, making a frown.

"I'm a horseman and a logger, ma'am. Out there, the timber is virgin, and it stretches for a thousand miles. Jake, my brother who moved out there, says a man can make his fortune in Oregon."

"So, is it your intention to find a wife and move to Oregon?"

"One thing I know for sure, there isn't much logging left here in Massachusetts."

Ida nodded. "Not going to be much of anything here soon in Lowell. They're not even upgrading the cotton mills here; instead, they've built new ones in the south where heating the buildings is less necessary. Their cotton is grown locally. The mills here in Lowell are dying, and the whole industry is changing. The mill girls formed unions years ago, and the companies are finding in the southern states they don't have to fight the union wages."

"You paint a pretty dim picture for things here in Lowell."

"Oh, don't get me wrong," she said, back pedaling, knowing she had probably said the wrong thing to a boy who might marry her daughter. The last thing she wanted was for Lucy to move away. "Lowell is a wonderful city. I've been talking to our friend, Dan Gage; we call him Old Dan. He needs a good horseman, and of course, Mother wrote to him and told him you were coming."

Edwin fell silent, not knowing how to respond to having someone plan his life. He hadn't even seen Lucy yet. What if she wasn't the right girl for him?

"What time will Lucy get home from work?"

Just then, they heard footsteps at the front door.

"Mama, I'm home," came the voice of a young woman.

"In the kitchen, Lucy. I have a surprise for you."

"Surprise?" the voice said curiously as a bright-eyed, dark-haired girl came through the kitchen doorway. "Well, Joseph Dowling, if you are not a sight for sore eyes. Look at you–you are all grown up into a handsome man."

"No," said Edwin, standing. "Look at you; you have grown into a beautiful young woman!" Lucy wore a long, pink dress and lace-up boots with heels. She had her long, dark hair pinned in a bun, and her slender nose and high cheekbones made a striking image that nearly took his breath away.

"Well, you certainly know how to impress a lady," she laughed.

"He goes by Edwin now," said her mother.

"Okay, then, Edwin. What brings you to town? Are you here for the labor demonstrations?"

"I came all the way here because your grandmother insisted."

"Insisted for what reason?"

Edwin paused, searching for the words so as not to mess this up.

"She said she had a granddaughter she thought I might like to meet."

"You came all the way here just to meet my sister Ida, did you?" laughed Lucy, and Edwin broke out in a laugh along with her.

"It would be a shame to come all this way and not take you for dinner."

"Where are you staying?" asked Ida. Edwin lifted his eyebrows at her question.

"I guess I will have to make some arrangements to find a room."

"We have a spare room here. You are welcome to stay. The mill is open tomorrow, and Lucy will have to work. I will take you to meet Dan Gage. For now, Lucy, show him to the guest room."

"Where would you like to have dinner?" asked Edwin as he followed Lucy out of the room.

"Now, Lucy," Ida called after them, "take him to an affordable place. Heavens, the man spent all he had just getting here. You need to go easy on his pocketbook."

"Come on, Edwin," Lucy giggled. "I'll show you to your room, and I'll go freshen up."

As Edwin followed her, he could not believe his good fortune. Every minute of the journey had been worth it.

Chapter 2

The Horseman
and the City Girl

Edwin had his best clothes in his bag just for the occasion: heavy, brown corduroy pants, a white shirt cleaned and pressed by his sister, Bell, and a short-waist brown tweed jacket. He freshened up in the bowl of cold water left in the room, splashing it on his face and drying with the towel. Stepping up to the mirror on the dressing table, he used the brush lying near the bowl to straighten his hair. He felt glad that Bell had insisted she cut his hair and trim his mustache before he left home. He stepped back to admire himself, knowing he would never be any more presentable than this. He took a deep breath to clear away the butterflies, then turned for the door and headed for the parlor.

When he stepped into the room, an older man sat quietly in a chair as if he were waiting for Edwin. He had just taken a puff on his cigar, and Edwin took a pause while the man blew the smoke from his lips, then grabbed the arms of his chair to pull himself up.

"You must be Joseph?" he asked, reaching out his hand with a piercing stare, as if sizing him up. Edwin took his hand in a firm grip, not too hard so as a man might think of it as a challenge, but firm enough to let him know he meant business.

"It's Edwin, sir. I go by Edwin."

"You might have guessed I am Lucy's father, Simeon," he said, taking another long puff on his cigar. Warren knew Simeon to be about forty-five years old and, at almost thirty himself, they were pretty close in age. Simeon was a robust man, not fat by any means, but big-boned and a half head taller than Edwin. He wore his hair short and his face clean shaven. He dressed casually in dungarees and a gray hickory shirt, and had a glass of whiskey next to his chair.

"I hear you are a horseman."

"They say I have a knack for it."

"What is the most important thing about being a horseman?" Edwin knew a trick question when he heard one. He took a minute to formulate his best answer.

"It's about leadership, of course, but most importantly, it is about listening. You need to talk to your horse and communicate. They want to work for you, and they want to have a relationship with you. A good horseman needs to be a good listener; that is how you build trust and respect."

"That's a good answer," Simeon said, putting his finger to his chin. "All the same skills will do you well in a relationship." Simeon smiled, taking another puff. "Do you indulge?" he asked, holding up the cigar.

"I do, but when I start one, I like to finish it, and I believe your daughter will be down any minute."

"You don't know much about women, do you?" He belly laughed and handed Edwin the cigar, knowing Edwin would have plenty of time to finish. "Have a seat; would you like a glass of whiskey?" Edwin nodded eagerly, accepting the cigar Simeon took from his breast pocket. Simeon struck a match and held it so Edwin could get his going. Then he poured Edwin a shot of whiskey, handing him the small glass.

"Shall we drink to your health, and that my daughter will find you to her liking? Have a seat," he said as Edwin took a sip of the whiskey, then held up his shot glass and nodded to his newfound friend.

"Interesting that you would say that listening is the most important part of horse training. My name, Simeon, means 'God listens.' Are you a man of faith, Edwin?"

Edwin gulped whiskey before answering.

"I believe there is a God, but I am not so sure He listens to me. My mother died six years ago when I was twenty-three, and I am still having a hard time with God."

"I don't know what to tell you about that one. Life sure can sucker punch you. But having faith in something bigger than yourself always makes it a little easier."

The two men made small talk for another thirty minutes, talking horses, logging, and war.

"Did you fight in the Civil War?" asked Edwin.

"When war broke out in 1861, I was only fourteen years old. I waited patiently to get called up, and I never did. I told my parents I wanted to enlist when I was seventeen, but that was right after Gettysburg. With the numbers dead, my mother refused to let me go. Finally, when I was eighteen, the war ended. So, that was that; I never picked up a rifle."

"Probably a good thing. You might have gotten killed, and you wouldn't have a beautiful daughter. My father told me he wanted to go but my mother refused. He was too old for the draft, but he needed some adventure in his life. Besides his grandfather had fought in the revolution and he would be following his roots. But, I guess he listened to my mother."

Simeon nodded his approval and Edwin lifted his glass and took another sip. Just then, Lucy walked into the room with a shy smile. She had braids tied up on her head with tight little curls lying flat against her forehead, and small white flowers tied in. She wore a long, red dress with a high neck and puffed sleeves. Her brown eyes, thick dark brows, and long lashes filled Edwin's heart with a feeling he could not describe.

"My goodness," said Edwin. "You were more than worth the trip. You look beautiful."

"Do you like the dress?" asked Lucy, spinning a little. "Mama got the fabric from the neighbor and started sewing this winter, just for such an occasion. When we heard you were coming, Mama finished it. This is the first time I have worn it."

Edwin glanced at Simeon, and they made eye contact. Neither man said a word. The look from her father said it all: *Look, but don't touch*. All Edwin could do was nod.

"Let me get my shawl, and I'll be ready to go."

Edwin had smoked the cigar down to a nub, and he stood up, placing it in the ashtray*.

Lucy re-entered the room.

"We'll be back before dark," said Lucy as she grabbed the door handle and whisked Edwin out the doorway. Edwin could see she was a spirited one. Edwin didn't know much about women, but he knew about horses and thought this couldn't be much different. If Lucy had known his thoughts then, perhaps she would not have been so eager.

🌲🌲🌲

"C'mon, hurry up, and we can beat the trolley." Lucy took Edwin's hand, and his heart nearly skipped a beat. She held on to her wide-brimmed hat as they crossed the cobblestones, then stepped up to the sidewalk.

"I wanted to take you to the French restaurant, but Mama says it is too expensive," said Lucy as she led the way across town.

"I would have gone anywhere you wanted."

---

*It was common etiquette to never crush a cigar in an ashtray as it would give off an offensive odor; instead it was polite to place it in the ashtray and let it go out on its own gracefully.

"I know, but I'm taking you to Kilpatrick's. Papa knows Mr. Kilpatrick, and his restaurant is a good place for a date."

"Oh, then it's a place where a man can get acquainted with a lady."

Lucy looked back, and her cheeks turned pink as she batted her eyelashes. The walkway was a flurry of activity, with people walking every which way.

"For heavens' sake, how many people live in this place, anyway?" asked Edwin, holding on to Lucy's hand for dear life.

"Papa says the population is pushing eighty thousand."

"What?" exclaimed Edwin. "That's crazy."

"That's Lowell; they say it's the cradle of the industrial revolution."

Edwin could tell he was falling fast for this beautiful young woman. But her ease and love for the city made him pause. *Would she ever want to leave all this?*

"This is it, Kilpatrick's café. Papa said it's the best in town. Good thing we got here early; I think we beat the rush."

"Table for two," said Edwin, stepping up to the man behind the counter at the entrance and letting go of Lucy's hand. The restaurant sat tucked along a line of businesses like a hole in the wall. It had large picture windows on both sides of the entryway and the inside, where lots of folks were sitting around various-sized mixed and unmatched tables.

"Let me check; we are pretty busy," the man said, disappearing inside. Edwin looked at the bill of fare posted on the sandwich board to see the prices and the selections.

"What's good, Lucy?"

"The clam chowder is good. Papa always has the pork steak." Another man appeared, dressed in a dark suit coat with a yellowing white shirt and an open collar.

"Victor said he thought that was you, Lucy."

"Good evening, Mr. Kilpatrick," responded Lucy with a slightly self-conscious smile. Clearly coming to dinner at this restaurant, accompanied by a man, was not something she did regularly. "This is a friend of mine, Edwin Dowling from down east Maine."

"Good to meet you, sir. I will show you to your table; follow me. Where at down east? I have a sister in Bar Harbor."

"I'm from the same place Lucy was born—Gardner Lake in Whiting."

Edwin reached down and took Lucy's hand, guiding her across the busy establishment. He could feel the eyes of everyone watching him with the pretty young lady in the red dress.

"I hope this suits you. It's the last table in the place," said Mr. Kilpatrick, pulling out a chair for Lucy. "Say hello to your father for me. I haven't seen him in a week or so. I hope he is in good health."

"Yes, he is. Thank you."

"The waiter will be here shortly to take your order. It's good to see you, Lucy. You certainly look lovely. It seems like yesterday you were just a little girl." Mr. Kilpatrick winked at Edwin, then turned and walked toward the kitchen. Edwin could see how comfortable Lucy was in this town and he thought about how he could never fully let his guard down in a busy place like this.

"So, Edwin, Mama says your brother went west to Oregon. You're not thinking about going West, are you?"

"Maybe. What would you think about that?"

"It's a long ways away. I might think about it if I could take my mother and father with me."

Just then, the waiter came to the table with water glasses. "What are you going to have for supper, young lady?"

"I would like a bowl of the clam chowder."

"And for you, sir?"

"I would like the rib steak."

"Coming right up. I will get this order into the kitchen."

"You ordered the rib steak. That's thirty-five cents, you know, big spender," Lucy said slyly.

"I haven't eaten all day," Edwin replied, good-naturedly defending his appetite.

The waiter brought their drinks.

"All right then, Edwin, where do you see our first date going?"

Edwin smiled. "I don't rightly know. I guess I just respect your grandmother and aunty enough to pick up and come down here and get to know you."

"Was your trip worth it?" she chuckled.

"I already said it was. And I came all this way before I knew anything about that red dress," he laughed. "Let's drink to where this might go." Edwin picked up the glass of beer as Lucy picked up her water glass, and they tapped them together across the table. "I might just see if Dan Gage is looking for a horseman tomorrow."

A week later, Edwin found himself running a horse cart, delivering ice for the Dan Gage Ice Company. He found a place to stay in an apartment building in the city. His dinner with Lucy had gone well.

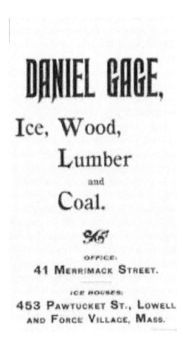

DANIEL GAGE,

Ice, Wood,
Lumber
and
Coal.

OFFICE:
41 MERRIMACK STREET.

ICE HOUSES:
**453 PAWTUCKET ST., LOWELL
AND FORCE VILLAGE, MASS.**

Chapter 3

Hopes and Dreams

The second week of May, Lucy made her way down the cotton mill's front steps after work one afternoon, and there she saw her mother waiting for her.

"This letter was in the box for Edwin," said Ida. "I got one from my mother as well. Edwin's father has died. You will need to take this to him."

"He's out delivering ice; how am I going to do that?"

"Go see Dan Gage. Edwin needs to read this immediately." Lucy took the letter from her mother's hand and started to turn to head down the street.

"He's going to take you away to Oregon, Lucy."

"Mama, we haven't even talked about marriage."

"Why can't you just find a nice young man here in Lowell? You could raise a family here, and we could all be happy together."

"Mama, Edwin needs me."

"What about Broadrick, that nice young boy from school? He wants to be a banker."

"Broadrick? Oh, Mama, his sister hates me."

"Lucy," said Ida as she closed her eyes and shook her head. "Run along now and take the letter."

Lucy walked the three blocks up town to 41 Merrimack Street, Dan Gage Ice Company's headquarters. She clutched the letter tightly so as not to lose it in the wind. A dark cloud toward the west spelled rain. She walked up the front steps and opened the heavy oak door with ornate glass.

"Good afternoon, Lucy," said the receptionist, Mabel. She was what they all called a "spinster," and had worked with Lucy in the cotton mill the year before.

"Are you here for Mr. Gage?" Mabel asked, looking over her glasses. She had her hair piled on top of her head in the latest style and wore a high-collar dress.

"Yes, ma'am," Lucy answered.

"I will tell him you are here." Mabel got out of her chair and walked toward the big office on the main floor. "How's things going at work?" she inquired, stopping at the closed door and looking over her shoulder.

"Nothing much has changed. But remember that girl they call Fancy? She got married to some man up in Wisconsin."

"I bet the place is much quieter now that she is gone," laughed Mabel, opening the office door. "Miss Lucy Cook is here to see you, sir."

"Lucy, oh for heavens' sake," exclaimed Old Dan. "By all means, tell her to come in!"

"He will see you," said Mabel with a smile. Lucy approached the office, and Old Dan met her at the doorway.

"What can I do for you, Lucy? My lands, dear. Have I ever told you how much you remind me of my Alice?"

Lucy smiled. Old Dan's daughter had passed away a few years before from consumption.

"She was just a bit older than you, but my goodness, your mannerisms and your look. Sometimes I have to take a second look. What brings you to my office, dear?"

"I have a letter for Edwin." Lucy held the letter up so he could see it.

"Is it important?"

"Mama said his father has passed, and it can't wait."

"Edwin said his father has been failing."

"Mabel," said Old Dan as the receptionist poked her head back in the doorway. "Find out what route Edwin Dowling is on. I'm going to take Lucy in my carriage so she can deliver a letter."

"Yes, sir, and I will notify the teamster to get your buggy ready."

"He's on Route 17, Mr. Gage," said Mabel as Old Dan grabbed his coat.

He helped Lucy step up into the carriage's front seat and take her seat as the teamster made the carriage horse ready. Then Old Dan pulled himself on board, sat down next to her, and grabbed for the reigns.

"I put the canvas up; it looks like rain. You can take her away now, sir," said the teamster, backing away from the mare.

Old Dan slapped the reigns, and the horse pulled the buggy out of the yard. The old mare's feet clip-clopped on the cobblestones as they came up Merrimack Street and headed toward the ice house on Pawtucket Street, along the Merrimack River. They passed under the old stone Pawtucket Bridge on Moody Street. Lucy pulled the heavy woolen coat around her neck as the wind picked up along the river, and the horse made her way to Pawtucketville on the other side.

"When they built this bridge, they called it an engineering marvel," said Old Dan, breaking the silence. Lucy nodded, but the wind and the knowledge of the bad news she was bringing to Edwin kept her silent.

"He's a good man, Lucy. I don't know when I have been so taken by a lad such as Edwin. Are you considering marriage?"

"Heavens, he's only been in town for a month. But now that his father has passed, I don't know what he will do. I suppose he will go home. The only thing he has here to hold him is you and this job, and, hopefully, me." Lucy's cheeks turned pink at the thought. "But, Mama thinks I should marry a banker or a lawyer."

"You could do a lot worse than a man with a work ethic like Edwin. He's got something special. He could go a long way. Have you seen him with horses?"

"No, sir."

"I've watched him. He has a sixth sense when it comes to them. It's almost like he can talk to horses. A man like that could run my company. Keep your eye out; he's got to be at the end of the route. It will be dark soon enough. I have one place to check first, and if we don't find him, then we'll just head back to the ice house and wait for him there."

"There he is," Lucy said, spotting the cart up the street. Dan gave the horse a little encouragement and trotted her up the block. Edwin spotted them coming down the road as he walked off the front porch of a house.

"This is a surprise," exclaimed Edwin. "To what do I owe this pleasure?"

"A letter came for you," said Lucy. "It's urgent."

"Urgent enough to bring the boss man?"

"I didn't know what else to do, Edwin. Here it is." Lucy held the letter out as Edwin pulled off his heavy leather gloves and took it from her.

"It's from Bell," he said, looking up. He tore the letter open, unfolding the single page then pausing as he read the words.

"My Pa has died."

Edwin was silent for a moment as he tried to hide his emotions. Then, seeming to come to a resolve, he looked up at Lucy.

"You are quite the gal, you know. Nobody has ever cared enough about me in this life like you, except maybe my Mama. I would be a fool if I didn't spend the rest of my days with you."

"What are you saying, Edwin?" Lucy asked, knowing full well what he meant.

"I guess I am asking if you would be my wife."

"Just like that? Aren't you supposed to get on your knee?"

"Well, I've never done this before. I just figured since you were up there sitting high in that buggy, if I took a knee, I would have to shout, and that didn't seem right either."

Lucy reached out her hand, and Edwin helped her to the ground.

"Okay, then, now I can do it properly if you like."

"That won't be necessary. You don't have to ask me twice, Edwin Dowling. You had me the first time."

Lucy put her arms around his neck, and he planted a kiss on her lips. Just then, Dan cleared his throat.

"I suppose you will be riding back with him?" chuckled Dan. "It seems to me that some days are full of the worst of news and the best of news. I am honored to be a part of it all. Maybe you'll make me your best man, eh?"

"Would you really, sir?" asked Edwin in all seriousness.

"Look, I never had a son, and you don't have a father now, for that I offer my sincere condolences. But, just a word of fatherly advice. Before you go making marriage plans, you might want to ask Simeon for her hand first."

"That won't be a problem," said Lucy with a wide grin. "My father loves Edwin. Their great-grandfathers both fought in the Revolution, they love horses, and they love cigars even more. It's a match made in heaven." Edwin knew she was right about her family, but her mother might take a bit more convincing.

⇞⇞⇞

A year and a half later, on September 2nd, 1892, the day came for Edwin and Lucy to be married. Pastor Alexander Blackburn presided at the First Baptist Church in Lowell, Massachusetts. Lucy wore a long, white dress with puffed sleeves and a red collar, with a matching red bow tied up in her hair.

"What about the corset?" asked her mother. "How tight do you want it?"

Lucy paused a moment before answering. "You know, don't you, Mama?"

"Oh yes, I can see it in a woman's eyes when she is with child. I don't think we should tie the corset too tight."

Louisa sighed. "Okay, you know best. I know we need to be discreet. I wouldn't want our guests to notice. You know how people love a scandal and how women talk over a cup of tea." Lucy looked anxious as she waited for her mother's response.

"How long have you known, child?"

"A few weeks. I think I am about two months along."

"I wish you could have waited until after the wedding."

"I know; me too. But what is done is done, and we will make the best of it. Right, Mama?"

"Yes, we will, but it won't make me feel any better about that scoundrel you are marrying today."

"That scoundrel is the father of your grandchild. Look, I know he is no prince, but I have no choice. It is either this or marry some man who makes me sick. Being with child is just a little insurance that a man will go along with the wedding plans and not get cold feet. He would be seen as a real true scoundrel by other men if he were to walk away from a woman he made pregnant."

Ida buttoned up the last buttons on the back of Lucy's dress, then spun her around to look at the final product and take the creases out with her palms.

"What will you do after the child is born and folks start counting their fingers?"

"I will just tell everyone the baby came early."

"Women will know just by looking that the child is full term."

"I guess I will cross that bridge when I come to it."

Just then, they heard the sound of a knock at the door, and it creaked open slowly. There stood her father at the doorway.

"It's time to walk, little girl. Are you ready?" Ida fussed with the ribbon in Lucy's hair to make it look perfect. Simeon took her hand as he escorted her out to the foyer. The pews were sparse but enough folks to make things appear as if there were a crowd. Lucy could feel her heart pounding, and her hands trembled as she took her father's arm. At the altar stood the Reverend Blackburn between Edwin and his best man, Old Dan Gage. On his left was Edwin's sister, Allie Bell, whom everyone called "Bell," and Lucy's best friend, Sarah.

The wedding march began to play on the organ, and her father began leading her down the aisle. To Lucy, the scene felt surreal. She wanted to remember everything from this day, but it felt like the day was slipping by like a muddy slope down a ravine in heavy rain.

The music stopped, and the Reverend asked her father if he gave his daughter to be married.* Acknowledging this, Simeon handed off his daughter to Edwin. His little girl, in the snap of a finger, was now another's man's responsibility. He knew he would still see her, but it was hard not to feel as if she was lost to him forever.

Within twenty minutes, Lucy and Edwin found themselves in the crowd of friends who wished them well. Lucy knew what this meant for her. If she had had any dreams of her own, she had now just given them away to a man with his own hopes and dreams, and her life would now be in his hands.

⚹⚹⚹

The couple had one month together before Edwin had to leave for a long winter in Maine, working in the logging camp where he dragged logs from the woods with his team of horses. Lucy took him to the train

---

*It wasn't until recently that fathers began the tradition of saying, "Her mother and I," in response to the officiant's question, "Who gives this woman to be married . . . ?" when a daughter was married. By practice dating back hundreds of years, a daughter was the father's property, and marriages were arranged and paid for by the groom to elevate the father's status. The origin of the word "wedding" has its roots in the German word, *Wette*, meaning to make a bet or a wager.

station in her father's carriage to say her goodbyes. A light rain fell as she huddled under the carriage awning to stay dry.

"I certainly hope this isn't going to be a sign of our life together," said Lucy, wrinkling her brow as she spoke. "Me with our children in one town, and you working in the woods and living in a logging camp far away for months on end."

"Lots of men do this, Lucy. My job is to provide for you and our family, and I will do what I have to, to keep a roof over your head."

"There must be plenty of jobs here in Lowell."

"For heaven's sake, Luce, we have been over this a hundred times. Let's not plow this field all over again. The days go quickly, and it will be springtime before you know it, and I will be home in time for our first child to be born."

"I will put on a good face just for you. But you have to promise to answer my letters."

"I promise to write you on Sundays–every Sunday," he said begrudgingly, knowing he had made a promise he was not sure he could fulfill.

"I'm not getting out of the carriage. So kiss me goodbye right here," she said, as she could see the train depot up ahead. Edwin leaned over and planted a kiss on her lips that would have to last all winter.

"Edwin, you make me crazy. I know we have been over this a hundred times, but I will say it one more time for the record. I wish you didn't have to go." Edwin climbed out of the carriage and grabbed his duffle bag, putting it over his shoulder.

"I love you . . . take care now."

Edwin tipped his hat and turned, walking away down the cobblestone street toward the depot. Lucy sat there for a few minutes, watching as he walked away into the hustle and bustle of Lowell. Lucy saw couples walking arm in arm and carriages coming to and fro. She heard men shouting at their horses, and a boy hocking newspapers shouted from the street corner. Lucy smelled the aroma from the food vendors serving hot meals from pushcarts mixed with the familiar fragrance of horse manure from a man scooping a fresh pile in the street. She kept her composure as she watched Edwin disappear through the grand depot entry. She sat frozen in time just for a few moments with hope above all hope he would come running out of the station with a change of heart—but to no avail. She slapped the reins and turned the carriage around in the street without looking back.

The following spring, after a winter of her longing and waiting with eager anticipation for Edwin's Sunday letters to arrive, the day approached for his return.

"It has been a long cold winter without him."

Lucy knew not to complain to her mother, but some days she couldn't help it. Despite Lucy's fond praise of Edwin, Ida had never grown soft on the man. His ever-present dream of taking her daughter West made her nervous. While she felt terrible for her daughter, being separated from her husband these long months, she was glad to have her still close.

"Well, at least you know he loves you dearly; look at all these letters!" Ida attempted to straighten Lucy's stack of letters that sat on the mantel.

"There's not much else to do when you're pregnant and jobless."

"I still can't believe they fired you at the cotton mill just because you got married."

"If they hadn't fired me for that, they certainly would have fired me by now in my condition. We do live in a man's world, don't we?"

"That is true, but remember it wasn't all sunshine and roses at the mill. I remember many a day when you would come home with hair-raising stories."

"Yes," said Lucy with a shudder. "Pinched fingers are the most common. But I've seen even more serious things from operators with long hair. We were supposed to wear it up, but I saw a girl get tangled in the warp and had her scalp pulled away. It was awful. The mill's noise is so loud from hundreds of looms on the floor, you couldn't hear screams for help. I had friends at the mill, but it was also pretty cutthroat. It was easy to get another woman fired; all they had to do was start a rumor. Two sure things get you fired: getting married without being pregnant, or getting pregnant without being married."

"That's so unfair; men don't have to worry about getting fired just because they get married or have a crush on a girl."

"I knew a girl once who got fired just because she got caught kissing a boy in the alley." Lucy sighed. She may not have missed her days in the mill, but she did miss her husband. With her baby on the way and Dan Gage counting on Edwin to help deliver ice in the summer, she knew Edwin would be home soon.

"Do you think Edwin will go West to be with his brother?" asked Ida.

"Oh Lord, I hope not. I'm going to do everything I can to nurture our friendship with Dan Gage and see if Edwin can work with him. Old Dan treats Edwin like a son."

Edwin returned home from the logging camps just before Lucy gave birth to a healthy boy, whom they named Warren. In fulfillment of Lucy's hopes, Edwin began working for Dan Gage, and he and Lucy settled into the city. Old Dan began to count on Edwin more and more and, after a few years, Edwin was running all the teamsters and deliveries.

Chapter 4

Gold Fever

In the winter of 1897, news reached the East Coast about the gold strike on the Klondike in the Yukon Territory. In the spring, Edwin received a letter from his brother, and opened it in his kitchen.

"What is it?" asked Lucy, holding their young daughter Etta, now eighteen months old, on her hip. Warren, four, was playing with a miniature on the floor nearby.

"Jake has connections . . ." Edwin mumbled, skimming through the letter.

"What sort of connections?"

"The gold rush in the Klondike." Edwin put the letter on the table. "He wants me to join him."

Lucy turned white, and her mouth dropped.

"You are not serious."

"This is our chance, Lucy, don't you see?"

"Our chance for disaster. You're not seriously thinking of going, are you?"

"Of course I am. It's my brother, and he needs me."

"What he needs is a good psychiatrist."

"What we need is to strike it rich, and Jake has done all the leg work."

"So you are going to take our whole life savings and put it on a roulette wheel."

"It's not a gamble. Jake knows the people, and it is almost a sure thing. "

"No, Edwin. You are even considering this? What about our family?" Lucy stomped her foot in anger. But Edwin stood, resolved. Lucy turned her back on him, fuming. She already knew it was a lost cause. Once his mind was made up, he was as stubborn as a mule. Nothing, not her or their children, could change his mind.

"How much is it going to cost us?"

"Don't worry about that. When I get back from the Yukon, I'm going to buy you a house so big you'll get lost in it." Lucy did not respond to his attempts to placate her.

"How long will you be gone?"

"Not sure, but I'll write you when I find out."

"When will you leave?"

"Just as soon as I am done with Old Dan this fall, and I feel like he is in a position to let me go."

"What about the gang up in West Fork at the logging camp? They will need you to run the team this winter."

"They'll have to get along without me. I'll be in the goldfields with Jake."

Lucy gritted her teeth and pulled her daughter closer. "There is no stopping you, is there?"

In the weeks that followed, Edwin made plans to leave in early November, 1897. When the time came, the family gathered at the train station to say their goodbyes. Lucy held Etta in her arms and Warren by the hand.

"I wish I could be happy for you," said Lucy with a heavy heart.

"When you all see me again, I'll be wearing fine clothes and a top hat." Edwin turned to Lucy and took their small daughter from her arms. "This will be worth it, I promise. I will buy you as fine a house as you deserve."

People around them were bidding friends and family final farewell as they boarded the train.

"You were smart to buy this heavy Mackinaw jacket here," said Simeon, grabbing Edwin's shoulder. "It would have cost you twice as much in Seattle."

Edwin looked over Simeon's shoulder, and his eyes brightened as he spotted Dan Gage making his way down the platform.

"Over here, Dan!" shouted Edwin, and Old Dan acknowledged him with a wave.

"I only have a few minutes, but I wanted to see you off," he said, out of breath as he approached and extending his hand with a wide grin.

"I won't forget our bargain and our handshake," said Edwin.

"Make me proud with the thousand dollars I invested in this venture. You hear me? My forty and your sixty, but that's not why I came, Edwin. You are like a son to me. I'll see you when you get back, and I'll carve out that place for you in my company. And don't worry about your family. I'll look after them while you are gone." Old Dan looked at Lucy and smiled.

"If my Papa wasn't here, I might say you were like a papa to me," laughed Lucy, looking at Simeon for approval.

"All aboard!" shouted the smartly dressed conductor from the lead coach near the engine. The locomotive began to spew smoke as the fires were stoked to build up steam.

"I hope this gets the West out of your system," said Ida, as she raised her eyebrows, clearly communicating her disapproval.

"I'll be home quick as I can, my love," Edwin whispered to Lucy, handing back young Etta to her waiting arms. He turned and shook his son's hand and gave his daughter one last kiss on the forehead. Lucy hugged him again and whispered in his ear.

"I'm probably going to be having a baby by next spring, so get home quick just as soon as you strike it rich."

"You better get on the train," said Simeon.

Edwin grabbed the handrail and pulled himself up in the coach as the train lurched forward and began to move. The smell of coal smoke filled the air, and the piercing roar of the steam pistons pounded their eardrums.

Lucy stood with a pit in her stomach, wondering if she would ever see him again. She thought how cold and inhospitable the Yukon Territory could be. A shiver overcame her at the thought of her husband trekking in that frozen land. She couldn't believe Edwin was leaving her again and once again she would go through a pregnancy alone. He was always leaving. First, to work at the logging camps most of the year and now all the way across the country. He had never even asked once if Lucy would like to join him.

Lucy watched the train as it lurched forward, the couplings thundering down the line like a base drum roll. She stood in quiet desperation, clutching her two-year-old daughter on her hip and hanging on to her four-year-old son by the hand, tears rolling down her cheeks.

"What will become of us, Mama, if he doesn't come back?" said Lucy. Ida held her tongue, nearly biting a hole in her cheek. Ida couldn't say what she thought about Edwin's selfish decision to chase some stupid dream, drain his bank account, and leave his family for a veritable roll of the dice at the crap table.

"This is just the beginning, dear heart," said Ida. "Mark my words. That man will get a taste of the West, and if he comes back at all, he will take you and my babies with him next time."

"Gotta run, Lucy," said Old Dan, tipping his hat. "If you need anything, just come see me." Lucy forced a smile and wiped another tear off her face with her gloved hand.

"C'mon," said Simeon, "Let's go home." Lucy glanced one more time down the long narrow track to see the last train car disappear around the bend, leaving a hole in her stomach.

Despite Lucy's hopes, the letters from Edwin we sparse over the next year. Of course, Lucy didn't expect to get much correspondence from him while he was off in the Canadian territories searching for his dream, but she had hoped for more. She had also once dreamed that he would return as a wealthy man, but from the increasing vagueness in his letters, she was almost certain he had lost everything.

"Have you thought about what you will say to him if he ever gets off the train, my dear?" asked Ida as the two women stood in the kitchen one late morning in the fall of 1898.

"That I love him, and I am glad he is home."

"I would be giving him a piece of my mind if I were you," said Ida, as her cheeks turned red and she began to tap her toe.

"That would be a great idea if I wanted to lose him forever, Mama. My guess is he's coming home like a dog with his tail between his legs. I suspect he has lost everything. He all but said it in his last letter. This is no time to beat a dead horse, but a time to nurture and support him. There are many challenges ahead for our family, but as the father of my children, I have chosen to love and support him."

"You have a strong love inside you, my dear."

"Oh, Mama, I learned it from you."

"I know, but sometimes my anger gets the best of me."

"I am angry, Mama, but there is nothing I can do now. Edwin is my husband, and I have to choose to love and support him. And you, Mama, you are his mama too. He doesn't have another one. Please love him like I do. He is not perfect, but he needs love right now."

"I don't know why he couldn't just tell you in the letter about what happened." Lucy shrugged her shoulders with no response. She finished washing the dishes and hung up her apron. Making her way to the table with a cup of coffee, she continued, "I know Dan will take him back as a driver. He doesn't care about the money; he will just be happy to get Edwin back. I hope nothing ever happens to Old Dan because his daughter Martha has always been resentful. I just know she doesn't want Edwin working with her father and the possibility of getting it all when Old Dan dies. Old Dan has taken Edwin and me under his wing; he has told me often I remind him of his other daughter that passed, which I think makes Martha jealous."

"There ain't nothing you can do about that," said Ida.

"I know. But if Edwin loses his job at the ice company, just as sure as I am standing here, there will be nothing to hold him here in Lowell."

Just then, she heard the front door squeak the familiar sound when it opened.

"Did someone just come in the front door?" asked Lucy sharply, looking up from the table. "I'll go check; maybe the wind blew it open." She jumped up from the chair and headed for the hallway, and then shrieked at the sight.

"Edwin, it's you!"

Edwin stood there with a wide grin and threw his arms around her.

"You came home early. Why didn't you write me?" she exclaimed, backing away to get a look at him.

"It was last minute; besides, the mail goes on the train, and if I wrote to you, the letter wouldn't arrive for a few more days."

"You must be famished. Come sit down; we just brewed a fresh pot of coffee." Lucy pulled a chair out, and Ida poured him a cup of coffee.

"Can I get you something to eat? We just had lunch," said Ida.

"Oh, no, coffee is fine. I had a big breakfast."

"You certainly have some explaining to do," said Ida putting her hands on her hips.

"Mama, can you give us some time alone?" Ida tightened her lip then nodded her reluctant approval.

"It is good to have you back," said Ida begrudgingly, heading for the hallway.

Lucy waited for her mother's footsteps to disappear, then pulled a chair out next to Edwin and sat in it, waiting for him to speak.

"What can I say, Luce, that you don't already suspect?"

"You must have an explanation, Edwin. What happened?"

"It's such a long story, I'm not sure how to start," he said tiredly, putting his elbows on the table and cradling his cheeks in his palms.

"Maybe this isn't the time," said Lucy.

"No time like the present, I suppose." Edwin paused, taking a deep breath. "Jake said he met these boys in Oregon, all his letters were so certain, it all seemed so legitimate. It's a long train ride across the country, and when I arrived in that little town, Mayger, in Oregon, there wasn't nearly time to breathe before we left for Seattle. Our spirits were high—we were like a couple schoolboys on vacation. It seemed like the adventure of a lifetime." The words were spilling out of Edwin. He seemed to Lucy like a guilty child trying to explain himself to a parent.

"Those two blokes met us in Seattle at the station, just as planned— Harvey Smith and Jason Snodgrass. Everything seemed to go like clockwork. We paid them the money and visited the boat at the docks. We were set to go for the following morning at daylight. We got a room, and I don't think either of us slept a wink from the excitement. We were up early and all packed and ready to go. We made our way to the dock, and the boat was gone."

Edwin let out a sigh and Lucy remained silent.

"I knew immediately we had been swindled like a couple of suckers. It took Jake a bit longer to admit it. I called on the authorities, but they just rolled their eyes. The constable said, unless we had some other proof, there was nothing they could do. He said that Harvey and Jason probably weren't even their real names. He said many folks were being tricked and cheated, and the merchants were the biggest culprits. He asked me if I thought the police should arrest all the merchants in Seattle, then laughed in my face."

"You should have written me and told me."

"I wanted to tell you face to face. I was so ashamed. I lost all the money Old Dan Gage gave me and . . . all of our savings. I would have felt better if at least we had made it to the Yukon." He began to cry. "All our savings, Lucy, they are all gone."

"There is nothing we can do now. It will have to be okay, you will see. I know Dan has been waiting for you, and I am sure he will take you back."

☖ ☖ ☖

On August 24th, 1900, Louisa Marion Dowling came into the world. Now the Dowlings had four children: two boys and two girls. Just as Lucy had predicted, Old Dan welcomed Edwin back with open arms and forgiveness. He offered him a job again delivering ice for his company. That February of 1901, however, Old Dan Gage passed away*. He caught pneumonia and died a week later. A day after the funeral, Dan's daughter Martina called Edwin into her new office on 41 Merrimack Street.

"Thank you for coming on such short notice," she said primly, as her secretary escorted him. Edwin had been in Dan's office many times before and had always admired the stately room with its large oak desk, matching chair, and red-padded cushion. The room still smelled of the old man's cigar smoke. He had never been in the office when he wasn't invited to smoke Dan's favorite cigar. He could see the Merrimack River and the Boot Cotton Mill in the distance through the large picture window. Martina stood up behind the desk and reached out her

---

*Daniel Gage was born in 1828 and died in February 9, 1901 of pneumonia at age seventy-two. His wife, Abiah Smith Hobbs, joined him in death seven years later at age eighty-two. They had two daughters, Martina Abiah Born in 1862, and Alice Lilian born in 1868 who died at the age of fifteen in 1883 of tuberculosis.

hand in a polite gesture. Edwin tried to read her eyes, wondering if she would be presenting him with the signed will.

"I know that you and my father had a special relationship. He always talked about you as the son he never had."

"I have always considered him as a father as well." Edwin took a gulp, unsure of the conversation's direction, but the tone didn't seem good.

"As you are probably aware, the daily operations of this enterprise has fallen on my shoulders. I know my father took a risk on you some years back in some random gold venture that ended in a disaster for you and your family. I know that was of great disappointment to him and to me."

"I was always grateful that he never held that against me." Edwin paused for a moment.

"I want you to know that your name does not exist in any legal form in any of my father's papers. Apparently, his relationship with you was nothing more than that of an employee. The reason I have called you in today is to let you know how pleased we are here at the Daniel Gage Ice Company for your diligent work for my father. But I regret to inform you that after today, I won't be needing your services here any longer."

"Just like that, Martina? Don't you know that we have four children?"

"Of course, I know you have children. There are many people in this town who have children, and lots of people in this town don't have jobs. You may soon be one of them if you don't find employment somewhere else."

"Your father would not be happy right now."

Edwin turned and walked out of the office, not giving Martina the satisfaction of having the final word. He could feel the anger boiling up like a volcano in his chest as he walked out the front doors onto the red bricks of Merrimack Street.

Edwin made his way back to the stable where his horse and his cart had been put away for the day. He didn't care if he never saw Martina again, but he couldn't bear to say goodbye to his horse. Molly had been a company horse since she was two years old and had been Edwin's partner for five seasons. She felt like a comfortable pair of slippers, and the two of them knew and trusted one another. He stood in front of the horse, caressing her nose.

"Goodbye, sweet girl; we have been an incredible team together. I know you won't understand, but I have to go away and leave you now. I won't be back in the morning to spend the day with you."

Edwin could feel the wet tear coming down his cheek, and his heart ached. He wiped his face with his sleeve and hoped in some small way Molly might understand. Her big round eyes looked into his with the unconditional love they shared. He patted her on the cheekbone, then turned to walk away toward the doorway. Molly gave out a loud whinny that echoed through the large stable, as if to say goodbye on her own. Edwin knew horses like the back of his hand and recognized the whinny as a sign of separation anxiety. He stopped and looked back.

"It will be okay, girl; you will be just fine." His words were more of assurance for himself than they were for her as he turned and walked out the wide double doors hearing her nickers as he went.

⇞⇞⇞

That evening, after the children had gone to bed, Edwin talked to Lucy.

"I had a discussion with Martina this morning," said Edwin.

"Are you out of a job?"

"Yes."

"I could see this coming," huffed Lucy. "I swear that woman has always been jealous of both you and me. Old Dan would be furious."

"What will we do?"

Lucy closed her eyes and bit her lip. "We will just pray and let God work out the details." Edwin didn't respond. He had lost everything once before and didn't trust that prayer would help them now any more than it did then.

"I'll write to Jake and see if he has work out West."

"You will do nothing of the sort," Lucy almost yelled.

"Lucy, then I suppose you would have me go to work in the cotton mill?"

"There have got to be more jobs around here for a horseman."

"Oh, yes, but not at the rate Old Dan was paying me. If you want me to make that kind of money, I'll need to head West. Jake already said a bloke can make a whole dollar a day more out there."

"You know I can't do that to my mother. It would kill her to take these children away. And Papa, too; I just won't do it." The argument was getting heated.

"You have to understand the logging industry. It's changing right in front of our eyes. Steam power is about to change the world. The trees are disappearing year by year. These forests are thousands of years old, and once they are gone, they're gone. The trees won't return in our lifetime."

"I thought you might have gotten a belly full of being gone so long when you went on that gold adventure. But, it only seems like it made things worse," Lucy's voice rose as she talked. "Edwin, I am a city girl; you knew that when you married me, and a mama's girl too. I just won't do it, Edwin. I just can't go West with you and leave my family."

"You don't understand, Lucy," said Edwin, putting his foot down. "I'm afraid we don't have any other choice but to head West. As the head of this household, that is my decision. I hope you feel you can support me in this. I'm going West, Lucy. Maybe not this year or next year, but mark my words, we are going West, and you and the children are going with me."

Lucy ran out of the kitchen and slammed the door behind her. Edwin had an urge to go after her, but stayed where he was.

Chapter 5

Five Years Later

On Tuesday morning, May, 15th, 1906, Edwin and five-year-old Louisa got ready to leave for Oregon. The family loaded everybody up into the family carriage, all except baby Edith, to whom Lucy had given birth in April. Lucy left her at home with her sister, Ida. Edwin's sister, Bell, had come from Machias to say goodbye, knowing she may never see her brother again.

With everyone loaded up and squeezed in, Edwin made a clicking noise to get Molly going.

"This time, you will have to say goodbye to Molly for good," said Simeon.

"She's in good hands with you, Pa. I'm just thankful that no one they brought in at the ice company could handle her. I guess Martina must have felt guilty for giving me the boot. It turns out Molly was my retirement gift."

Lucy sat with Louisa on her lap, holding her daughter tightly.

"Edwin," said Lucy in a stern voice, "You have to watch over this little pumpkin like a hawk."

"Now, Lucy, don't go a harpin' on me. I won't let her out of my sight; you know that."

"I know that; you know that," said Lucy in a stern voice, "But does Louisa know that?"

"I'll keep my eye on her," said Edwin. "How many times do we have to go over that?"

"It's dangerous out there. There are Indians and gunfighters too," said Ida.

"No, Mother," said Edwin, "The Northwest is tamed now. It's 1906 and all civilized."

"I still don't see why you have to go and take all my children with you," Ida said. "You know that's going to be the death of me."

The family piled out of the buggy while Edwin tied it to the curb. Lucy watched Edwin with Molly as he stroked the mare on the cheek and talked to her softly. He pulled a carrot out of his pocket and put it under her nose, and she crunched it in her teeth.

"I will miss you terribly," said Lucy as he turned his attention away from the mare. "I hate being apart. I just don't seem to do so good when you are gone."

"It's just for a few months," he answered. "Time always passes quickly."

"For you," said Lucy. "Just please be careful, you have a child with you this time."

"It's not dangerous, my love," said Edwin.

"I know men are dying in those camps, but you never tell me. I see it in the papers, you know. Besides, you have told me about those loads you tote. What happens if a cable breaks and that whole load comes down?"

"Now, don't go worrying about me," he said. "What am I going to do with you? You know I know horses better than most. I know how to run those teams. The only thing I know better than horses is you, darling. No matter what I would do, you would worry. If I were a ship captain, you would worry I might drown; if I were a banker, you would be afraid I might get shot in a bank holdup," Edwin laughed.

"Okay, so you have me pegged," said Lucy. "I am a worrier." Lucy looked at Edwin with a forced smile and sadness in her brown eyes. They hustled into the station, and Edwin showed his tickets.

"This train leaves for Chicago in twenty minutes, sir," said the porter. "Folks been boarding carriages for the last hour or so. Go make your way to the east platform and find Coach 10. Are you going to keep that travel bag with you, sir?"

"Yes, I'll keep this with me on the train," Edwin answered.

They followed his instructions and fell in with the crowd as they made their way to the carriage.

"There, that's Coach 10," said Ida. Edwin handed his traveling bag to a porter who was getting on the train, and the man said he would place the bag on Edwin's seat. The locomotive whistled, and someone called out, "All aboard!"

Up and down the line, passengers were making their way to the rail cars, and families were bidding their loved ones a final goodbye. Lucy looked back at her mother, standing behind her, holding Louisa tightly in her arms, then she turned around to Edwin.

"Now give me a kiss goodbye," he said. "One good enough to last six months." Lucy melted in his arms, and began to cry. The hug lingered as they made their goodbyes, remembering the goodbyes they had made the night before.

"I'll take her now, Mother," said Edwin pulling away and reaching for Louisa. He lifted her into his arms.

"Mama, I will miss you all day," said little Louisa. Lucy kissed her on the cheek, then wiped the tears away from her face with her sleeve.

"Don't cry, Mama."

"Take good care of Luce, sir," said Edwin as he extended his hand to his father-in-law.

"I'll have a smoke for you, son," he said. "Hope to see you again one day."

"I love you, Papa," said eleven-year-old Etta in a broken voice, trying to control her crying. She threw her arms around Edwin, and he struggled to hold Louisa while Etta clung to his waist.

"We will see you in the fall," he said as he shook the hands of his two sons, thirteen-year-old Warren and seven-year-old Loring. He rubbed the top of Loring's head, fluffing his hair. "Obey your mama now, boys."

Edwin turned and lifted his little girl onto the train, setting her on the top step, then grabbed the handrail to hoist himself aboard. He stopped and turned back, realizing he had forgotten to bid goodbye to his mother-in-law.

"Mother," said Edwin, "I will take good care of them in Oregon. You know I will. You take care now, hear? We will look forward to you and Pa coming out soon."

"Goodbye, Edwin," she said with a stiffness that seemed to melt to a caring softness as they looked into each other's eyes. Then she nodded, giving Edwin the approval he had sought from her for sixteen years.

"We will all miss you, Edwin."

"Oh wait, Edwin," said Lucy, "don't forget the cake." Lucy took it from Warren, who had been patiently holding it as each bid Edwin their goodbye, and handed it over to her husband.

"Don't worry, Mama; I will take good care of Papa," said Louisa from the top step, waving her hand. Just then, the train whistle blew, and the locomotive let go a massive puff of steam. The black smoke from the stack came down on the crowd, and everyone held their nose from the smell of burning coal. The cars lurched forward, causing the couplings to clank from the front clear to the back. Both the train and ground shook.

Edwin grabbed a handrail as the carriage began to move. Bell and Etta cried and embraced each other. Lucy could hear her mother crying behind her, and she turned back and placed her hand on her mother's shoulder, knowing her tears were for Louisa. Lucy began to sob as reality set in. Simeon tried to comfort the boys, who stood in shock as the train moved slowly down the tracks. Though the boys fought to remain stoic, small tears ran down both of their cheeks.

The train left the station, and they stood watching and waving as it rumbled out of the yard, vanishing out of sight in a cloud of smoke.

"We best get back to the baby," said Ida.

🌲🌲🌲

"You know why he took Louisa, don't you?" asked Ida, making a frown.

"To make it easier on me when I travel next fall with one less child," said Lucy.

"If that's what you want to think," retorted Ida. Ida knew well that if Lucy changed her mind about going now, Edwin had an ace in the hole.

"What are you saying, Mother?"

"Louisa is the funny one; she always brightens our day. Edwin knew how much you would miss her. He knew you would move heaven and earth to travel West to be reunited."

Ida shook her head. She had always known that if Lucy married Edwin, he would one day take her grandchildren away to the Wild West, where she might never see any of them again.

"Why did he have to go?" asked Etta.

Lucy hesitated to go into all the details with an eleven-year-old. Still, she felt she needed her children to understand.

"Men like your Papa make a good living working in the woods, especially out West where there are more trees and much less competition. Here in the East, old-growth timber is getting scarce. Even in upstate Maine, the trees are getting cut away, and the logging crews are getting thin. Your father said the young men are taking over the woods and forcing the older ones out. I guess even at age forty-four, men like your father are considered past their prime."

Lucy paused, lost in thought.

"Mama, did you hear me?" asked Etta, patting her mother's hand to bring her back from the blank stare.

"What, dear?"

"Papa loves us more than his work, doesn't he?" asked Etta anxiously.

"Of course, darlings, of course. But Papa only knows one thing, and that is driving horse teams. He is one of the best horsemen around. So he's going to a place where he can make a good living and support us."

Lucy knew that everything her husband had worked for, everything he knew, and his whole livelihood was disappearing before their eyes in a mist. It was a new century, and everything seemed to be changing.

Logging companies were going to steam power and on the verge of making horse hauling something of the past. The whole world was in an extraordinary move toward using machinery and motor power. No one had prepared for the changes, especially men like Edwin, who had invested their whole careers in running horses. In just a few years, once the railroads took over, horse hauling in the logging camps out East would be a thing of the past.

But in the West, the world was still fresh and needed cultivating. Men like Edwin were in short supply, and the world seemed unlimited. Edwin told Lucy that he could not imagine ever running out of timber in the West.

"I thought Papa only logged in the winter," said Etta.

"It's different out in Oregon. It doesn't freeze like it does here. That's why Papa left now, because your Uncle Jake got him a job all summer in the woods. We will join him when your baby sister is old enough to travel."

Chapter 6

Whose Is That, Anyway?

Edwin began to get settled in the carriage with Louisa. Voices throughout the carriage murmured from personal conversations. Louisa cozied up next to her father as she watched out the window.

After a few minutes, she turned to him with a straight face and asked, "When will we get there, Papa?"

"Just relax, Pumpkin," Edwin laughed. "We have a long way to go."

"Papa, Grandma Ida made my bow too tight. I can't hardly wink."

"Let me have a look," he said, turning her and feeling the knot in the pink satin bow. Edwin pulled one end, and the whole thing came untied in his hand.

"Now, I know your mother showed me how to do this. Let's see here." Edwin fumbled in his satchel to find the hairbrush Lucy had given him. Edwin began to brush Louisa's hair, careful not to pull too tightly before he brought it back into a ponytail and then tied it up again with the bow.

"Tell me again how you learned to do this, Papa." said Louisa.

"Your Mama showed me, remember?" he asked.

"But you said you learned it from the horses, right? Did they show you?" Edwin had to hold himself back from busting out in laughter.

"Oh no, Lou, I learned it from tending my horses. You see, the horse's tail has to be tied up, so it won't get caught up in the load. So you have to braid the tails and tie them up all pretty."

Edwin looked down at her, knowing that in her mind, she still thought the horse had taught him how to fix hair. She still thought that her father could talk to horses, and Edwin wanted her to hold onto that magic for as long as possible.

"Now, let me have a look at you. How's that feel?" he asked. Louisa blinked her eyes and felt her hair all pulled back neatly, all tied up in a bow.

"Wow, Papa, the horses taught you good." Edwin laughed, a deep belly laugh, but Louisa had a curious look about her.

"Mama said you could talk to horses."

"Well, it's different than talking to people." Edwin scratched his forehead, wondering how to explain it to a five-year-old. "Most people don't think a horse can talk aside from nickers and whinnies, but a horse talks with his ears and his tail, with his neck and his head, and his nostrils and his eyes. If you aren't listening, he will try to get your attention with his teeth and his hooves. You have to listen carefully, not with your ears, but with your eyes and your heart. You don't control a horse with a whip or a bit, but you control him by your feelings, your friendship, and your care. You get that right, and you will get along just fine."

He could tell Louisa was trying to listen intently. Still, her eyes kept sliding over and eyeing the thickly frosted chocolate cake on the tin plate beside him.

"It will ruin your appetite for supper," he said, following her line of sight.

"I won't let it hurt me," Louisa insisted.

"Well, I guess your mother isn't here, and she did bake the cake special for us."

Edwin took his knife off his belt and cut her a small piece. He handed it to her carefully, along with a cloth napkin Lucy had packed for the very purpose.

"Now, don't get it on your pretty new dress, young lady."

Louisa's eyes were as big as saucers as she took the piece of cake in both hands. Edwin cut a piece for himself and took a bite. He watched Louisa carefully to make sure she didn't drop crumbs.

"Is it good?" he asked.

"Oh, Papa, it is so good. How can chocolate not be good?" she exclaimed as a big chunk of frosting fell off the cake and bounced off her dress onto the floor. Louisa's eye widened, but Edwin just reached over and brushed off her dress and kicked the frosting under the seat with his boot.

"You are going to ruin the child's appetite with that dessert, sir," said a woman with a red hat, leaning over her seat to interrupt them.

"Oh, I know. And it is the most delicious way to ruin an appetite."

Edwin was being cheeky; he did not need a stranger judging him for his parenting choices, but he thought it better to kill them with kindness. No sense in making enemies on a long train ride. The woman harrumphed and turned back around in her seat. He could hear her whispering about him to a fellow passenger, but he couldn't make out what she was saying.

"She is a nice lady," said Lou. "She reminds me of Grandma Ida."

Edwin let a chuckle. He could see the resemblance.

"Papa, is Grandma Ida your mama?" Edwin almost choked on his cake, thinking of Ida as his mother.

"My mama passed on before you were born," he explained. "A long time before you were born . . . sixteen years."

"Passed on where?" she asked, looking out at the trees and farms moving across the landscape as the train rumbled down the tracks.

"Oh sweetheart, I lost my mama."

"Where did you lose her?" asked Louisa curiously, squinting and staring into her father's eyes. Children saw the world so differently.

Edwin had never spent much time with his children, he'd spent most of their lives away logging. Now he was beginning to realize that holding a conversation with a five-year-old may be more challenging than he had expected.

"Up to heaven, for heavens' sake!"

"Where is that, Papa?" she asked, still frowning.

"Okay," he said, trying to gather his wits about him, knowing this would be a long conversation. "You see when a person gets sick or old or has a terrible accident . . ."

Edwin paused for a minute, thinking about all the horrible things he had seen in the woods from logging accidents: men cut near in half from broken cables, smashed flat from falling trees, trampled under horse teams, and with broken skulls from dead limbs. These visions continued to haunt him, keeping him awake in the night.

"You see, when that happens to a person, they die and go to heaven. Hopefully, they go to heaven if they have lived a good life, that is."

"Mama told me about that. It's a place like the church where she sings. Oh, Papa, I hope Mama doesn't die because I would miss her. I miss her already."

The train continued to roll along the tracks, clickity-clack, clickity-clack, clickity-clack. Louisa finished her cake so carefully as not to drop another crumb and watched out the carriage window, not wanting to miss a single sight.

"What was she like?" she asked, pulling her attention back to her father.

"Who?" asked Edwin.

"Your mama," she insisted.

"Oh, yeah. You were named after her, you know? She was a Crosby," said Edwin.

"What's a Crosby?"

"That was her last name before she married my Papa—Louisa Keyes Crosby. She had beautiful brown eyes, just like you, dear, and dark brown hair, and a warm heart. My Papa always called her 'Princess.' If she could have only seen you, she would have been amazed."

"When will I see her?" Louisa asked, looking at Edwin expectantly. "Mama said we will see everyone someday. And those who aren't there we won't miss."

"I'm not the one to ask about that, Pumpkin."

"Then who?" she said.

"That's a Mama question for sure."

"Well, just because they lived in a different time doesn't mean we aren't supposed to know them forever."

Edwin pondered his daughter's statement, wondering how a little one could be wiser far beyond her short five years of life.

"I'm going to see them all again, Papa, because I have Jesus in my heart, Mama said!" Louisa folded her arms across her chest just to make a statement. "What about your Grammy and Grampa? Do you have some of those?"

"That would be John Dowling, Junior, and my grandmother, Deborah Libby. He died fifteen years before I was born, and she died ten. Then there was Daniel Russell Crosby; he died young, and my grandmother, Hannah Woodward Eaton, who married Ichabod Ramsdell. She is still living up in Lubec and is almost ninety-one."

"How do you know all these names, Papa? It seems like too much to know."

"My father told me; it was always important to him. And it will be important to you someday too, Pumpkin."

"I like it when you call me 'Pumpkin,' Papa," said Louisa, smiling.

"You are so sweet; you remind me of pumpkin pie."

It was several days before they arrived in Chicago. When they pulled into the station, Louisa had her eyes glued to the window, watching the hustle and bustle of the big city. On the platform stood hordes of people waiting to board or waiting for loved ones to get off.

"Are we getting off the train, Papa?"

"Yes. But I wish we didn't have to, Pumpkin."

"That's good; I feel like a chicken at a market, all cooped up." Edwin broke out laughing.

"Okay, my little chicken," he said as he grabbed his travel bag.

As he gathered their things, Edwin noticed a police officer walking briskly in their direction, pulling out his billy club from his belt. Edwin stood frozen as the constable approached.

"Come down out of that coach, sir," demanded the officer.

"What seems to be the problem?" Edwin took Louisa in his arms and stepped down to the platform.

"What is your name, and where are you from?"

"I am Joseph E. Dowling from Lowell, Massachusetts."

"Are you carrying any sort of papers?"

"My name is in the family Bible up in Maine, but that isn't going to do either of us any good. Oh, perhaps this," he said, reaching for his leather billfold tucked in his inside coat pocket.

"Easy, sir," said the officer suspiciously, raising his club. "Now, nice and slow."

Edwin pulled out his pocket wallet, found his union paper, and handed it to the officer.

"The International Brotherhood of Teamsters, aye. You shouldn't go flashing union papers in my face with all the trouble they caused here in Chicago last year." The officer clenched his fist around his billy club and seemed itching to use it. "Who is this young 'un?"

"This is my daughter, sir. Our family is headed out West. My wife just had a baby and will be joining us soon."

"Is this your father, young lady?"

"Of course he is," said Louisa resolutely.

"This is quite the young lady you got there, Mister Joseph Dowling," he said, looking at the name on the union papers. "I guess I will just have to take your word for it, my dear," he said as he shook his head and handed Edwin back the paper.

"There is one thing," said Louisa putting her finger to her lips. "My Papa's name is Edwin."

"Folks call me by my middle name; it's Joseph Edwin."

"Well, there ain't no law against that, I guess," the officer said, much more kindly now that his suspicions had been laid to rest. "Have a nice trip," he said, touching the brim of his cap as he walked away into the crowd.

"Good thing they didn't find out I stole you from the gypsies," Edwin whispered in his daughter's ear, and Louisa giggled.

⫙⫙⫙

A haze hung low over the city of Chicago from all the coal and wood-fired cookstoves, steamships, and locomotives. The sun rose high overhead, but the smoke seemed like a heavy fog.

"Where are we going, Papa? Why we are we leaving our train?"

"We have to change trains here in Chicago from the New York Central Line to the Northern Pacific. We came into the La Salle Street Station, and the Northern Pacific leaves from Grand Central Station in four hours."

"How far is that?" Louisa asked, putting her hand on her cheek.

"It's a quarter-mile or so, about as far as you walk with Mama to church on Sundays."

"I'm tired. Why don't you ask one of those horses to give us a ride?"

"It's not that easy, Pumpkin."

"Papa, you said you could talk to horses."

"I can talk to them, but it is still going to cost ten cents, and besides, it is such a nice day."

"Can you carry me if I get tired?"

"We're a team, remember?" he smiled.

"Sure, you carry the bag . . . I'll carry me," said Louisa." What about our trunk?"

"The railroad takes care of all that. They load the baggage on a wagon and take them all to the next train," said Edwin, holding on tight to Louisa's hand as he made his way through the crowd.

"Where are all these people going?" asked Louisa. "And where did they all come from?"

"They all live here, I suppose," said Edwin.

"Where is their house?"

"They live in apartment buildings; that's why there are people here by the hordes," he said. "That's why we are going to Oregon, to get away from all this hustle and bustle."

"Oh . . . look, Papa, there is a carriage without a horse!"

"That's why we are heading out West," said Edwin, "to get away from those."

Suddenly, something in a window caught Edwin's eye, and he stopped dead in his tracks.

"Will you look at that," he said, pointing to the Brown Bess flintlock musket leaning against the wall inside the plate glass window of a curiosity shop.

"That's a musket, just like my great-grandfather used when he fought in the Revolution. That thing is its twin, I swear. I looked at a musket just like that one every day as a kid growing up, hanging over our fireplace mantle, and I would swear . . ." Edwin stopped short of accusing his brother of selling the family heirloom. There was a price tag of sixty-five dollars hanging from the trigger guard. "Who would pay sixty-five dollars for an old rifle like that?" he muttered aloud. "They were so inaccurate you couldn't hit the broadside of a barn with that thing."

"You should buy it, Papa."

"Oh heavens, your mother would kill me. But then again, if she tried to shoot me with that thing, maybe she would miss," he laughed. "Besides, I would have to work every day for two months to buy that thing. Come on, Pumpkin, let's get going." Edwin pulled on Louisa's hand, looking over his shoulder one more time at the musket.

"When are we going to get there, Papa?"

"Not much farther to the next station."

"No, silly, to Oregon, so I can meet my Uncle Jake and Aunt Anna," she said, looking up at him with a bright smile as they walked up the street.

"We've still got another two-thirds to go."

Their train left on time at four o'clock sharp that afternoon, and Louisa and Edwin were in their seats on the sleeper carriage, ready for the long train ride to Portland. The Northern Pacific Railroad went west through Illinois, Iowa, Nebraska, Wyoming, Colorado, and the Rocky Mountains, then Idaho and Oregon.

A few days out from Chicago, Louisa gazed out the window as the train came to a stop at a station.

"That's a nice-looking team," said Edwin, watching beside her as a man with a team of horses passed by, pulling a wagon.

"That's what we are, Papa."

"What is that?" asked Edwin, scratching his chin.

"We are a team, you and me," she said, looking up with a bright smile.

"That's what we are, Pumpkin; we are a good team together, that's for sure. A team on a grand adventure."

Chapter 7

Torn from a Mother's Arms

Did you get it all settled?" asked Ida as Lucy walked into the kitchen.

"Yes, I had to tell the railroad a little fib, though."

"And what fib was that?"

"It would have been another one hundred and seven dollars if Loring were eight years old, so I told them his birthday wasn't until next year. I didn't lie, because his birthday IS next year!"

"You are a sly one. That is a staggering amount for a train ticket!"

"The entire cost was three hundred and twenty-two dollars, to be exact. Thirty-two for the fare to Chicago, sixty-five from Chicago to Portland, Oregon, and ten dollars extra for a bunk. And that is not even including the exorbitant train meals we will have to buy along the way!"

"Where did you get that kind of money?" asked her mother, her hands on her hips. "Your husband is a horseman!"

"Ever since Edwin returned from . . ." Lucy didn't need to continue. Her mother was well aware that Edwin had lost all their savings on his previous trip out West. "I have been in charge of the money and

I save like the dickens. I cut corners where I can. I make all my own clothes, and we don't go out on the town."

"So much sacrifice just to take you away."

"I know it's expensive, Mama, but you will visit us, won't you? You just have to." Lucy's eyes welled up at the thought of being separated from her parents, and a tear rolled off her cheek.

"I'm not saying I won't come," said her mother. "Who knows what life dishes out and how situations change? You just don't lose hope, now, hear?" Lucy wiped her face and returned to her task. She was making and packing snacks that would help her family save money on the trip.

"Does Edwin know your plans?"

"I will write all this down in a letter with my itinerary."

"Why don't you send a telegram?"

"Oh heavens, a telegram transcontinental is seven dollars and fifty cents; a letter is two cents. How do you think I saved all that money for the train? It departs on Sunday the 21st, the day after tomorrow, and we will arrive in Portland one week later, on the 27th. I told Edwin to meet us in Portland."

↟↟↟

The morning of their departure had a bitter chill in the air as a light rain fell. Everyone wore long woolen coats to keep warm. The air had a heavy coal smell as the steam engine sat idle, and the black smoke from the stack lay over them like a thick blanket.

Lucy's father stood quietly behind his wife, biting his cheek to keep his emotions at bay. Simeon's heart broke at the thought of never seeing his beautiful, thirty-three-year-old daughter again. She brought such life to their household.

"Well," said Lucy, "the time has finally come for our grand adventure."

"Spoken like a true Dowling," said Ida, putting her hands on her hips. She turned to Lucy's eldest son. "You'll be good to your mother now, won't you, Warren?"

"And you, young man, better obey her," said Simeon as he shook his finger at Loring. "If you don't, I'll catch the next train, and when I catch up with you, you'll have hell to pay."

"Oh, Papa," Lucy laughed, "it's Etta I have to watch out for."

"What did you say, Mama?" asked Etta innocently, holding the baby in her arms.

"Oh, you heard me," laughed Lucy.

"You better get going now, or you will miss your train," said Ida, throwing her arms around her daughter one final time. "Not that I would mind in the least if you missed that damn thing."

"Come along, children," called Lucy. "Let's go find our seats." Lucy stood aside as her tribe boarded, then stepped up and turned to wave.

"Goodbye, Mama and Papa; I will miss you terribly."

The train whistle blew. The couplings from the front to the rear clunked one at a time like a significant movement in a powerful symphony as the train stretched out, then began to move slowly. Lucy jumped up and opened the window, looking back at her family on the platform. She waved wildly while they shouted and waved back. She could feel the warm tears coming off her cheeks and struggled to see through her blurred vision. The figures in the distance grew smaller as space separated them. She knew in her heart that it was very likely the last time she would ever lay eyes on her parents in this life, and the thought ripped her near in half.

She watched until they disappeared in the distance, then pulled back inside the car and closed the window, sinking back into her seat. The children sat quietly with wide eyes as they watched their mother. She wanted to turn back, but knew the time had come and gone for that. She wanted to break down and cry, but she bit her lip and calmed her spirit with a silent prayer. Sitting stunned, almost in shock, she wondered how this day had finally come. It seemed the fabric of her life hung limply in shreds, blowing in the breeze.

⚘⚘⚘

Lucy and the children shared a train compartment with her friend Peggy and Peggy's husband, Pete, who were also headed West, at least part of the way. Peggy had decided to accompany Pete on his business trip to Chicago to help Lucy with the children.

"I don't see how I will sleep on this contraption," said Lucy to her friend. Peggy was sitting across from her, holding baby Edith in her lap.

"Well, the baby seems perfectly happy," laughed Peggy.

"She is such a good baby," said Lucy. "I think the vibration on the train is good for her."

"It must be mesmerizing to her. I have never seen her so content,"

"Oh Mama, this is glorious," said Etta. "I feel like I am soaring."

Warren and Loring sat glued to the window, watching every sight.

"Look at that man's string of trout," said Loring. "Let me off this train right now. Is there a string I can pull?" Loring pretended like he was going to pull the emergency ring.

"Don't you dare pull that ring," warned Lucy. Loring smiled and laughed mischievously.

"You wait till we get to the Columbia River," said Lucy. "You know that canned fish you like. That's where that fish comes from. You just wait, little man."

"Mama, they tricked us," said Loring.

"What do you mean?" she asked.

"You said there was a place to sleep. All they have in here is seats!"

"Here is how it works. After dinner, around nine o'clock, the porter will come through and pull down the upper bunk. See that latch right there," said Lucy, pointing over his head. "That whole thing comes down and makes a bunk."

"What about the seats. I can't sleep in a seat."

"They fill the spot where our feet are and then fold the back cushions down and make the two seats into one bed."

"What about privacy, Mama?" asked Etta.

"There are curtains that come down when they fold the upper bunk down. You'll see."

Just then, the porter, an older black man, stopped by, asking if they needed anything. Lucy asked his name and informed him that she and her children would do their very best to not be a nuisance. He laughed and assured her that her children brought a joyful presence to the train car.

"He is such a nice man, isn't he?" said Etta as the porter walked away. "I never talked to anyone with dark skin before. He said his name is Mr. Sinclair, but I thought all the porters were named George."

"They call them George after George Pullman. He invented the sleeping train car like we are in now. He hired only black porters, known as Pullman Porters and many people refer to them as George. But every porter we see, we are going to ask him his name and call him by his real name."

⚑⚑⚑

On the morning of the second day, the train passed by Lake Ontario. Lucy could see the blackened fields where the farmers had burned last year's crops. The children were amazed at the sight of water as far as they could see with no land in sight.

"We will be in Toronto soon," remarked the porter, making his way down the aisle.

"Mama, look at the roundhouse where they turn the trains around," said Warren.

"And the shipyard," exclaimed Loring. "Just look at the size of those ships!"

"When I grow up, I'm going to be a ship captain," Loring pronounced, glancing over his shoulder and then looking back toward the ships.

Warren struggled to pronounce the names: Le Ayuga, Bellville, and the Steamer Aurania from Cleveland.

"Pete said we are stopping for twenty minutes," said Warren. "Can I get off with Pete and go have a look around?" Lucy looked across the aisle at her friend's husband, who nodded his approval.

"Don't go far," warned Lucy, "and make sure you get back on the train because they won't wait for you." Warren jumped out of the seat and followed Pete toward the exit.

"He's such good company for Warren," said Lucy to Peggy. Lucy was holding the squirming baby Edith in her arms. She looked on jealously as Warren and Pete left the train car. She wished she too could get out and stretch her legs.

Peggy, noticing Lucy's struggle, reached out and took the baby out of her hands.

"She is a handful, isn't she?" Peggy said as she tousled Edith's hair.

"I don't know what we are going to do on our way to Portland without you, Peggy."

"We will be just fine," Etta declared, trying to console her mother. "You'll see."

"I know, but I wish my Mama were here. Something about this train journey is making me feel ill."

Soon Warren and Pete returned, and the train continued toward Chicago at a slow pace.

Just then, the porter, Mr. Sinclair came by the seat, and Lucy stopped the man with her hand on his arm.

"Yes, ma'am, what can I do for you?"

"Why is the train in such as slow creep?"

"It's a new bridge, and they are still putting the finishing touches on it. They are putting a million dollars on the railroads, building them up all over the route."

"Thank you, Mr. Sinclair; I just thought it was odd." He tipped his hat then moved on down the car.

"Etta, can you just imagine having a million dollars? What would we do then? I know I would never have had to leave Lowell, that's for sure," said Lucy.

198

"What's all the fuss?"

"We should be coming to the St. Clair tunnel soon; they say it will be so dark they will have to light the lamps."

"We are just a few minutes out, and everyone on the train is all in a tizzy."

"What is all the fuss? It's just a tunnel."

"Yes," said Pete, "but the tunnel goes under the St. Clair River. They had a ferry that took the train across the river and loaded it back on the track in the mid-1800s. But now they don't have to mess with all that. They dug under the river and the tunnel opened in 1891. They say the miners started at each end and met in the middle, and they weren't off more than a fraction of an inch. Just imagine that?"

"Under the river?" exclaimed Lucy. "We are going underneath the river? How far is it?"

"A mile long."

"Just think what would happen if it sprung a leak," laughed Peggy.

Pete reassured them, "It's completely safe; just unique, that's all. We have nothing to worry about."

"That's easy for him to say, but I worry."

"Oh, look, they are lighting the lights," said Etta as she looked around at the other passengers sitting in the dim light from the lamps, some of whom were holding their nose from the smell. After a couple of minutes, the light burst forth as the train flew out of the tunnel.

"That was something," said Lucy. "I'm glad that's over with."

Pete opened his window to let some fresh air in the car.

Loring was wide-eyed. "It's like a new day, Mama. We were in the night, but now it's day again."

Chapter 8

A Hand Up

The train stopped at Port Huron, Michigan, as they came back across the American border. Everyone waited patiently as the customs officers worked their way down the car, talking to every passenger and asking the same question.

"Are you a United States citizen?" asked the officer as he stood imposingly over Lucy and her children.

"Yes, sir."

"And where are you headed?" Loring began to speak, but Lucy glared at him and put her hand on his knee.

"We are headed to Oregon to meet my husband, who preceded us by six months. We plan to live in Oregon."

"Can I inspect your bag, madam? "

"Yes," she said politely, grabbing her bag from under her seat and presenting it to the officer. The customs officer began pawing through it and chuckled out loud.

"There must be enough baby clothes in here for ten children."

"Everybody I know gave me baby clothes for a going away gift. But you are right, I didn't have the heart to leave any behind, and she is going to grow out of them before she can wear them all," laughed Lucy as baby Edith gurgled pleasantly in her lap.

"Do all these children belong to you?"

"Yes, sir."

"We have another sister, but she is with our father," said Loring. Lucy looked back and gave Loring another frown.

"Well, I suppose I won't throw you in jail for being short one kid," the officer laughed. "Have a pleasant trip, ma'am. I can't imagine my wife traveling by herself with three children and a baby all the way across the country. You are a stronger woman than most."

Loring glued his eyes to the window, waiting for the train to move again. In just a short while, they were off and running.

"This train must be trying to make up time," he said.

Lucy watched out the window and could see things flying by as if they were on the wings of a bird.

"It sure seems we are going awful fast."

"The engineer is trying to make up some time. I asked about it, and the conductor said we are traveling at sixty-seven miles an hour," announced Pete, who was always a bevy of information. Lucy was glad to have him to answer all the boy's questions.

"That is faster than the wind!" exclaimed Warren.

"That's a mile every minute," said Pete. "We have two hundred and fifty miles to Chicago, and at this rate, we will be there in four hours. It is necessary to keep on time. If we are not on time, we could mess up the whole system. That's how you end up in a head-on crash with another train from not being on time."

"Good to know," said Lucy, envisioning a train wreck. "I just hope those men who drove them spikes in the ties hammered them down tight."

"They are checked by railroad men quite regular. You don't worry about that."

"There is always too many things to worry about in life, isn't there?"

⇑⇑⇑

Lucy looked up and saw Peggy coming down the aisle.

"Pete said he talked to the conductor, and we won't get to Chicago until after midnight."

"I'm going to miss my train connection. I have a mind to march up there and tell him to get back up to speed!"

"Oh Lucy, I am pretty sure they know what they are doing."

"I can't miss my connection; that will put us a day late to Portland if there even is a train the next day. I may have to wait three days, or who knows how long. What is the matter with these people? Don't they know that people have connections to make and a husband waiting for them in Portland?"

"Probably not, Lucy. That is probably the last thing on their mind."

"I hope they honor the tickets, for land's sake. What would happen then?"

"Don't worry; things always work out for the best, you'll see."

⇑⇑⇑

The train pulled into Chicago at twelve-thirty in the morning. The railroad allowed passengers to spend the night on the train and provided breakfast in the dining in the car morning. As they ate, Lucy looked out the window at the Chicago streets and took a drink of her hot coffee.

"We will be leaving you after breakfast, my dear," said Peggy.

"I will never forget you, Peggy. You will always be in my heart."

"And you too, my darling . . . you too."

The two families packed up after breakfast and departed the train. Lucy went to the ticket office to see about her connection, and Peggy and Pete followed her just to make sure she made her connection. Lucy stepped up to the counter and explained her situation.

"Sorry, ma'am, but the six o'clock is completely booked now. We won't have another train to Portland until Friday morning." The man had thick glasses and a ruddy complexion. His cheeks were red, and he had bushy eyebrows and a bald head. He had an arrogance about him that Lucy found distasteful.

"That is completely out of the question," she said, stomping her foot on the wooden floors. "I should be put at the head of the line; it was the railroad that caused us to miss our connection. Honestly, what sort of circus are you running here? Where do I make a formal complaint?"

"Just give me a minute," said the trainmaster, picking up his telephone receiver. Lucy tried to make out the conversation, but the man muffled his voice.

Lucy smiled, thinking it might matter. She looked back to the waiting bench where the children were sitting. Etta held little Edith, who was starting to fidget. Pete started to approach, but Lucy made a hand motion and mouthed the words, "I've got this."

"Excuse me, sir?"

"What is it, ma'am?" he asked, holding his hand over the mouthpiece.

"When that baby starts crying, she gets so wound up she just won't stop. I just wanted to let you know what you are in for. Can you take a crying baby on that waiting bench for two days?"

"Just one moment, please. I'm doing all that I can." He put the phone back to his ear and turned with his back to the counter, continuing to try and silence his voice. Lucy tapped her toe, and she straightened her hat.

"It's all set," he said, turning back toward her as he put the receiver down, then straightened his coat.

"All set for what?"

"I have seats for you on the six o'clock. We had a last-minute cancellation."

The man pulled the slips out of the drawer, stamping them one at a time, and pushed them across the counter.

"You will need to find a coach that will take you over to the Union Station. It is about a twenty-minute ride from Grand Central. Have a nice trip to Portland, ma'am."

Pete and Peggy helped Lucy gather the children and their bags, and they made their way out onto the busy streets of Chicago.

"I'm not ready to say goodbye, Peggy." They stood on the street corner as the bustle of Chicago moved around them. Lucy fought to hold back her tears, with no success.

"You will be just fine in Oregon, my dear. Who knows, Pete and I may even come out for a visit next year."

"Do you really mean it?" smiled Lucy through her tears.

"My goodness," said Peggy, "look at us, two pitiful old women crying in public. I'm sure glad we don't know a soul here in Chicago, or else they would be talking about us."

Lucy laughed, and then Peggy joined in.

"It will be good to be with Edwin and my little Lou in just a few days now. How I do miss them so. I think that's our carriage coming now to take us over to Union Station."

"Well, dear," said Peggy. "I will write to you just as often as I can to let you know how things are doing at home, and I hope you will do the same."

"We just have to, Peggy. It's not like I can just jump on a train and come home anytime I like. This trip cost us our whole life savings."

"This is just a little something from us," said Pete, handing Lucy a white envelope.

"What's this?" asked Lucy with a suspicious voice. "If it's a handout, Edwin will send it right back to you."

"That's precisely why we didn't send it," said Peggy. "It's not a handout; it's a belated birthday and early Christmas gift." Lucy paused before taking the envelope.

"You will offend us if you don't accept it, my dear," warned Pete.

"How much is it?" she asked.

"Just a very small token of our love for the both of you. Take it," urged Peggy, taking the envelope from Pete and placing it in Lucy's hand. "We love you, dear heart. Use the money to get ahead, sort of like a nest egg. You don't even have to tell Edwin if you don't want to."

"It is surely not a handout," said Pete. "Think of it like we are giving you a hand up."

Lucy folded the envelope and shoved it in her coat pocket. She gave Peggy one last hug.

"Thank you for coming with me this far. It means to world to me." Lucy turned and climbed in the buggy with her waiting children.

"Goodbye, dear friends," said Lucy as the driver closed the door behind them.

Lucy felt in her pocket and pulled out the envelope. She opened it discreetly so her children wouldn't notice, just enough for a peek, and saw three shiny new twenty-dollar bills staring her right in the face.

"What's in the envelope, Mama?" asked Etta, trying to look inside as Lucy folded it up quickly to hide the contents.

"Just a private letter from Peggy for me to read later," she answered.

🌲🌲🌲

When they got to the train station, Lucy stood in a line waiting to show her tickets to a man behind a cage. When her turn came, and she gave them over. He began to fidget, then called another man over. He looked quickly and then started to wring his hands.

"Where did you get these from, ma'am?" asked the man with thick-wired glasses, red hair, and freckles.

"You see, sir, our train was late into Chicago, and we missed our connection," explained Lucy. "They gave me these slips and said to show them, and everything would be fine."

"Well, I don't know how to tell you, dear, but we cannot accept these. You have changed railroad companies, and we cannot honor these. I'm sorry," he said, handing them back to her. Lucy knew she would have to control her temper and remain calm.

"I'm sorry to trouble you, good sir," said Lucy trying to calm her voice. "But this is not acceptable to me. I demand to see your supervisor."

"He is indisposed at the moment, Madam. I will take the next person in line."

"You will not take the next person in line," she said, putting her fist on the counter. "I will see the supervisor above him then. And if I have to, I will take this whole matter to Edward Harriman, President of the Union Pacific!" Lucy remembered seeing his picture as they walked in the front entrance of Union Station.

She glanced behind at the crowd of people waiting to see the clerk. They seemed more annoyed with the clerk than with her, so she turned back to the man. "Do you see those children sitting patiently on the bench over there? We are going to meet their father in Oregon. We haven't seen him in six months, and if we don't show up, he will be quite annoyed." Lucy paused, thinking of a plan, and put her finger to her lip. "My husband is a schoolmate of President Edwin Harriman and a personal friend. I am sure Mr. Harriman would love to hear about this mess."

"Just a minute, ma'am," said the clerk. "Let me see if I can find a supervisor for you. Can I have your tickets back?" Lucy held them out toward him with a tight jaw.

Lucy stepped aside, folding her arms and trying not to show her nervousness while the other man stepped up to the counter. All the time, she kept her eye on the goings-on. Then, after a bit, she spotted the pale-skinned man in a brisk walk with a more senior-looking man dressed in a white shirt, suit coat, and a tie. He had silver hair and a warm, friendly smile as he stepped up behind the counter.

"Sorry for the mix up, ma'am. These tickets are more than adequate for you to catch your train. They are personally signed now with my approval, so you shouldn't have any more trouble. You may take your children and board at Gate 2. Make sure her bags are taken care of, Sidney."

"Thank you, good sir, for straightening this out so quickly," said Lucy putting her hand on her chest. "My heart nearly skipped a beat, thinking about my husband's disappointment and all."

"You have a pleasant trip out West," he said with a smile. "And give your husband our best wishes from the Union Pacific."

Chapter 9

Arrival

Lucy settled in her bunk next to Etta, just as the lights went out in the train car. She was nestled with the girls into the bottom bed—the day seats transformed—while the two boys whispered in the bed above.

"Just look at that beautiful sight," said Lucy as the train made its way along the edge of the city of Chicago. "The lights seem like stars in the sky, too numerous to count."

"You are going to miss Peggy, aren't you, Mama?" asked Etta.

"Yes, my darling, I will. However, we will make new friends."

The lights were dark and the car went quiet except for the clickety-clack from the tracks. Lucy had just dozed off in the bed when the movement on the train woke her. She tried to get comfortable without waking the baby nestled between her and Etta, but her side ached. She had been feeling a little sick since they began their journey, but it seemed to be getting worse. She felt her side and a sharp pain shot through her like a knife.

Lucy was growing frustrated with the long journey. Her arms ached, and she couldn't seem to get any sleep on the train. Every delay felt like an added torture.

Not only did her body ache, but her heart ached as well at the thought of being torn further away from her mother, minute by minute. She tried to stay focused with the sense of excitement of seeing Edwin and Louisa.

The porter, whose name was Earl, stopped by just then to talk. They had grown friendly over the past few days and he often checked in on Lucy, for which she was grateful.

"I know you were anxious about our arrival in Portland, but with all this snow we won't be arriving now until Sunday. I am so very sorry to have to tell you because you and your children look so travel weary."

Lucy smiled and tried not to be offended by his comment.

"I already suspected that might be the case," Lucy answered.

Then, as they watched outside, the train began to slow and then came to a stop.

"What now?" said Lucy, shaking her head. "We are not going to make it to Oregon for a month."

"Is it okay if I walk up the car and see why we stopped?" asked Warren.

"Go ahead; I want to know." Warren jumped out of his seat.

"I want to go, Mama," said Loring.

"You wait here, Loring, and keep me company. Go ahead, Warren." He turned and headed up the aisle.

"I just don't want to make a big fuss up there. One is enough," Lucy continued. After a minute, Warren came down the aisle, making eye contact with his mother and sliding into his seat.

"They are up front with shovels; I think they are shoveling the snow! The conductor said it will be a while and said if we wanted to get out and walk in the snow we could."

"I wanna go, can we Mama?" asked Loring.

"Go ahead, but tell those crew men to hurry up and clear the way."

"Really?" said Warren.

"No, I'm Joking. Don't you say a word to them."

↟↟↟

The boys ran along as Lucy and Etta sat quietly. Out of the blue, a snowball smacked the window startling Lucy from her thoughts, and the girls looked out the glass through the snow plastered in a big splotch.

"That devil," said Etta as she spotted Loring outside standing in the snow, giggling. "If I were out there, I would toss one right back in his face!"

Warren let go of his snowball as it smacked the window as well.

"I would too," laughed Lucy.

Loring began making another snowball, and Lucy shook her head and waved her finger. Warren pelted his little brother, and Loring threw a snowball at him.

"Hey, Mama, I was afraid that snowball was going to come crashing clean through your window," said Loring with a big grin as he ran down the aisle, Warren at his heels.

"You are a rascal, young man."

"Is it cold out there?" Etta asked.

"Cold as the dickens," Warren laughed as Lucy touched his nose.

"Feel mine," said Loring. "It's cold too."

"I can see from here; it's all red."

"There is a man from the dining car making his way with toasted marshmallows," said Loring.

"That will be a treat, won't it?" said Lucy. "We'll have to get some."

The train got going again, and the boys were once again watching the window. A man from the train crew came strutting down the aisle, pounding the floor with his boots as he came. He had a stern look on his face, as if he were angry. As he approached, Lucy saw the crest on his cap: "CONDUCTOR." He wore a long black coat with a white shirt and black bow tie. His handlebar mustache, bushy eyebrows, pointed nose, and strong chin gave him a daunting air of authority. He stopped at her seat and put his hands on his hips.

"Are these your boys?" he asked, as his cheeks turned red and he squinted with one eye.

"Yes, they are, sir," said Lucy, rising from her chair to challenge him.

"I was told they tossed snowballs at the window. These windows are fragile, and they will bust right through. If you can't control your boys, I will have a crew member put them over his knee and give them a wailing."

The conversation in the car went silent as all eyes were on the situation brewing.

"You will do nothing of the sort," Lucy said firmly, standing her ground and putting her hand on Loring's shoulder.

"If you won't control them, we will."

Lucy wrinkled her nose and gritted her teeth. "How dare you accost a woman with her four children riding alone on the train? Why, if my husband were here, you would find yourself in a fix."

"Well, ma'am, I . . ."

"Don't you 'ma'am' me!" Lucy pointed her finger at him as she spoke. Just then, the man and woman sitting behind Lucy stood up behind her to back her up. Lucy glanced over her shoulder and looked, as more folks got to their feet.

"Maybe you could have approached me like a gentleman and explained the situation in a civil manner instead of coming at me like a bulldog. These boys have been perfect gentlemen cooped up on this train."

"The matter is settled then," said the conductor as he cleared his throat. "See that the boys behave themselves." The conductor tipped his hat, then turned around and walked off up the aisle. Lucy turned back at the folks standing in their seats. She smiled. Her boys were watching her with big round eyes as if they had just witnessed a prizefighter in a ring deliver a knockout punch. Lucy turned and slithered into her seat.

"That was something, Mama," said Warren.

"There will be no more throwing snowballs at the train. You understand me?"

"Yes, Mama," muttered Loring.

"We're sorry," said Warren.

When the man with the toasted marshmallows reached their car Lucy bought all the children, including herself, a treat. She took a small bite but struggled to swallow. Her body aches were getting worse, and now she could hardly get any food down her throat.

"Mama, are you okay?"

"Yes, I'm fine," said Lucy as she felt her neck and swallowed.

"Look," Warren shouted eagerly, "we are passing Laramie. Earl said it's the highest point of our trip; the elevation is over eight thousand feet!"

"There is no wonder I am having trouble breathing," said Lucy. "I can feel it in my chest."

"That sign said sixty-five miles to Portland," announced Etta. "That must be a relief to you, Mama!"

It wasn't long before Earl came around and began helping Lucy gather her bag.

"It's been a pleasure serving you all these days since we left Chicago, ma'am. I don't know when I enjoyed passengers so much as you and your children."

"You have been a wonderful host for us on this trip." Lucy reached in her handbag and pulled out three quarter-dollar pieces. "I know this is nothing, but I hope this will help and give you something to remember us by."

"Oh, you don't have to do that," said Earl.

"Well, I don't, but I am," she smiled, putting the coins in his open hand.

"I'm gonna miss you, ma'am. Nobody treats me like you have."

"Maybe someday we will live in a world where the color of your skin doesn't matter."

"It would be a good world for sure," he said, tipping his hat and turning away to continue his work. He looked back one more time, and said, "I think there is a place like that, but they call it heaven. I hope to see you there someday." With that, he gave Lucy a wide grin and tipped his hat.

The train arrived in Portland at three o'clock on Sunday afternoon. Edwin was not at the station. Disappointed and exhausted, Lucy could not tell if her body was getting worse or her heart was just so tired from the journey. After sitting at the station for four hours, she and her children left the station for Mayger. It took another two-hour train ride up the Columbia River to reach Mayger. The train stopped every ten minutes up the line, and by the time they arrived, it was late into the evening.

"I don't know if my heart can take this," said Lucy holding her chest. "We've been traveling for so long; I can't believe it is over. Now I'm filled with so much anticipation for this reunion with your father and our little Lou. Honestly, Etta, I can hardly breathe."

"Keep breathing, Mama," said Etta.

"It's just another ten minutes now, according to my watch," said Warren. Lucy tried to watch out the window. From the darkness, she could see trees passing by like ghosts floating on clouds. With every clickity-clack, her heart pounded with exhaustion and anticipation. Suddenly she heard a hiss from the steam locomotive and felt the train begin to slow.

"This is it, Mama," said Loring, trying to see out the dark window.

"There will be no rush for the doors, ma'am," laughed the porter. "This will just be a brief stop. You and your children are the only passengers getting off here."

"What does that tell me?" laughed Lucy. "I guess Mayger ain't a place folks come to for a vacation."

"It's not one of our more popular destinations, that's for sure," he said. The car lurched as the breaks squealed, and the porter held the seatback to steady himself. "Your trunks are in the hold. Is someone meeting you here? The engineer doesn't like leaving folks to fend on their own in the dark."

"Oh yes, my husband will be here. We haven't seen each other since last March," said Lucy, grabbing her things and counting the heads of her children.

"Take care of that little one," he said. "She is awfully cute."

"I'm just glad we all got here in one piece." Lucy made her way down the aisle and stopped to bid Earl farewell, then headed for the doorway. She could see people on the platform with lanterns.

"MAMA!" came a shriek as Louisa came barreling toward her mother. Lucy bent over, still holding Edith in her arms and carrying her handbag while at the same time trying to give Louisa a proper greeting. Then she looked up, not seeing Edwin but instead an unfamiliar couple.

"Where is my husband?"

"He went back to the camp," said the man, who looked like Edwin. The woman reached out her hand.

"I am Anna, and this is Edwin's brother, Jake."

Lucy could feel the rage boiling up in her innards and fought to contain her emotions in front of her children. Jake reached down and took her hand.

"It is so nice to meet you after all these years."

Lucy's eyes welled up, and she quickly rubbed her face with her gloved hand before anyone could see her emotion leaking from her eye.

"You would think he could at least be here to greet his children," she whispered.

"He spent all day in Portland yesterday waiting for you to arrive, and no one could change his mind that you were not coming at all."

"I wrote him when I left."

"How do you think the mail travels," said Jake. "That letter is probably in the mail sack on this train. They only deliver once a week."

"Well, I'm glad to meet you. I'm thankful someone came to meet us." She glanced down the line and saw men pulling her heavy trunks out of the baggage compartment and stacking them on the edge of the track. Jake left to go grab the trunks.

"I am so thrilled you are here," said Anna. "We will have so much fun, the two of us. I just can hardly wait to get to know you."

"What do you have in here?" said Jake as he loaded the first trunk on the wagon. "You didn't bring one of those cast iron kitchen sinks, did you?" he laughed as he walked back down the tracks to get the second one.

"ALL CLEAR!" shouted the trainman as he pulled the door closed on the baggage compartment. The train whistle blew and echoed off the hillsides through the darkness, and the men ran for the steps to board the train. The engine hissed and bucked like an unbroken stallion; the cars shook as the couplings buckled from the front to the back. It began to move, and then it was all over. Their journey was done. They had arrived. Lucy watched as the last car with a red lantern disappeared down the tracks. The noise of the iron monster subsided in the darkness.

Part IV—Edwin and Lucy Dowling, Cont'd.

Edwin Joseph Dowling
Born: February 17, 1862, East Machias,
Washington County, Maine

Lucy Delia Cook Dowling
Born: November 27, 1872, Maine

Edwin and Lucy's First Five Children

Warren Henry Dowling
Born: April 30, 1893, Lowell, Middlesex, Massachusetts

Bertha Etta Dowling
Born: January 18, 1895, Lowell, Middlesex, Massachusetts

Loring Estes Dowling
Born: May 26, 1898, Lowell, Middlesex, Massachusetts

Marion Louisa Dowling
Born: August 24, 1900, Lowell, Middlesex, Massachusetts

Edith Hill Dowling
Born: April 2, 1906, Lowell, Middlesex, Massachusetts

Part IV

Chapter 1

Little House
on the Columbia

The night was black, with a heavy cloud cover shading the stars and the moon. Lucy looked around at the dark night sky and wondered what new life awaited her family. Her brother and sister-in-law were so kind, but she wished Edwin could have been here. She had traveled all this way for him to not be there when she arrived.

"Here, sweetheart, let me take that baby," said Anna. Lucy gratefully handed her over.

"She is everybody's favorite. We all got tired of the people on the train gushing over her," Etta piped up.

"It is so nice to meet you all," Anna said. "Lucy, you must be exhausted. Come get in the wagon."

"Are we very far from the ocean?" asked Warren. "I hope I get to swim in it."

"You will be doing plenty of that when summer comes," said Jake as he loaded the second trunk. "There is a lot to do here. We hunt deer and waterfowl, and we fish. We get ocean clams, oysters, and crab, and pretty much live off the land."

"What kind of fish do you catch?" asked Loring. "At home we have trout. Or, what used to be home, I guess."

"We catch salmon here, and sometimes we get them on a hook and line, but usually with a gill net at night or seine them and pull the net out with horses. The canneries will buy a good chinook for a whole dollar. But it ain't like it used to be; twenty years ago they say you could've walked across the river on the backs of the fish."

Loring wrinkled his nose.

"Not really," laughed Jake. "But there ain't near the fish in the river there used to be."

As they all got settled, Jake turned to put out the lantern so the horses could see better in the dark.

The children were giggling and excited as they continued to pump Louisa, Anna, and Jake with questions. Lucy could tell that Louisa was proud to be such a wealth of knowledge for her siblings. Lucy felt exhausted and just wanted to get settled in her bed for the night. Then she spotted a house light along the road.

"We're here," said Anna. "This is your little house. Come on now, let's get you all settled in for the night. Jake will go to the camp tomorrow and fetch Edwin. But for now, I want all you kids tucked in bed so your mama can get some rest."

"She looks awful tired," whispered Jake in Anna's ear.

"Louisa, honey," said Anna, "why don't you stay with us tonight, and we'll come get them in the morning and have a nice breakfast at our house."

"What time?" asked Lucy. Jake relit the lantern so they could see to get out, and he walked up to the front porch. Lucy looked him in the face in the light and could see her husband's resemblance in his eyes. He wore a grey felt hat and had a wide bushy mustache, just like Edwin. She had heard so many stories about the two of them growing up on Gardner Lake, and she could see from his face that his fifty-six years had been hard on him. She peered in the windows of the tiny house. She saw a red glow from the fireplace and the low, flickering kerosene lamps.

"This is my house?"

"Yes, ma'am," said Jake. "Edwin made it nice for you, and we came over this afternoon and made sure it would be all warm and toasty for your arrival. There is hot water on the stove and a full bucket of coal on the back porch and the outhouse is right out back."

"And the bed linens are freshly cleaned," said Anna as Jake opened the front door and turned up the lights. A soothing warmth came flowing out as they entered the front room. Lucy set out a sigh. This wasn't the home she had ever wanted or imagined for herself, but at least for tonight it wasn't a moving train and it was warm and clean.

"Welcome home," said Anna, beckoning Lucy and her children inside. Anna had turned forty-one that year but looked far beyond her years. Lucy wondered if this is what a life in the country did to people. She wore her greying hair pulled back in a bun, and her nose had a hook on it. Lucy had heard the stories of abuse from Anna's former husband. She remembered hearing that he had broken her nose with his fist. But Anna had a kind face and a pleasant smile that went a long way.

The wood floors of the home were spotless, and a wool braided rug brightened up the living room. The flickering light of the flames from the river-rock fireplace cast shadows that danced on rough-cut cedar walls and ceiling. Lucy peered into the kitchen and took in the new dishes on the shelves, and the iron cook stove. She asked Anna about the rooms.

"It has three. One for you and Edwin, and one for the boys and one for the girls."

"This one is ours, Warren," announced Loring as he made his claim.

"Can someone carry me?" Lucy laughed. "I feel like a dog after a long day's hunt."

"We'd best get her trunks in the house," Jake said quietly to Anna. "Smells like rain."

Anna handed Lucy the lantern as they went down the hall to her room. "We will get out of your hair, darling, and see you in the morning. Lou, are you going to come with us?"

"Good night, Mama. I missed you so much. I never want to let go."

"You don't have to, dear. I won't ever let you out of my sight again. Run along now with Anna, and we will be over in the morning."

After they left, Lucy undressed, getting free from her corset and lace-up boots, and sliding gratefully into the covers of her bed. The comforter smelled slightly musty, as if it had been in a trunk for some time. Even though there had been a fire in the fireplace, the little house felt cold. She could feel the stress from her trip welling up in her throat, along with her anger at Edwin for not meeting them at the station.

Lucy woke as the sun poked through the window, and she could hear someone up, stoking the wood stove in the kitchen. She hurried around to get dressed. As she came into the kitchen, Etta was sitting at the table holding Edith, and Warren was tending to the stove.

"I don't remember when I had such a restful night," she said. "Well, you are all up dressed and ready to go, I see."

"We wanted to let you sleep," said Etta.

"How'd you keep baby Edith quiet?" Lucy asked, surprised. Etta didn't answer but just smiled. "Sometimes I wonder about you, girl. You have such strong mothering instincts." Etta's cheeks turned red.

"Mama, looks like Jake is here," said Warren, peering out the window.

"What time is it, for heaven's sake?" she asked.

"A quarter past nine," he answered.

"Quarter past nine?! You should have woke me before now. Where is Loring?"

"He said he was going to take a walk," Etta chimed in.

"And you let him go?" Lucy could feel her face getting flush.

"I'll go find him," Warren declared as the front door opened and in walked one of the most pleasant surprises Lucy had ever seen.

"Edwin!" she shrieked, running to him and wrapping her arms around his large frame. "Oh, Edwin," she said, smelling his hair and his work clothes that always had the familiar odor of horses mixed with cigar smoke. She had so longed for that smell these past six months.

"I can't believe we are finally together. And now you won't have to live in the logging camp anymore. You can come home every night and be with the children and me."

Edwin did not respond. Warren and Etta held back, respecting their parents' moment together.

"Papa, we missed you," said Etta, anxious for a hug from her father.

"You all look pretty good to me," replied Edwin as he counted heads and came up two short. "Where's Louisa?" he asked.

"She stayed one more night with Jake and Anna," answered Lucy. "Warren, go fetch your brother."

"Hi Papa! I'll be right back," Warren announced as he ducked out the back door.

"Where'd Loring go?" asked Edwin in his gruff, backwoods voice.

"They let him go outside," said Lucy.

"Who's they?" he asked.

"Warren and Etta . . . I was asleep."

"I'll go, but if I know Loring, that kid is probably on a boat headed downstream by now," muttered Edwin, shaking his head. He seemed annoyed at Lucy for letting an eight-year-old go off by himself.

"I'm coming with you," said Lucy, taking her coat off the hook by the door, "Etta, stay here with the baby."

They stepped outside in the cold and damp morning air. The sun had risen over the mountains and poked through the puffy white clouds mixed with patches of blue.

"Hold up," said Edwin, calling to Warren.

"Yes, Pa," he answered, stopping dead in his tracks as Edwin hurried to catch up. Lucy followed several steps behind, fighting to get her coat on.

"Look up at that mountain," said Edwin, looking east to the hills, gazing at a white-capped cone poking up above the foothills like a giant ice cream cone. "That's Mount St. Helens, son."

"It looks like a volcano. Is it a volcano?"

"I suppose it was a volcano once, but I can assure you it's dormant now and will never erupt again. But never mind that; take a look at the ground, what do you see?"

"Grass?" he said, shrugging his shoulders.

"Here is the boy's track right over here," he said, pointing off the other direction. "See here, the tracks are trailing off to the river where morning dew has been knocked off the grass."

"Okay, yeah, now I see," Warren said with surprise. The three of them rounded the bend, and there came Loring up the hill, holding a huge salmon by the tail.

"Papa!" shouted Loring, "Look what I got!" Loring ran and gave his father a hug, trying not to let the wet salmon soak Edwin's clothes.

"There are many things I need to teach you boys about living in the country. I'm not going to be too hard on you today, but next time tell somebody where you are going," said Edwin grimly. Then his face turned into a smile. "That is one fine-looking fish you have there. Where'd you get 'im?"

"Some guy named Charlie," he said with his eyes as round as saucers. He was still a bit out of breath. "He knew my name!"

"This is a small place," laughed Edwin. "Everybody knows everybody, and everybody's business is free game. So, old Charlie tossed you a fish, did he?"

"And a big one, too," said Loring, trying to hold it up by the gills.

"You'd a thought he woulda picked out an ol' black one to give away," said Edwin. "but this one will be good eating. Were you going to pull his entrails, or are you planning to eat him whole?"

"I don't have a knife on me, Papa. But, it's just like cleaning a trout, only bigger, right? How much do you figure it weighs?"

"Near twenty at least," said Edwin. "Almost as big as you! What grade in school are you in now?"

"Third grade," said Loring. "Did you forget?"

"No, I didn't forget; you just have to remind me, that's all. Two more years, and you should be done with all that."

"Mama said I have to go till the eighth grade." Edwin looked over at Lucy; this was a longstanding disagreement between them.

"That's your mother for you. But there is plenty of things to learn about life that don't come from book learning. Who cares if you know about the War of 1812; that thing has been over for ninety years. A man needs to know enough about words to read a book, write a letter, and enough about numbers to keep track of his money. Everything else that comes down to what he does with his hands and his wits."

"As long as that's good enough for me to become a ship captain," said Loring.

"A ship captain? Since when did you decide to become a seaman?"

"Since I saw those ships on Lake Michigan coming out West."

"I'll take Loring back to the river and clean our supper," said Edwin. "We'll be up in just a minute."

Somehow, Lucy was sad to see him go, as if in letting him out of her sight she might lose him again. But seeing how confident and at home he seemed in these woods, she wondered if she already had.

"Warren and I will head back to the house and get ready to go," said Lucy. "My feet are soaking wet." Lucy had run out in her nightgown slippers, which were now covered in mud. She was happy to have Edwin home, but looking down at her wet feet, she somehow felt foolish and out of place. All she had wanted was to be together as a family, but now that she was here, she didn't know if she could make it in this rural life.

Chapter 2

Family Heirloom

Lucy and the children were bundled up tight as Edwin drove the wagon down the road past a store and a little white church.

"This isn't much of a town, that's for sure," said Lucy.

"But smell the air," Edwin offered encouragingly. "It's nice and clean and it will be good for your health and recovery from having Edith. The scenery is spectacular, and it will be a good place for us to raise our children—near the river and the mountains."

"If we decide to stay, that is," Lucy interjected as Edwin looked over and caught her eye.

Edwin parked the wagon after pulling up in front of Jake and Anna's farmhouse. "Their house is quite a bit bigger than the one you landed me in," said Lucy. The children all piled out of the wagon and headed for the front door, leaving Lucy and Edwin on the driver's bench.

Lucy went on, "I heard tell Anna got an inheritance from her father after he died; that's how she was able to run off from her first husband and steal away her girls. Makes me thankful for you, Edwin Joseph. A man who loves me and works hard to take good care of us. Even though you do seem to like to work away most of the time, you still come home eventually."

Just then, Louisa came bursting out of the front door. She climbed up on the wagon crawled into her father's arms.

"What about me, child?" Lucy exclaimed. "Am I chopped liver? You have seen your father almost every day for the last six months, and you jump into *his* arms?"

"Here, Mama, take me," she said, reaching for her mother. Lucy picked her up and struggled to carry her in the house.

"You are getting too big for me to carry," Lucy said. "Something is hurting my back, probably just old age."

"Old?" laughed Anna as they walked through the door. "You're not a day over thirty-five; don't you be talking about old."

Anna ushered them all into their home. The whole house had the smell of sweet smoked bacon and fresh bread. There were knick-knacks on every shelf and a fancy red brick fireplace that gave the old farm-house class. Lucy admired the surroundings.

"We have a country breakfast ready for you. I baked fresh bread, and there are plenty of eggs, bacon, and fried potatoes. The coffee is black, and the tea is hot. Find a seat and relax."

Anna never skipped a beat but stopped to put her hand on Loring's shoulder. "You can wash up in the kitchen; you smell like a fish carcass," she chuckled. "Have you been out fishing this morning?"

"I didn't go fishing, but I got a fish. A guy named Charlie gave me a great big salmon."

"That Charlie," said Jake. "Consider yourself chosen. Charlie never gives any of his fish away."

Anna led the children to the wash bin, taking the tea kettle off the stove and putting steaming water in the pan.

"But first, let's get names proper. You all can call me 'Annie'; that's what everyone calls me. Now hold on and let me cool it off first before you go dipping your hands in." Anna ladled cold water from a bucket in the pan.

"You are quite the cook there, sister," said Lucy. "I hope I can measure up. I've always been a better seamstress than I have a cook."

"If you teach me to sew, I can teach you to cook."

Edwin pulled Lucy's chair out and scooted her in tightly, close to her plate. She put her hand on the seat next to her, coaxing Louisa to sit by her. Anna laid out a plate of fried potatoes, another with crispy bacon and pork rinds, called cracklins, a bowl of fresh-cut tomatoes and cucumbers, sliced bread still warm, and whipped butter, and then she came with another plate of fried eggs.

Loring reached for a slice of bread, but Lucy gave him her eye since not everyone had sat down yet. He snatched his hand back, giving her a sheepish grin.

"Now, if you don't see anything you want, don't ask because we don't have it," laughed Jake.

"Will you take coffee or tea, Lucy?" asked Anna.

"Tea, please," she replied, holding her saucer while Anna poured hot water into her cup.

"Quite the beautiful china, my dear," said Lucy.

"I had it shipped out some years back. It belonged to my mother; God rest her soul."

"Well, it is awfully pretty, I must say," said Lucy, checking out the expensive kitchen table and chairs, and the crystal water goblets.

"Would the children like milk?" asked Anna.

Lucy watched the faces of the loved ones sitting around the breakfast table as they began to settle in, waiting for Jake to take the lead on saying a blessing, but he picked up the plate of bacon and started passing it to Edwin. Lucy dared not say a word about reminding him to pray, but then thought again. Anna handed her the plate of bacon.

"Shall we say a blessing?" Lucy blurted out. Edwin looked at Jake for a response, and Jake looked at Anna, and Anna looked at Lucy.

"I don't know what us heathens were thinking," said Anna with a smile as she spoke.

"Well, I didn't mean . . ." Lucy stopped her words before she dug herself any deeper in the hole.

"It doesn't mean we don't believe or that we don't go to church on Sundays," said Anna, putting her hand on Lucy's arm. "Will you do us the honors?" Lucy set the bacon plate in the middle of the table and caught Etta's eye for some needed inspiration. Lucy took Louisa's hand with her right hand and took up Loring's on her left.

"Shall we all join hands and give thanks?" she asked.

Lucy opened her mouth and her words began to flow, speaking to God as if He were in the room. She gave thanks for their safety and all the wonderful people in their lives, her voice breaking as she thought about her Momma and Papa back home, wondering if she really would ever see them again. She gained her composure and finished by asking God to bless their first day here on the mighty Columbia River.

"That was real nice, Luce," said Edwin, taking up the plate of fried potatoes and continuing to dish up as Jake nodded his approval. Anna patted Lucy on the hand and gave a warm smile, seemingly thankful that Lucy had stepped up to do what no one else would.

"Is that knucklehead still trying to do you out of your team up there?" Jake asked Edwin.

"He sure is! He's been there a whole month longer than me, but they gave him the mules. He thinks it's all about seniority, when it's about how you treat the animal. Old Dennis, the camp boss, gave me the best horses he had. If that jackass don't stop mistreating those mules, he's gonna end up with a dent in his head."

Lucy tried to show her disapproval toward Edwin, but she couldn't catch his eye. "Edwin, that's enough of that talk."

"Okay . . . okay, I'm just saying. Logging out here is just like it was up in Maine twenty years ago. You just don't find old-growth like this anymore out East. They cut a tree last week six feet across the stump. It took three teams just to pull it down the skid road where they could get it hooked up with the steam lines.

"You are happy again now that you are logging, aren't you, Edwin?" asked Lucy, trying not to talk with food in her mouth.

"It's what I know, Luce, and all I am. Sure is a world of difference from darned ice deliveries and trying to put on some happy face for somebody else's customers. When I get those logs to their destination, I don't have to be some happy-pants' so people keep buying my logs. I just go get another load."

"You like folks, Edwin. You don't have to pretend," said Lucy.

"Oh, I like 'em too much to try to hoodwink em into thinking I'm their best friend so they keep taking my ice and not the competitor's."

"How did you like your house, Lucy?" asked Anna.

"Oh my goodness . . . so cozy and inviting. You can even see that Saint Helens Mountain out the side window."

"We love it here," Jake beamed.

"I wouldn't leave either if I owned a farm like this one," remarked Edwin, almost enviously.

"This place is a good start," said Lucy, covering up for Edwin, "I have a dream to one day have a big house of my own in the city. I know it will happen for us, Edwin. I just know it."

Edwin sat in silence, not knowing how to answer or wanting to burst Lucy's fragile bubble. Anna set her fork on her plate and put her finger to her cheek as she spoke.

"I know you are a city girl. I just don't know how farm life is going to suit you."

"I haven't seen very much of your city yet," said Lucy.

"You went right through the heart of the town on your way here. That was it. Did you see the store and the church?"

"I saw that, but I must have missed the city," replied Lucy.

"What you see is what you get here," chuckled Jake. "That was the big city of Mayger."

"Edwin, you said there was a city," she said, pursing her lips.

"Now Lucy, you know I have to go where the work is."

233

"But you said . . ." Lucy stopped in mid-sentence, looking at all the eyes that were on her.

"It's going to be just fine," Edwin said. "We have a store, a school-house, and a church. What more do you need than that, except a bunch of standing old-growth and a good team of horses. I'll make it good for you, Luce, just you wait and see."

The conversation went slack around the table as they finished up the meal. It seemed no one wanted to get Lucy upset.

"I want to see the Musket," said Warren, chiming in out of nowhere. "Papa, you said Uncle Jake had it, and you would show it to me when we got here."

All eyes were on Jake as he sat in silence, and his blank face told the story.

"The Musket." Jake paused and gritted his teeth. "You mean Great Granddaddy's musket?

"That would be the one, Jake."

"Edwin, now what was I going to do with that old thing, anyways?"

"You were entrusted by our father to be the steward of the family heirloom. What did you think you were going to do with it?"

"We can discuss this later, Edwin. This isn't the time nor the place."

Edwin had a strong suspicion the musket he had seen in Chicago was the one belonging to the family. Edwin didn't want to start a fight with his brother, but now the cat was out of the bag.

"This is a family matter, and we are going to discuss it right now."

"Would you feel any better if I told you it just came up missing?"

"I wouldn't feel any better about a lie than if you just told me the truth." Lucy could see Edwin's face turning red as he spoke. "You sold it in Chicago, didn't you?"

"How would you know that?"

"Because I saw that damn thing sitting in a window of a curiosity shop. I swore that was the rifle, so tell me the truth, Jake."

"You don't know what it was like for me coming West after Mom died in eighty-five. That musket weighed ten pounds, and it was like a rock in my knapsack. Worse yet, everyone in Chicago gave me creepy looks, packing that thing down the street." Jake paused, feeling uneasy about telling the rest of the story.

"Okay, then what?" Edwin folded his arms across his chest. He felt as if he were pulling an abscessed tooth out of his brother's jaw.

"A guy offered me ten bucks for it." Jake closed his eyes, feeling the guilt for what he had done.

"Ten bucks, Jake! For HEAVENS' SAKE . . . ten bucks?!" Edwin shook his head, and everyone at the table sat silently watching the exchange.

"I was broke, and I was hungry. I know–I feel terrible, and it has bothered me for twenty years."

"Do you know what the musket represents? And you went and sold it for ten bucks." Edwin could feel the anger building up in his stomach, and he stood up. "That musket wasn't yours to sell. It dates back to the Battle of Culloden and the Jacobite uprising in 1745, besides being a symbol of our family's part in the Revolution and a young John Dowling coming to America." He stood up. "Come on, Lucy, let's go home."

Jake didn't say a word. He didn't even know where to start or how to defend himself. He just stood there, silent, as Edwin took his family and headed out the door.

Chapter 3

A Need for Change

Over the winter, Lucy tried to make the best of what she had grown to consider as a bad situation. She liked her little house to a point, but most days it felt small and isolating. Sometimes it made her sick to her stomach just thinking about living in Mayger all the rest of her days in a pitiful little house. She saw Edwin a few nights a week, but since that first breakfast with Annie and Jake, things had grown tense and most days Lucy was alone with the children.

One day in early spring, Lucy took a walk in the afternoon to the General Store. The clouds were dark, and the air smelled like rain again; it had been pouring nonstop for a week. She tried to avoid walking in the muddy street and stepped up to the boardwalk, making her way to the large store with big plate glass windows. Written on the windows were the words "Drugs and Dry Goods" on the left side and "Groceries and Hardware" on the other. On the front door glass, it said, "Post Office." This one building had become her city.

"Good day to you, Lucy," said the storekeeper as she closed the door behind her. Lucy looked around at the now-familiar surroundings. The shelves were filled with canned goods of all sizes, shapes, and colors. There were flour sacks stacked five high on the floor and burlap sacks of beans and dry corn.

"You're looking good today, Clancy," she said.

"I've been waiting for you; got two letters here for you today."

"Two . . . I've never gotten two letters in one day," she said. Clancy turned and retrieved the letters from her box and handed them across the counter.

"Who are they from?" he asked.

Lucy held them in her hand as if they were gold. "This one is from Edwin's sister, Bell, and this one is from my very good childhood friend, Sarah Arnold."

"Where's that little one?" he asked.

"She's home in her bed, sleeping."

"Need a letter opener?" he asked, handing it in her direction.

"No, thank you. I'll take them home and savor every word."

Lucy walked out the front door. Just as soon as it closed behind her, she ran down the street all the way home. As her feet stepped on the front porch, she stopped to catch her breath before going inside. She had never really gotten over whatever had begun bothering her on the train, and short bursts of energy took longer to recover from. She gazed once more at the envelopes just to make sure she hadn't been dreaming. Then she stepped inside, listening to see if Edith had woken from her nap. Lucy peered through the crack in the bedroom door and found the child still fast asleep. She turned and walked into the kitchen, laying both letters out in front of her on the table, trying to decide which one to open first.

"Family first," she whispered, slitting the envelope with a kitchen knife to pull the folded papers out with Bell's beautiful handwritten words covering the page. Lucy sat in the quiet of her house as she poured over the words, gobbling every one like pieces of chocolate. It warmed her heart to know that Bell missed her so much, and it thrilled her soul to read the promise that Bell and Jewell would come for a visit the following year. The rain began to pitter-patter on the roof. Glancing out the window at the rain falling, she wondered how wet the children would be when they got home.

Taking up the second letter, she slipped the knife under the seal and ripped the envelope open. Lucy hadn't seen Sarah for two years, since Sarah had left Lowell to come out West to live in Everett. Lucy had written to Sarah soon after Sarah left, in the summer of 1904. When she hadn't heard from her friend by Christmas time, she wrote to her again. She had penned a letter out soon after Edwin left in the springtime the year before, and again when she had arrived in Mayger. Lucy had all but given up on her, thinking the address had been incorrect, and she unfolded the letter with great anticipation.

Everett, Washington
April 21, 1907

My Dearest Lucy,

Please forgive me for not writing to you sooner. I did receive your letter last fall telling me that you now reside in the state of Oregon with your family. I have never heard of this place called Mayger, but I hope this letter finds you well. I know I should have written to you long before this, and shame on me. I don't want to start right off with my woes, but if I get them away early then I can fill the rest of this letter with happiness. I was pregnant last summer and carried the child half term until I lost it. It was a boy this time. The other miscarriage shortly after we arrived in Everett was a girl. I am sorry to share so much sad news, but now it is off my heavy heart.

Everett is a glorious city growing by the day. There are many churches here, and people here are from all over! I don't know if Mayger is a big city; maybe you are experiencing the same things. The men here all strut around in their derbies and fine clothes with their women dolled up, just the same to show off their money. We don't have money like that, but we are comfortable enough, and we are buying a house.

I always remember when we were girls, laughing together at the boys who tried to impress us by wearing their fancy duds. That's why I remember you married Edwin, because he wasn't one of those.

Why I am writing is because William said that he could help Edwin find work here if he was a mind to it. There is a little house that just came open down the street where your family could fit. I am not meaning to meddle, but Lucy, it would be so wonderful to have you here with me and hear you laugh again. I know that would do more to lift my spirits and be a breath of fresh air to my soul. If not permanent, then maybe you could come up for a visit, and I will even pay the fare. The weather will be nice here soon, and we could talk about old times and maybe even visit a park. I would love to see your children.

Please think about it, Lucy. I know it would do me good to have a friend nearby and to help you take care of your children.

I will wait for a reply with great longing.

Sarah

The thought of having a home in the city made Lucy's heart fly like a bird. She folded the letter and put it back in the envelope, then went into her bedroom and placed it in the bottom of her sock and undergarment drawer face down. She would not say anything about it for now.

She heard the children clambering on the front porch home from school, and she rushed to greet them. The front door burst open, and laughter filled the house with four bubbling children all soaking wet.

"Louisa couldn't keep up, so Warren carried her," laughed Etta.

"I wanted him to carry me too," giggled Loring with a big smile.

Just then, Edwin came through the front door, and everyone turned in amazement.

"Off early today?" asked Lucy, trying to examine the look on his face.

"Now . . . now," she said to the children, trying to break up the mad rush for his attention. "Give your Papa some air. Children, listen, your Papa needs some quiet time. You have been cooped up all day at that schoolhouse; I think it's going to stop raining. I want you to change out of your wet school clothes, put on your playthings, and go outside. Run along now, you hear me?"

"Yes, Mama," said Etta as the boys backed away, leaving Louisa clinging to Edwin's neck.

"Are you okay, Papa?" she whispered in his ear. Edwin gave her a nod and kissed her cheek then put her down. Louisa gave her mother a nod then ran off to the girls' room.

"Why are you home early?" she asked.

"I quit," he answered.

Lucy stiffened.

"I'll put on some coffee." She headed for the kitchen while Edwin followed closely behind. She opened the door to the firebox on the cook stove and tossed in a few pieces of wood from the wood box to get it stoked up again, pulling the damper open to give it some air and then ladling water into one of her teapots.

"Here, wash up."

She poured some of the warm water into the wash pan and handed him a clean towel. Then, cranking the coffee mill, she took the grounds and put them in the top of her drip coffee maker. Edwin washed his hands, then took his hands full of water and splashed his face, feeling around for the towel to dry himself.

"That's better," she said, kissing him encouragingly on the cheek. "Now, sit and tell me what happened."

Edwin pulled the chair away from the table and sat down. Putting his elbows on the table, he held his chin in his palms. "They up and sold my team, Luce, right out from under me, near four weeks ago. I didn't say anything because I know how you worry. Then they brought in more oxen and expected me to run 'em. They changed boss men on me too, and Howard left for Napavine up north, in Washington."

The fire in the woodstove began to crackle, and the kettle started to vibrate from the boiling water.

"Keep talking." Lucy got up and grabbed the teapot, pouring the steaming water into the top of her coffee pot.

"See here, Luce, you know I can't run oxen." Lucy watched as he spoke, seeing a man defeated.

Then a thunder of humanity came bursting in the kitchen, laughing and chortling like a herd of wild horses. "It's time to go out and let some of that stink blow off you," she chided. Lucy checked out the window and reported, "See, it has quit raining, so now shoo, you hear me . . . shoo! Before I have to get the broom!"

The children made their way outside and Lucy set a cup on the table in front of Edwin, pouring out fresh hot coffee.

"I gave it my best, but those damn oxen are stubborn, and they won't talk to you. You know what I mean. I just won't run oxen, and that's it. They got this tunnel down there that comes through a ridge top and cuts off a half-mile of dragging to the dump at Hungry Hollow Camp. Now there is talk about pushing a railroad through it."

"A tunnel," she answered, squinting her eyes at him. "You said nothing about a tunnel."

"I never said because I knew you would worry."

"I would worry because I would have something to worry about. Where is it?"

"It's down at Westport. They say the founder, Captain John West, had it dug before he died in eighty-seven. They are building the railroad, that's for sure. The writing is already on the wall. They will do away with all the animals once that happens."

"What are you going to do, Edwin?"

"Do you know Spike?"

"No, I don't think I have met anyone named Spike," she answered.

"Well, no matter, Spike has a boat, and he is heading across to Washington tomorrow and going up the Cowlitz River to Kelso. He said

I could throw in with him, catch the train at Kelso, and then head on up to Napavine and find Howard. He said I would find him up there."

"Sounds like you have this all planned out." After everything, he was leaving her again to find work.

"Where will you stay?"

"They have a hotel up there, and I have a little money . . . enough, I suppose."

"I've been putting money away too," she said.

"You been holding out on me?"

"Not holding out, but I know you wanted to get your own team, so I have been saving up. I call it Edwin's horse fund."

"Lucy, a good horse team that ain't all broken down and overused with all the tack and harnesses will run nearly eighty dollars. Just where are you going to come up with that kind of money?"

"Don't you worry none about that, old man. You just figure out where to buy them, and you let me worry about the finances."

"I just don't know, Luce. The damn trains are running us horsemen right out of business. The whole world is changing right in front of us with automobiles, trains, and now aeroplanes. Things that have made sense for centuries don't seem to make sense anymore. Steam power and gasoline engines are going to ruin everything. Everybody is in a hurry these days. It's like they are trying to cut the last tree or catch the last fish. My job is evaporating in the mist, right in front of my eyes." Edwin sighed defeatedly, his shoulders sagging.

"Don't get down on yourself. You are the best damn horseman in the state, probably in the whole Northwest."

"Luce, watch your tongue." Edwin smiled at her, but Lucy could not manage a smile back.

Chapter 4

A Fine Team

I want you to find a team you like and buy it. Not an expensive one, but a good solid team."

"Are you sure?" smiled Edwin as he took her hand in his. "I don't know where you got that kind of money, but I'm not going to ask. You didn't rob a bank, did you?" Lucy laughed, and Edwin burst out laughing with her.

"It will stay my little secret, then," she said, still laughing. She knew there was no way she could tell him that Peg and Pete had given her the money. He would have made her give it back, even if it meant giving up his horse team. She prepared herself to make up a convincing lie.

"How much do you have, Luce?" he said, looking deep into her big, brown eyes. Lucy paused, thinking she should take out ten dollars from the eighty she had saved.

"I have seventy dollars," she exclaimed.

"Seventy dollars, you little sneak." Edwin smiled and paused just for a minute. "No, I take that back. You are a big sneak. I know you want to buy a house. I know you got that money from your parents to help us get one." Lucy looked away, glad he had filled in the details on his own and she didn't have to lie. She would let him believe what he wished. She steeled herself to bring up the conversation that might be a way out for her family.

"What would you say about me looking for a place up in Everett?"

"Everett?" Why would you possibly want to go to Everett?"

"I wasn't going to tell you, but I got a letter from Sarah Arnold today, and she wants me to come up for a visit, and if I like it up there, she will help us get a house. It's time to move on, Edwin. This place is just a little too country for me. You knew that about me when you married me. I have to have shops and bakeries and churches and such. I need to be in a place there where there are people all around me. A place where there is hustle and bustle and things going on. I need to be in a place where my children have opportunities more than just fishing, logging, or feeding cows."

"What's wrong with being a logger?"

"Nothing . . . nothing at all," she said, trying to back away from offending him. "But you are the one who said it was drying up under your feet. I just want our children to have it better than we did. I know there is logging up in Everett."

"Don't we have it good, Luce?" he asked, putting his arm around her neck and pulling her close.

"Yes, we have it good, Edwin. You have always supported us, I know that."

"I hate it when I am away from you, but you know I have to be away. I have to leave you where you are safe, and I know here in Mayger you will be safe. I will have peace of mind knowing that Jake and Annie will take good care of you. Besides, just quick like, Austin and Bessie are likely to move out here. If I know Austin, he will find somewhere here close to Jacob. Don't you want to be together with the family?"

"If that happens, I may find a home here; you know how much I love Bessie. But Anna and I have just never clicked. She is nice and all, but she is seven years older, and she treats me like I am a little girl. At least if I move up to Everett, I will be back in the twentieth century. We are still cutting wood to heat with, hand pumping water out of a well, and using these kerosene lamps. I feel like I am living like I was back down east in Whiting twenty-five years ago."

"That's how you feel?" asked Edwin, taking a sip of his coffee.

"Yep, this is how my grandparents lived, but we don't have to live like this. There are modern conveniences in the city. I need my flush toilet back; I am sick of walking out in the cold and rain to use that outhouse."

Edwin and Lucy sat quietly. Neither talked for some time. They could hear the faint laughter of the children playing in the yard. Edwin cracked the silence first. "Lucy," he began. "If you want to go for a visit up to Everett, then I think you should go."

"If I go up to Everett to visit Sarah, I don't think I will come back here."

Edwin took a deep breath. Lucy knew his response would change her life. She had tried to make sacrifices to support Edwin, but now it was his turn to support her. She held her breath as he began to talk.

"Okay. I will head up to Napavine and find Harvey, and you will head to Everett. If you find a place up there, just send a note to Napavine in the care of Harvey Casper. I'll go to work to find the proper horse team. Harvey said they are clearing stumps up there to make farmland. If I have my own team, I can make good money, enough for us to save up to buy a house. When I get something going and get a break in the work, I will jump a train and meet you up in Everett. Then we will see what happens. How does that sound?"

"It sounds fantastic. Oh, Edwin, we are good together because we can talk like this, openly, like a couple of old friends."

"When you go talking like that you give me other ideas right here in the middle of the day." Edwin held her hands and winked at her.

"Yeah, well, don't be getting any ideas like that in your head." Lucy shoved him on the shoulder, and they both smiled.

"That bean soup sure smells good," said Edwin.

"Oh, my soup!" cried Lucy, jumping up.

⚡⚡⚡

Edwin left the following day, April 30th, catching a boat across the Columbia and then up the Cowlitz River for Kelso. Every time Edwin left, Lucy had a pit in her stomach; she always worried about him and wondered if she would see him again. Three days later, Lucy had packed all of their things, confident she would not come back to Mayger except to visit. Jake and Anna took her and the children to the train stop to catch the southbound.

"You don't have to go, you know," Anna remarked.

Jake concurred. "I don't see why you are leaving when you have a perfectly good house here."

"I'm just going up for a visit," Lucy said, knowing full well she hoped to never come back to this place she could hardly call a town.

"Lucy, I know you are not coming back," replied Anna soberly. "You may be able to fool Edwin, but you can't fool me. I know you don't like it here; that's no secret."

"I'll be back," she said. "Even if it is for just a visit." The children sat quietly at the train stop, waiting for the sound of the steam engine to pierce the river corridor.

"We just have to come back to see my Annie," said Louisa, clutching her aunt's waist.

"I hear it coming," announced Loring.

"I don't hear anything," Jake responded.

"You wouldn't," laughed Anna. "You never even hear me when I am in the same room."

"I am pushing fifty, and with all that dynamiting I have been around over the years, and the duck shooting . . . I'm surprised I can hear at all." Jake's face grew serious and he turned to Lucy.

"I know Edwin's leaving here has a lot to do with me selling the family heirloom all those years ago. I wish he could forgive me, but I know he won't let it go."

"You know Edwin." Lucy shrugged her shoulders and wrinkled her nose. "Lord knows I can't change him."

They could hear the sound of the steam engine echoing across to the north side of the river. Then they saw the smoke from the stack shooting up above the trees. Then the headlamp came bursting around the corner as the black iron monster made its way through the trees and around the bend from the West. The train rumbled and snorted as it began to slow, and the engineer rang the bell. The locomotive went past in a puff of steam while the coal smoke settled on them. Everyone held their sleeves over their mouth and nose, trying to shield themselves from the foul smell of coal smoke. The breaks squealed, and the engine let out a puff of steam as the train came to a stop.

"Those are my trunks on the wagon," Lucy said as the trainmen approached. "The second one is the heavy one; it has all my china from back East, so please be careful."

"You better get on board, children," said Anna as she handed Edith over to Etta, and Loring grabbed Louisa by the hand.

"Louisa, you better give your Annie a big loving hug to last a while," Anna said as she embraced the child she had come to love like her own. "If your mama ever casts you off, then you come back here, and I will always be your other mama. I'm gonna miss you something terrible, child."

"I will miss you already, Auntie," said Louisa, soaking in the last bit of love from her. Anna took her by the hand and helped her up the steps of the coach. Lucy reached down and took Louisa's hand and wished Jake and Anna goodbye.

The whistle blew, the train bucked and lurched forward, and just like that, they were gone from Mayger. She had closed the book on her country life and was excited to begin her new chapter as a city girl once again.

They rode the train seventeen miles to Goble, a place along the Columbia River where there was a ferry landing. Lucy had to get off the train heading toward Portland to catch the ferry to Kalama.

Lucy thought there would be plenty of folks traveling with them, and was surprised when she disembarked to find they were the only ones heading to Tacoma and Seattle. Porters unloaded her trunks, and the men put them on a baggage cart. There was a comfortable waiting room at the station, enabling passengers to get out of the rain. Stepping in the front door there, she found a man sitting behind a counter.

"What time does the train to Portland arrive?" she asked.

"It will be here within the hour, ma'am. Do you have tickets?"

"No, sir, I need them."

"Name please?" asked the man, who wore a wrinkled white shirt with dirt marks on the sleeve. He had a bushy mustache and a shiny bald head that appeared waxed. His thick eyeglasses sat low on his face, and he took his finger and pushed them back up his nose.

"I am Lucy Dowling and, as you can see, I have five children."

"Let's see," he said, rubbing his chin. "Under eight rides free, and you and the older ones pay full fare."

"Under eight?" exclaimed Loring. Lucy grabbed his shoulder tightly, and he looked up at her with big round eyes.

"Yes sir, I have three under eight, so I need full fair for three of us," she said, knowing full well Loring had turned eight years old last September, and she was lying through her teeth. The clerk scrutinized Loring, looking him up and down.

"I'll take you at your word, ma'am, but I know everyone fudges the railroad."

"We are coming from Mayger, where we have lived for six months, and we are moving to Everett. My husband runs horse teams and . . ."

"I didn't ask for your life story, ma'am," he said, cutting her off in mid-sentence and pushing his glasses back up his nose. "The train from Portland will be here as quick as a wink. I can sell you tickets to Everett, but it would be better if I just book you to Tacoma for this leg.

I have to charge you a ten-cent service fee, but if you get them straight from the Northern Pacific, there is no extra cost. When you get to Union Station, you will have to get tickets to Everett."

"Well, thank you, sir. I had no idea."

"So, heading off to the great Puget Sound, hey? It's beautiful. Did you bring food for your trip?"

"Yes, we are seasoned travelers."

"How seasoned are you?"

"We came out from Lowell, Massachusetts, in the fall, and rode the train all the way across the country."

"Yep," he said with a surprise in his voice, "you are well seasoned, well-seasoned indeed."

Chapter 5

The Ferry

Lucy watched out the window as the big steam ferry floated in closer to the landing, and men waited along the dock to link the train tracks on the boat with the ones on the shore.

Lucy sat back down and thought about how far they had come. She couldn't believe she was traveling once again without her family. Hopefully for the last time.

"Maybe we should buy a postcard to send to your grandma and grandpa," Lucy said and Etta nodded enthusiastically.

"I feel terrible that you children never met so many of our relatives. That's what's so terrible about moving halfway around the world. I am afraid I will never get back to Lowell in my lifetime and never again to Machias, and I will never see any of my family on this earth ever again as long as I live."

"I guess at least we got Jake and Anna, and pretty soon, Uncle Austin and Aunt Bessie will be here too," said Etta.

"That will be nice. If only I could convince your grandparents to come out and see this place. Just maybe they would decide to stay, once I get us all settled up in Everett. I can't wait for you all to meet Sarah. She and I have always been like sisters. I guess family is just what you make it."

"Do we have all their names written down somewhere?" asked Etta.

"I think the Gardner side might be in my Mama's family Bible, but we won't forget."

"What about my children and their children's children?" said Etta.

"Yea, what about them, Mama?" asked Louisa, looking at her with her piercing brown eyes. "Who is ever going to remember all this in a hundred years?"

"They won't forget, don't you worry," said Lucy. "There, I think I hear our train coming. But I suppose it would be a good idea to write this stuff down. Maybe we will get to it someday."

At that moment, the boys burst through the doorway.

"That man said we could walk on the ferry and board the train when we get on the Washington side, at Kalama," said Warren, half out of breath.

"We should wait until the clerk returns for instructions," declared Lucy.

"No, Mama, that *was* the clerk. He told us to tell you," said Loring. "He said to go right down the gangplank, and there are real nice passenger quarters on the ship."

"And from there, he said when we land to go straight to the depot on the bow of the ship, and they will load us on the train on the Washington side," continued Loring.

"Okay, I believe you," replied Lucy. "Who's got Edith; Warren, will you carry her?"

"I've got her, Mama," said Etta.

"Can you make it down that walkway carrying her?" Lucy asked anxiously, gathering her things and looking around to make sure they hadn't left anything behind. The brisk morning air blew in her face with a gentle breeze off the river as she went outside. She held the brim of her hat as they made their way on the ship. Lucy kept a careful eye on

Etta. She could just imagine her slipping and then dropping the child in the Columbia River.

The family made it safely to the passenger area, where a crewman appeared to be waiting for them to arrive.

"Welcome aboard the Tacoma, ma'am. You must be Mrs. Dowling," he said, looking at his ledger. The man had a clean and pressed uniform, and was clean shaven with a well-trimmed haircut. He wore a white shirt, black wool jacket, and bow tie. If Lucy had to guess, the man appeared to be just her age, around thirty-four.

"Yes, sir," she answered.

"It says here you are traveling to Tacoma, is that correct?"

"Yes, sir."

"Would you like a cup of tea?"

"Oh, thank you. I would love a cup of tea."

"Just relax; it is just over a quarter-hour run across the river, and then we will get you loaded on your coach once they unload the train." He poured hot water into a cup, put in a tea strainer, and then handed it to Lucy by the saucer.

"That is quite the accent," he commented with interest. "You must be from the East Coast?"

"I am born in a little place down east in Maine called Machias, and then raised in Lowell, Massachusetts."

"That explains it; your accent suits you well."

Lucy gazed out the window as Kalama began to get close.

"Done with your tea, ma'am? We are almost there." Lucy took the last drink and handed him her cup. Then the big ship lurched as the paddle wheels reversed, slowing the ferry as it came into the landing. "I can escort you down to the depot if you like."

"That would set me at ease for sure," smiled Lucy as she extended her hand.

"Come on, children, make sure you have everything you brought," coaxed Lucy as the man opened the door, and they made their way toward the front of the ship. "Oh my goodness, this is a huge ferry. How long is it?"

"She is three hundred and forty feet," said Loring.

"He wants to be a ship captain," laughed Lucy.

"If you want to be a captain, then you will have to do good in school and listen to your teachers."

"My Pa said it's better for a man to find a job than it is for him to waste his time going to school. He told me if I want to work on a ship, then it's best when a boy reaches the age to work to find himself a job and learn from the bottom up."

"That used to be true twenty years ago, but I never went to school past the fifth grade, and now I wish I had gotten more school because I could never be a ship's captain. I would have to go back to school, and Lord knows, I am too old for that now." Loring pursed his lips and looked up at Lucy.

"See what I have been telling you, Loring. You have to apply yourself in school if you want to get ahead in this world."

"Look, Mama, how they lined up the tracks to the ferry, so they can scoot the train on the tracks."

Lucy watched as the engine on her right came to life, and made its way off the steamer and up the steep grade where men switched the track to get it out of the way of the main road. Then another black steel monster, smoke belching out of its stack, started its wheels, moved out onto the dock, switched to the middle track, and backed on board to grab hold of the coaches. Lucy and her children hustled off the boat and walked up the planks toward the small station building. Looking back, she watched as they began to pull passenger coaches up the steep grade; passengers and all went up the bank with an air of ease.

"It's time to board the train," said a porter. "They loaded your trunks into the baggage car when you were riding the ferry. Would you like to follow me?"

"I don't have a choice, do I?" she asked, trying to make light of his request.

"Not unless you want to get left behind," he said with a smile.

Lucy and her children followed him outside to the train platform, and there stood the familiar sight of last fall: the glorious locomotive in all its splendor, the coal fires burning and the massive steam boiler sitting quietly as if she were napping and ready for the awakening.

"We rode out on the Transcontinental last fall," she said. "I'm glad we are only going a hundred and sixty miles this time."

"How long will it take for us to get to Everett?" asked Louisa.

"I don't know, Pumpkin; it depends on how many stops."

"I see you only have fare to Tacoma. If you are going to Everett, you'd better get that taken care of," said the porter, helping Etta on the carriage.

"What time do we get into Tacoma?"

"Somewhere around four o'clock."

"That's six hours. It takes this train six hours to go a hundred miles?" asked Lucy putting her hands on her hips.

"Do you have any idea how many stops there are between here and Tacoma?" he asked.

"No, I only know when we came across the country, we made much better time than that."

"Officially, there are twelve stops, and usually we stop for at least ten, maybe fifteen before we get going again, and so do your school arithmetic. That's over three hours just in stops."

The little station buzzed with activity, which seemed strange to her for being such a small town. The train whistle blew two long blasts, the cars shook, and they began to pull away. She tried to hold her excitement as the bell clanged, and then went silent as they slowly got up to speed. She felt excited to be heading north to a big city. She remembered Edwin telling her that, near Everett, there was a place called Lowell in an outskirt town nearby. She couldn't wait to get to Lowell and see if the people there were from New England. She hoped that maybe she might even recognize someone there from home.

"The engineer is running that engine cold this morning," said Lucy in a low voice to Warren and Loring, who were looking out the window. "Look at all that smoke; you can hardly see out the car. He needs to stoke up that fire."

"If the engineer drives the train, what does the conductor do?" asked Loring.

"The conductor gets his name from being the person who directs all the instruments in a symphony, and he is the one responsible for making beautiful music," she explained. "Do you hear all the noise the train makes—from the chug, chug to the whistles, and that clanging bell? All that announces it's coming, and keeps people and animals off the track."

Louisa looked at her mother with her big brown eyes as she spoke, and Loring nodded his acknowledgment of his question. "It's like a song to the train crews, and they have a conductor to lead them in the symphony."

"I don't mean to break into your conversation, dear lady, but if you would permit me, I might be able to shed some light," said the man across the aisle, taking his Derby off his head. He was an elderly man with a thick white mustache, thinning gray hair, and wrinkled face.

"Allow me to introduce myself. My name is Henry Sealey. I have been a railroad man for nearly thirty-five years now, and I know the whistles and the horn blasts quite well. You are right about the conductor, that it is like he is conducting a symphony. You will hear a series of longs and shorts that they use for communication with the train workers and those in the yard. Every time they come to a wagon crossing, the engineer will sound two long blasts, one short and then one long. That tells the crew there is a crossing, and is a warning for any wagons to stay clear. The origins are sketchy, but old train runners tell me it originates with the letter 'Q' in Morse Code, which was to say, 'here comes the queen.'"

"That is amazing," said Lucy. "All my life, I have heard train whistles, and this is the first time anyone explained it to me. I thought they were just blowing their darn horn to tell people to get out of the way."

"That's all most people know," he said as he started to laugh. "Most people just think the engineer likes to blow his own horn. I won't go into all the signals, but whistles instruct the flagmen to do certain things, like a whistle telling the crew they need to switch over at the next station to let a train behind them go ahead because of a schedule demand. Not all railroads use the same patterns, but mostly they try to keep them all the same."

"That is fascinating! Where are you headed, Mr. Sealey?"

"You can call me Henry. I am heading up to Everett to help a friend who is building a logging train. He wrote me, and he doesn't know the first thing about running a railroad."

"That's where we are going as well," Lucy answered. "I might just need to contact you when you get established to see if there might be any work there for a horseman."

"Who might that be?" he asked.

"My husband," she said, thinking that she was treading on dangerous ground, looking for work for Edwin without him knowing.

"Is he a good worker?"

"Oh, Edwin is a hard worker and a good provider. I think he would do anything if he could live in a big city and stay home with his family," she said, thinking how guilty she felt for telling an outright lie.

"Where is he now? Is he waiting for you in Everett?"

"Actually, no, he is in Napavine."

"Yes, Napavine," he answered. "Just a couple stops north of Winlock. Would he want to change occupations and run a train?"

"I could ask him. It never hurts to ask, right?" But she already knew the answer.

The train began to slow, the bell started to ring, and then the whistle blew.

"Are we stopping already? For heaven's sake, we just got going."

The train would stop in Kelso, Strander, and Castle Rock. At Castle Rock, they admired the stone pillar along the Cowlitz River, shaped like a castle, the inspiration for naming the town. The train then stopped at Olequa, Sopenah Station, also known as Little Falls, Ainslie, and then Winlock.

"That means Napavine is the next one," Lucy said just as the train began to slow. The engineer let out a long blast on the horn.

"Will your husband be getting on?"

"Not a chance," she said as the train came gliding into the tiny Napavine station. "He doesn't even know we are on the train."

Chapter 6

A Pair of Horses

There's Papa!" shouted Loring. Lucy spun to the window and sure enough, there stood Edwin with a pair of fine horses. She had not expected to see him for perhaps months, but there he was, waiting for them at the station.

"Papa!" shouted Warren as he reached over and unhooked the latch and slid the window down.

"Papa!" shouted Louisa. "Are those your new horses?"

"Stay here, children," said Lucy, jumping out of her seat and heading for the exit. A porter stood by the door, waiting for the train to come to a complete stop.

"This isn't your stop, ma'am," he said, trying to be as polite as he could.

"I need to get off the train; my husband is waiting to see me."

"You are not leaving your children behind, are you?"

"Who do you think I am? I am not leaving my children. I will be right back!"

"You better be quick; otherwise, you could get left behind," he said as he pulled on the door, and Lucy skipped down the steps. "Tell the engineer to hold the train," she said, looking over her shoulder as she walked briskly across the boardwalk.

"Now look here," he shouted.

"My kids and my baby are on the train. Don't you dare leave me," she shouted back. Lucy turned and walked hurriedly toward Edwin, who saw behind her that all eyes from the coach windows were on them. She wanted to run to him, but at the same time, she worried she might catch her foot on the planking and fall. Edwin held the reins on two glorious horses. They were both chestnut, one with a white face and white socks, the other with a white patch between his eyes and a thin white strip between his nostrils and white stockings.

"Edwin, you have outdone yourself," she said, approaching the horses cautiously and then slowly allowing one of them to smell her hand. "They look like pure-blooded Percheron. Are they ours?"

"You are half right," he answered. "Clydesdale and Percheron, but all ours."

"How in the world did you ever find them? They are some of the finest horses I have ever seen. So muscular and powerful, excellent conformation with an upright ready-to-go stance. The conformation is amazing. They are just perfect for your workhorses, Edwin."

"I can't believe I found them."

"What are their names?"

"This one is a mare with the white face, and she is called Cedar, and the other is a gelding called Alder," said Edwin.

"Seventeen hands?" asked Lucy.

"Not a bad eye for a city girl," laughed Edwin.

"Did you name them?"

"Oh heavens, no, those were someone else's idea. But I suppose for logging horses, the names are fitting."

"I'm glad you didn't name the mare 'Lucy,'" she laughed.

"How's the train ride, dear?" Edwin reached out and put his arm around her shoulder.

"How long before I will see you, Edwin?"

"I am just getting things going here. I found these animals just four days ago now and put forty bucks on the barrel head this morning. I took a chance that you would be on this train so you could see our purchase."

"Where are you staying?"

"I'll be pulling stumps for a farmer up on Pleasant Hill about five miles from here. He's got a shed out back he converted into a cabin. So for now, room and board are on him."

"How much is he paying you?"

"A dollar a stump, most of which are twenty-four inches at the butt. Two days ago, we pulled four stumps in one day."

"Not bad for a day's work. I'm going to find you work when I get to Everett. You know I have always been a good sport about being on my own, but I need you to come up to help me get settled in."

The conductor shouted, "All aboard," and the train whistle blew. Lucy looked over her shoulder and gave the man a wave, then looked back at Edwin. "Lady, this train is leaving," shouted the conductor.

"Just a minute, sir," she shouted. She turned back to Edwin. "I have to know, when will you be coming to Everett?"

"I'll write you, but you will have to write me first, so I have a post to send to you. You can just address it to me in care of Walt Anderson in Napavine." The train whistle sounded again, one long blast showing just how impatient the engineer had become. They heard the steam brakes go loose with a huge puff, and she could see the engineer would not be held up any longer.

"All right . . . all right," she shouted. "I'm coming, for heaven's sake!"

"You better go. The engineer isn't bluffing. Kiss me quick, or he'll take off and leave you standing here." Lucy looked back over her shoulder, seeing all the people on the train watching them. Edwin grabbed her shoulders and planted his lips on hers.

Lucy walked vigorously toward the conductor as he shook his head in disgust, looking down at his open pocket watch. She grabbed the handrail and pulled herself up to the first step, and made her grand entrance to the coach. Everyone began to clap as if they had just watched the final scene of a love story play out in the theater. She could feel her cheeks getting warm as she walked down the aisle, then stopped and took a bow and gave her best smile to everyone in their seats.

Edwin had approached the train and was reaching out to his children. Lucy had to grab Louisa to hold her back from jumping out the window into his arms. The porter slammed the door shut, and the train lurched forward and began moving. The bell clanged, and the engine chugged, both horses lurched, and Edwin grabbed hold of them to settle them down. Louisa extended her hand, trying to get her father's last touch as the distance between them began to increase.

"Bye-bye, Papa," she shouted. The black coal smoke came drifting through the open window, and Lucy fought to shut it quickly to prevent any more of the foul odor from coming in the cabin. Then she sat down hard in her seat and covered her eyes to hold back her tears. Life seemed to be just a series of ups and downs. Some moments were beautiful, like a chance meeting in a little town like Napavine. But these moments seemed few and far between as the two were ever torn apart by the lure of a few dollars and the money that never seemed to be enough to make their dreams come true.

The train whisked right past Eleanor Spur and Newakum, then rumbled on toward Chehalis at a fast clip. The fields were green, and the surrounding hills were full of alders and maples that had spurted up in the clear cuts from logging twenty years earlier.

"Next stop, Chehalis, Mama," said Warren.

"Seems like everything in the Northwest has an Indian name, and everything on the East Coast has an Irish or English name," said Lucy.

"Not exactly," said Henry, "you'll discover there are lots of British names out here, but we don't have much history at all compared to the

East Coast. I mean, even Lewis and Clark only came out West a hundred years ago. Then there was a guy named George Vancouver and his young lieutenant, Peter Puget."

"Is that why they call it Puget Sound?" asked Lucy.

"That's right."

The train stopped at Chehalis and then went on to Centralia. Both stations were busy with a bustle of people coming and going. Some of the passengers in Lucy's car got off, and new folks reoccupied their empty seats. All the time, Henry and Lucy talked on about the beginnings of the Pacific Northwest. Lucy drank in everything he told her as if she were a student in a classroom.

The train chugged north, and Lucy took pleasure in just watching the sight of people engaged in all sorts of activity, working in the fields and going to and fro on horse-drawn buggies. Every time she saw a team, she would compare it to Edwin's horses and think about the excellent team he had purchased. The thought crossed her mind that maybe she should just stay in Everett a short while and then write to Edwin to find a home in Napavine. A chill came down her spine at the thought, and she quickly got that notion out of her head. She felt positive she could find him a job up in Everett, running his team.

"Would it be out of the question to transport a team of horses on the train from Napavine to Everett?" Lucy asked Henry.

"I suppose not out of the question. They transport beef, but it might be pretty spendy. I suppose if you were rich and you loved the horses. But it might be more cost effective to sell them and buy a new team in Everett."

"Oh," said Lucy, "I was just thinking, you know."

Henry reached his hand across the aisle and said sincerely.

"Mrs. Dowling, when we get to Everett, where neither of us has any family, you will be comforted to know that you have someone like a father that you can count on." Mr. Sealey seemed sincere, but she didn't know anything about him; he was just a stranger she had met on the train. Lucy caught his eyes, and his smile said everything to her, and she knew instantly he was a papa who needed a family as much as she longed for a papa on this side of the country.

"That means a lot to me. If I said it once, I have said it a thousand times. My father is the best one a girl could ever have. But he always told me, you could never have too much family around you."

"You have a smart papa," said Henry with a wide grin. "My wife and I have lost two children in our lives together, and our daughter, Lisa, in Oregon, is the only one left. We lost our son to whooping cough at just a year old in seventy-five, and then our other daughter, Patricia, died at age twelve of the measles, back in eighty-two. That was almost twenty-five years ago, and it seems like yesterday." Henry's eyes welled up as he spoke.

"It's okay," said Lucy. "I think God made tears for a purpose to cleanse our souls and help us let go of the past. I think it shows you are a real man with real feelings. All this hogwash about being stoic and acting all tough inside is ridiculous. Women aren't afraid to show their emotions, and I think the world would be a lot better off if men could open up and learn to do the same."

🌲🌲🌲

The train headed north, stopping in McIntosh and Rainier to exchange passengers and then on to Yelm. Lucy watched out the window and could see small farms dotting the landscape. She looked for ducks sitting on the lakes and ponds.

"Sure don't see very much wildlife," said Lucy. "I would have thought the West would be full."

"If anybody sees one, it dies quick and goes on the dinner table, no matter what," said Henry.

"Do you think they will ever wake up to what they are doing with the fish and game in this country? They can't just continue on this way, or everything will become extinct."

"That's the least of anybody's troubles with this new land. Heck, they just settled the Indian wars, and everybody is so focused on trying to win a fortune that deer and salmon and such are the last thing anyone is thinking about."

Chapter 7

Tacoma

Through the clouds, the top of Mount Rainier was suddenly visible. The huge white mass towered majestically, like a Mount Olympus of the West. Lucy let out an audible gasp.

"You are lucky to see it. Most of the time, the mountain is covered in clouds. Most people have to buy a postcard just to see what it looks like."

"We have been here since the fall, and this is my first time seeing it," she said. "I don't know if I will ever get used to all the rain here. It is sort of depressing. I became so familiar with Mount Saint Helens poking up like a big ice cream sundae, but this mountain is spectacular."

"We are just going into the most beautiful part of living here in Washington State, which is the summer. Enjoy the long days and the beautiful weather, because the season is very short."

The train made a short stop in the town of Rainier, and then they were back clacking on the rails heading north. The train stopped in Yelm, Roy, and whisked right past Hillhurst without a stop, then sped on to Lakeview and Tacoma. By now, Lucy was hungry to see a big city, and when she laid her eyes on Tacoma, she became emotional.

"This is a glorious place." Lucy watched out the window as the train came into the station, looking through her tears. She had hardly a glimpse of the main street that ran parallel to the tracks, but she could see the buildings and the people visiting shops and restaurants.

"I just love the hustle and bustle of the big city," she said as Henry watched out his window as well.

"If you love this, you are going to love the downtown views. You haven't seen anything yet. I know you probably think Lowell is a big city, but when you see Tacoma, the Gateway to the Northwest, you will be impressed."

"I don't know if anything will impress me after seeing Chicago."

"Yes, Chicago, New York, San Francisco . . . those are all beautiful places, but nowhere in the world will you see a city perched on a more beautiful bay with a mountain view of Rainier like downtown Tacoma. Tacoma is the Indian name for the mountain. But Tacoma is not exactly the correct pronunciation according to what I know. The Puyallup Indians called their Mountain Tahoma. But the 'h' sound came out very hard in their throat when they spoke it, and so many people thought the letter 'c' more appropriate in the translation. Thus the name Tacoma became the official pronunciation and the English spelling."

The train stopped in south Tacoma only briefly and then pulled away. People stood on the boardwalk, waving, and Loring and Louisa waved back. As the train made its way north through the outskirts of town, Lucy could feel her anticipation growing.

She was once again amongst the living where there were soda shops and fine restaurants, places to window shop and grand hotels. She wished Edwin loved the city like she did. If he didn't have such a love affair with his horses, just maybe he would come home and find a real job where they could live as a proper family. Lucy felt again the sinking feeling that she needed Edwin by her side to help with the children. She was growing tired too easily these days and the children seem to look after themselves.

The train thundered down the hill and slid through buildings, almost like some back alley. The city stood majestically, like a crown jewel against the waterway with Mount Rainer looking down like a mother hen watching over her chicks. The buildings rose up eight or ten stories; such a sight she had not seen since Chicago.

"I have to purchase tickets for the train ride to Everett," she said, speaking across the aisle to Henry.

"Don't you worry your little head another thing about that. You just stick with me, and I will get you all fixed up."

"Don't you dare go and pay for me."

Lucy looked out the window to see if she could get a glimpse of the station, thinking surely for a city such as this they would have built something quite grand. The coach began to slow, and the breaks squealed; then the bell began to ring as they came to a stop.

"Where is the station?" she asked, raising her eyebrows then looking back out the window. "We are backing up?"

"Yes, I suppose I should have told you. The train has to back up to the station because there is no room for a turn."

"That's something I never saw before. A station they have to back into? Well, I never."

The train backed up several hundred yards into the station, and Mr. Sealey helped her gather her things and her children. Lucy adjusted her hat before going outside to make sure it was still pinned tightly to her hair. Henry adjusted his derby, positioning it smartly.

Henry went down the steps in front of Lucy. He took her hand, helping her and the children onto the boardwalk.

"This way, follow me," he said, heading toward the station behind the crowd of people going in the same direction. Etta carried Edith, and Warren walked with Louisa, holding her hand tightly. Lucy carried her handbag, and Henry had an attaché for his important papers. When they got to the station, the crowd had thinned as people made their way to the street. Lucy looked across the avenue over the rooftop at the eight-story brick storage warehouse and the sizeable wholesale grocery building. She turned a gazed toward the waterway and saw a furniture factory building perched on the side of the hill in line with the sight of the glorious mountain. The sign painted onto the side of the building said "Harmon Furniture". Henry held the door for her, and they walked inside the depot.

"Not much of a station for a city such as this," she said.

"Yes, but they have grand plans for a station fitting for the city of density. They are set to begin construction next year." Henry stopped at a bench and coaxed the children to wait for them as they got the tickets.

↟↟↟

After they had secured their tickets, Lucy was determined to use their short wait to get a look at the city. She felt rejuvenated as they stood on the street corner on the front side of the depot along Pacific Avenue. Folks were on the move with horse-drawn buggies and wagons, and everyone was dressed in fine clothes.

"Sure is a far cry from Mayger, where the men wear logging duds with suspenders, and they all chew tobacco." Lucy took a deep breath to smell the air. "What is that foul smell?"

"Why, that's the smell of progress, my dear."

"So that's what progress smells like. But that is quite the odor. I didn't know money smelled like rotten eggs."

"They call it the 'Tacoma Aroma.' It's a mix of low tide, sulfur from the lead smelter, sewage, and the rotting bark stripped from the trees at the sawmill. That's progress, and that's money."

"Look at that restaurant just down the street!" Lucy could only imagine what it would be like to sit with friends and have a fine dinner out on the town. *Wouldn't that be grand,* she thought longingly.

"Don't be disappointed when you see Everett."

"I know it won't be as grand as this, but if it's only half the size, I will be thrilled."

"I want to look at the boats," said Loring.

"We have to cross over on that bridge right there, and you will get a good look at them out the window of the car," said Henry. "Are you ready?" We should probably get back on the train. I doubt if you will get lucky twice in one day to have the engineer hold the train for you."

"I already got lucky twice in one day, dear sir. The engineer held the train, and the second stroke of luck was sitting next to you."

The whistle blew one long blast, and the steam burst from the boiler as the brakes were released and the engine began to chug. Crowds of people stood on the boardwalk waving to loved ones, and passengers on the train crowded the windows to wave back. Lucy watched the crowd with her hands folded in her lap, wondering if any of those people were from New England and watching their faces to see if anyone looked familiar. She thought about her Mama and Papa. She wondered what they were doing back home on this fine day, and fought back tears of loneliness.

Henry could see the sadness in Lucy's eyes, recognizing she was just a little girl who felt homesick. Henry gently asked her about her family back home and what she hoped to find in Everett.

"I have a dream to own a fine home with a large backyard where my children can play." She lowered her voice and whispered across the aisle, checking to ensure the children were all preoccupied with waving to the crowds. "With a loving husband who comes home every night and tucks his children in bed and reads them stories. That's the kind of papa I had growing up, and that's the kind I long for my children to have." Lucy paused, wondering how he might respond, but he said nothing.

"Anything else?" he asked.

"Not really," she answered. "I'm a pretty simple girl. Oh, I suppose I want to live a good long life and die an old woman at age eighty in my sleep. I want to see my children grow up and get married and have many grandkids who come to visit often and fill my big house with laughter. I want to be the grandma who bakes cookies and makes dresses, and we will even make gingerbread houses at Christmas time. I want to find a church in Everett, a place where I can sing on Sundays."

"Do you just sing along, or do you sing up front?"

"In my church back home, I always did a solo on special days, and sometimes I led the choir too."

"Maybe when we get settled, I will come and hear you sing when you find a church," he said. "Just as long as the minister don't go preaching fire and brimstone. That's what I grew up with, and it just ain't for me."

"Don't worry, Papa, I will find us a good church," said Lucy, looking at him with a big grin. Henry chuckled back, and the two had a nice laugh together. Lucy didn't know if he laughed out loud because she suggested the church would be theirs together or because she called him Papa. Either way, she didn't care because laughter filled her soul with life.

Chapter 8

Seattle

Along the way, the rest of that afternoon, the train stopped at every little station it could find to delay their arrival to Everett. They waited long enough for the lunch rush to pass, but not long enough for all the food to be gone. Many travelers, such as Lucy, were on a tight budget and avoided the railroad food altogether.

"Oh my," said Lucy as she strolled into the dining car. "This is an upgrade from the one we had on the Transcontinental last fall."

"Yes, this is a new dining car," said Henry. "Quite luxurious. The Northern Pacific has ordered several more of these. They will be stationed in Tacoma—due to arrive in two years. This car came up from Portland and is the first of its kind."

"I hope the food matches the surroundings."

"It will; I guarantee it. They have to put on the Ritz because there's other competition, such as the Great Northern and the Union Pacific."

A dark-skinned, impeccably dressed steward met them politely and showed them to a table set with fine linen and lined with polished silverware. Lucy took the menu to see what she might have for lunch and find out what her children might eat.

"The salmon sounds delicious."

"I think I will try the smelt," said Henry.

The steward came back, and he tipped the goblets up and poured water from a pitcher.

"Have you decided on anything yet?" asked the steward.

"Is the salmon fresh?" asked Lucy.

"The salmon is delicious, and we have had lots of compliments." Lucy knew he was dodging the question but felt satisfied that others on the train gave it a useful review. "I'll have the salmon."

After they had ordered and the steward headed for the galley, they were free to talk. "This can't be Columbia River salmon," she said under her breath.

"No, I'm sure it's sport-caught right here in Puget Sound," he said. "Puget Sound isn't like the Columbia where the fish only come up to spawn. There is a large population of fish that live here in these waters year 'round. Many salmon go out to the ocean and return during the run, but people come out here from New York and Chicago just to fish. They say a man can make a good day's wages here with just a fishing pole and a rowboat."

"Maybe I'll be a fisherman when I grow up," said Loring.

"You were going to be a ship's captain," replied Lucy drily.

"Either way, I will be on the water. I had a mind of being a teamster, but Papa said horsemen are a dying breed."

"Besides, horsemen who work in the woods don't get to be with their kids," remarked Etta.

"I don't suppose a ship captain is much better," said Warren.

"Don't matter, the sea is for me," declared Loring.

As they ate their lunch, the train passed Meeker, stopped in Sumner, Auburn, and Kent, and then headed north to the much-awaited city of Seattle. Lucy loved how much Henry knew about the area and invited him to share all he knew.

"Seattle has always had the idea they are the 'upper crust' of Washington State. There was a huge competition to win the Northern Pacific Railroad western terminus, which would mean lots of dollars to the city who got it. An eager crowd gathered at the Yesler Mill in July of 1873 to hear Arthur Denny read a telegram from Northern Pacific executives announcing their decision. When Denny opened the telegram and read it in front of the crowd, they were stunned—then angered—to learn that Tacoma had beaten them."

The children were all listening; Henry's voice was captivating.

"The reaction in Tacoma was completely different, as you can imagine. It was met with celebration and gaiety, knowing full well that Tacoma would benefit from the money. However, a group of powerful men decided to pool their money and build their own railroad. Executives at the Northern Pacific were not ready for that and began to try to appease them. Of course, it was too late, but Northern Pacific caved in and moved their western terminus to Seattle twenty years ago. Since then, there has been a sometimes bitter and quite difficult rivalry between the two cities."

"Everything comes down to money, doesn't it?" Lucy observed.

"It's always money, because money translates to power, prestige, influence, and lifestyle."

"Yes," said Lucy, "but in the end, it's just a chasing of the wind. It doesn't amount to a hill of beans in the grand scheme of life. The only thing that matters in this life is something a lot of people will never figure out. They are so busy chasing the things of the world they forget about the real treasure in life that has been hidden away in clay jars."

"Clay jars?" he asked. "What do you mean?"

"You have to be thirsty enough to look for it. If you're not, you never will."

"I think I know what you are getting at," he said with a suspicious smile. "I gave up religion long ago."

"Most people stop at religion, and they never realize that God is real," said Lucy earnestly. They look at the cross, and Jesus' death, and they don't realize that He is alive. So they have this dead faith."

Lucy could tell that Henry had become uncomfortable talking about matters of faith. Knowing that if she spent too much time on the subject, she might lose him altogether, she changed the subject.

The steward returned to their table. "Are you done with your lunch? Would you like me to take your plates and get you some dessert? We have orange sherbet, carrot cake, or a baked apple."

"I think the children will have the sherbet," she said, waiting for them to respond, and each eagerly agreed. "I will have the baked apple."

"And for you, sir?"

"I will have the carrot cake," said Henry as Lucy took a sip of her tea.

They finished their dessert while the train chugged along, and listened to the whistle, which blew every time the train came to a wagon crossing. Then they made their way back to their seats. Although Lucy had become very tired, she felt a certain measure of excitement mixed with a little resentment the closer they got to Seattle.

"What else do you know about Seattle?" she said, trying to pick up their conversation where they had left off.

"Do you remember hearing about the Klondike gold rush?" asked Henry. Lucy hesitated to answer and could feel her emotions welling up inside as those familiar words rolled off his lips.

"Yes, Henry, unfortunately I know more about the Klondike than I ever wanted to know." Lucy looked over at her children to make sure they were occupied. Henry looked at the empty seat next to him and then coaxed her to scoot across the aisle, and he moved over so they could sit together. The children looked up from their play then went back to what they were doing.

"I tried to tell him, but he wouldn't listen." Lucy looked across the aisle to make sure her children were busy. "My husband took every cent we had and came out West in ninety-eight." She proceeded to tell Henry her sad story, trying to not let her anger seep through her words.

Henry was understanding. "It sounds like your man made a good go of it, but—like a lot of folks—he got beat to the punch."

"He got punched, all right. He got sucker punched, and it nearly took all the stuffing out of him. I had to live with my parents for a year, and I know that took a toll on them. But Edwin never got the taste of the Northwest out of his system. A seed was planted in him that began to grow."

🌲🌲🌲

The train stopped for about thirty minutes in Seattle, just long enough to refill the water tanks and the coal bin. Lucy toured the new station, amazed by the beauty; it nearly took her breath away—twenty-five-foot ceilings with ornate woodwork, large hanging chandeliers, and oversized windows all around. There was a huge sitting area with oak benches and chairs for people to relax while they waited.

"What time is it?" asked Lucy.

"Didn't you see the big clock on the wall?" Lucy turned, and right in front of her face stood a grand, larger-than-life clock that said four-thirty.

"What time will we get to Everett?" asked Etta.

"Looks like we will be right on time, depending on where they take us. If we go on the Northern Pacific rail lines, it will be much later with all the stops, but if we take the Great Northern line, we will be right on time at six o'clock."

"This is going to be a long night of getting settled in Everett," said Lucy. "I hope Sarah received my letter so she will be there when we arrive. If not, I will have to find a hotel for the night, somewhere, and then try to find Sarah the following day. I'll need to hire a carriage and track down her address."

"Maybe she has a telephone?" suggested Henry.

"If she does, she didn't put that in her letter. I suppose if I can find a public phone, there might be a directory listing for her, if I get lucky." The thought came to Lucy that she should be praying and not relying on luck. "I heard it said once that the acronym for LUCK is to be

'Living under Christ's Kingdom.'" Henry laughed, and then Lucy laid back in her seat and closed her eyes.

"If that is true, Lucy, then your name means, 'Living under Christ's Yoke.'"

"I like that," she responded with a smile, and then she closed her eyes and fell fast asleep.

🌲🌲🌲

She awoke as Henry tapped her on the shoulder. "We are coming to Lowell," said Henry. "I thought you might like to see it. Besides, we are almost to Everett. Your children were very protective of you as your eyes got heavy, and you just took a nice little nap."

"We're here?" she asked. "I can't believe it. How long did I sleep?"

"About an hour and a half. Looks like we will be right on time, despite being a little behind schedule in Seattle. We switched over to the Great Northern track, which has far fewer stops. The Northern Pacific doesn't go through Lowell, but these tracks do. So you'll be able to get a good look at it."

"Who founded it?" asked Lucy. "Maybe our family knows them?"

"The founder's name is Eugene Smith; he was a logger and came out here as a young man from Massachusetts on a schooner. He named the town Lowell. He married Margaret Getchell, who was born in Machias. That's why they named a town here in Snohomish by the same name—Machias."

Lucy knew that name from her family history. She was excited to finally have information to share back to Henry.

"The Getchell family are a prominent family down east Maine, and they go way back and intertwine with the Gardners and the Dowlings. If my husband were here, he would tell all the stories about our lineage. John Dowling fought in the revolution with Joseph Getchell. And as I recall, he was one of those who fought to capture the Margaretta. I don't recall a Eugene Smith from Lowell, but I can write my Papa and ask. He or my Mama would know!"

"Sometime, you will have to tell me more about the battle over the Margaretta. Sounds like an interesting story." Lucy smiled, knowing she was not the one to tell it and that Edwin knew all the details.

Chapter 9

Everett, Finally

I told you not to be too disappointed about Everett. You have been to Tacoma and Seattle, and now don't expect Everett to measure up to those cities."

"I don't need a grand city. All I need is a city with schools and churches filled with friendly people like we have back home in Lowell. I know in a city like Seattle, a person could get lost, but if Everett is anything I have imagined, it will be just right for me. Not too big and not too small. Does Everett have a grand train depot?"

"They haven't built their grand station yet, only a station adequate for accepting the trains and moderate volumes. I am pretty sure the Northern Pacific has great plans to build something nice in the next few years. This is a very young city, only incorporated sixteen years ago, but it has a lot of growth potential. That's why I decided to come here. Even though I'm getting on in years, I believe this place has a lot of promise for me, and it will hold a lot of promise for you and your family as well."

Lucy sat with great anticipation, hoping with all hope and praying that Sarah would be waiting for her. She began to feel the lump in her throat as her worry mounted.

"What's the matter?" asked Henry looking at Lucy's face and her distress.

"Oh, I'm just tired, that's all." She wondered to herself why she always felt so tired.

"Are you worried about your friend not showing up?" asked Henry.

"I have so much to do . . . if I have to find a hotel for the night, I just don't know how I will do it."

"Don't you go worrying your head because I will take care of you, just like a proper papa. I will help you find a room for the night, and after my early morning business meeting, I will help you find your friend."

"I can't believe my good fortune to find you, Mr. Sealey. You have been a godsend." Lucy watched out the window as the train traveled across the city. She had put all of her hopes in this one place. People were bustling in the streets. There were horses and buggies and an occasional motor car mixed in. The train came down the hill, and Lucy could see the grand waterfront of the harbor.

"That must be Port Gardner," said Lucy.

"How do you know that?" asked Henry in surprise.

"Because Edwin has talked about Port Gardner being the main water port here in Everett. Of course, my mother is a Gardner. I am from a long line of Gardners—Thomas Gardner came to America on a ship right after the Mayflower. He became the first Governor of Massachusetts. So don't spoil it for me because Edwin said they named it for my family. I'm sure it's not, but I will prefer just to be naive and accept the myth as fact. I think he told me that just so I would want to come out here all those years ago," she laughed. Henry wanted to tell Lucy all that he knew about the British Admiral Allan Gardner, who had mentored young officers such as George Vancouver, Peter Puget, and Joseph Whidbey. Still, he refrained, letting her believe the Gardner name came much closer to her family tree.

The train pulled up to the station, and the whistle blew as it announced its arrival. Lucy scanned the crowd, hoping to see her childhood friend. The brakes squealed, the train began to slow, the cars clunked as the couplings clashed together, and the mammoth monster breathed its last sigh of the trip as the steam pressure went out of the locomotive.

"I hope she is here," said Lucy gathering her things. People began standing all around, anxious to get off, while up ahead in the car, some passengers began to depart the exit. "I'm so nervous," she whispered in Henry's ear.

"We'll be just fine, Lucy. Don't you worry about a thing."

The street was wet, and the air smelled like the fresh rain had just passed over. The sun had begun its journey below the horizon, and the sky was getting dim. People were shouting across the boardwalk and running to embrace their loved ones. Looking up the train and then back down the other way, she scanned the crowd for a familiar face— to no avail.

Not looking down but keeping her eye on the crowd, she took a step, and her foot caught on the metal rung. She grabbed for the handrail but missed it as she went flying down the steps and landed in a sprawl on the wet landing. The crowd gasped then went silent as all eyes were on Lucy. A porter ran quickly to her aid.

"Are you all right, ma'am?" said the man with concern, taking her hand. She looked up and saw a woman with her hand over her mouth in horror. Henry hurried down the steps behind her and helped the porter get her to her feet.

"Mama!" shouted Louisa as she flew off the train.

"I'm fine . . . I'm just fine," she said, pulling her hand away from the porter but wondering if she might have hurt herself. She tried not to look red-faced with humiliation from all the attention from the crowd.

"I just want to get out of here and disappear," she whispered.

"Don't you worry," said Henry. "I'll take care of you." Lucy quickly straightened her hat to regain her dignity.

"Come on, children," said Lucy, trying to brush the smudge off the front of her dress.

"Are you okay, really?" Henry whispered under his breath as they made their way through the crowd.

"I think I scuffed my knee. I just need to find Sarah."

Lucy's heart sank even deeper, looking around the platform and coming up empty as they made their way to the baggage area. She looked down at her dress, where her knee hit the bricks, and saw the fabric had a small tear. She wondered how badly she had scuffed it and reached down and rubbed it.

"Got your baggage stub, ma'am?" asked the porter as Lucy dug through her handbag. The only thing on her mind seemed to be Sarah and recovering from her embarrassment. Lucy looked at her wrist, and noticed she had a raw spot where she had landed.

"I have three trunks, sir," she said, handing him the slips.

"What happened to your wrist, ma'am?"

"Oh, it's nothing. I just slipped getting off the train."

"How about you, sir?" asked the porter as Henry passed his claim check. Men were unloading trunks and leather bags from the car onto hand-pulled flat cars. People began crowding in around them as everyone eagerly retrieved their things.

"With so many people here getting off this train, I wonder if it will be difficult even to find a hotel room," said Lucy.

"You wait here. I'll go hire us a carriage before they are all taken."

"Want me to go with him, Mama?" asked Loring.

"No," answered Lucy, "I want you to keep a grip on your sister, please."

"I'll go with him," said Warren. "And then I'll come back and help with the luggage." Both Henry and Warren disappeared through the crowd. Lucy tried to watch for her trunks but spent most of the time looking for her friend. She felt a stab of relief as she saw her things being taken off the train by porters, and saw Henry approaching.

"There is Mr. Sealey now," said Lucy to the children. "He must have found us a carriage." Lucy caught his eye coming down the platform with Warren following just behind, but by the grim look on their faces, she could tell they both seemed frustrated.

"The carriages are all booked, and the trolley just left full. We'll have to wait in line for them to drop off and return," said Henry as he came near. Lucy's heart sank, knowing she had almost reached the end of her rope. She was feeling quite exhausted from the long day and wanted to get the children settled for the night.

"How long is the wait?"

"An hour or so, maybe longer," answered Henry.

"What other choice do we have?" she said resolutely, trying to keep a good face for her children. "We will just have to wait."

"At least it's not raining," said Louisa.

"We have a lot to be thankful for, Pumpkin." Lucy watched as the skylight began to fade away into the darkness of the night and street workers began to light the gas lamps along the boardwalk. The baby started to fuss, and Etta tried bouncing her in her arms.

"I think she's wet, Mama."

"Nothing we can do now," said Lucy. "She will just have to wait until we get to a hotel if we can even find a room this time of the evening. I just don't want to be sleeping on the street somewhere."

Lucy watched as the railroad workers loaded her trunks onto a cart, along with several others. The men stacked some smaller leather bags that she had seen in the catalog, called "suitcases." Most people traveled with trunks, but she could see that the suitcase might just catch on for short-term travelers. They followed the porters as they pulled the heavy cart around the station out to the frontage street.

"I can't believe she is not here," said Lucy. "Anyone living in this town can hear the sound of that whistle blast, and you would think she would at least come to see if we made it. Something must have gone wrong."

They waited as a carriage approached in the dim light, hopeful it was one for hire so they could get along for the night before the baby made too big of a scene. Lucy's heart fell again, seeing that the carriage had a woman riding beside the driver and knew the cart would not be one for hire. She could see the horse favoring its front leg and wondered what could be so crucial for this driver to be pushing a lame animal.

She wished Edwin were here to take a look at the poor horse's front leg. Lucy focused her attention on the horse, trying to evaluate the seriousness of the injury, and wondering what Edwin might say about this unfortunate situation.

"Lucy!" came a shriek and the woman in the carriage began waving wildly at them. She bounded off the buggy and came running down the street.

"Sarah!" yelled Lucy, so excited that she wanted to dance. Sarah ran across the station platform, and they threw their arms around each other like long-lost sisters. "We would have been here sooner, but our little Tilly went lame. Albert thought we should turn around and go home, but I just had to come."

"Oh, Sarah, finally, we are together again," said Lucy.

"You have no idea. You don't know how I have waited for this day, for this moment."

"Let me look at you," said Lucy taking a step back from her. Sarah wore a red dress and matching red hat. Her facial features were stunning with her big round eyes, rosebud mouth, and high cheekbones. She wore her long, dark hair tied up and tucked under her hat.

"Everything will be fine now, Lucy, you just wait. I can't believe you are finally here."

"What's wrong with your horse?" asked Lucy.

"Oh, I don't really know; you'll have to ask Albert. Come on; I can't wait for you to meet him." They approached Albert as he parked the coach. "This is my husband, Albert."

Lucy reached out her hand to greet him, and Albert took her hand in his. He wore a long double-breasted woolen camel coat, black leather gloves, and a brown derby similar to Henry Sealey's. Albert had a clean-shaven face with a dimple on the end of his strong chin, dark eyes, a thin mustache, and a kind smile.

Lucy pulled her bonnet from her head, careful not to mess her hair, which was tied up and fastened with hairpins.

"Oh, that feels good to get that thing off," she said with relief, handing it to Louisa, then lifting her skirt to step off the curb and approach the horse. Lucy reached out, stroking the mare on the nose and talking to her gently, whispering in her ear. "Are you going to let me take a look at that leg of yours?"

Albert came around the front of the carriage to watch this strange sight as Lucy reached down and picked up the animal's foot, trying to see it in the dim light from the streetlamp.

"Look here," said Lucy. "She has a rock stuck on the edge of her shoe. Does anyone have a pocket knife?"

"I have one," said Henry, stepping off the curb as he pulled the folding knife from his pocket. He handed it to Lucy, who reached out and took it from him.

"You are going to get all dirty, Mama," said Louisa. Lucy went right on with her business as she held the hoof between her knees. She pried the sharp stone away from the edge of the shoe and the pebble bounced in the street. Lucy put the horse's foot down, then stepped back and brushed the front of her dress off. "There, that's all it was, dear Tilly." Lucy rubbed the side of the horse's cheek. "Just a rock in your shoe." Lucy looked back to Albert, who raised his eyebrows.

"Not bad for a city girl who knows her horses," said Henry.

"Oh, I am a city girl, all right, but my husband is a horseman. Oh, how rude of me. Sarah and Albert, this is my friend, Henry Sealey. We road up from the Columbia River together on the train. And this is my oldest, Warren, then Etta, Loring, Louisa, and the baby is Edith."

"Lucy, you have gotten your dress filthy," said Sarah.

"No, not just from that," she explained. "You see, when I got off the train, I tried to fly, but my wings gave out, and I crashed on the platform." Sarah gave a smirk to Henry, and she shrugged her shoulders.

"What do you mean?" asked Sarah as the children began to giggle.

"Mama took a tumble," laughed Loring. "She is so graceful that she thought she could fly."

"It was our mother's grand entrance to this magnificent city," laughed Etta.

Warren and Albert struggled with the heavy trunks and fastened them to the back of Albert's carriage while Sarah and Lucy got the children settled. Henry spotted a carriage for hire coming down the road and waved it down.

"Henry," said Lucy, "I know this is the end of the line for us."

"I certainly hope not. You are like family to me now. When I get settled, I will come and visit, if that's okay. And when Edwin comes to Everett, I should hope that you will contact me so I can come and meet him."

"Here is our address," said Sarah, pulling the slip out of her coat pocket and jotting it quickly on the paper. "Here you go."

Henry stepped onto the street, greeted the teamster driving the hired horses, and told him he needed to go to the Grand Hotel. The driver stepped down and took Henry's suitcase, then opened the door for him. Henry turned and tipped his hat, then got in the carriage, the driver securing the door shut behind him. Lucy had a lump in her throat, and a tear came down her cheek as she quickly wiped it away with her sleeve so no one could see. She had finally arrived in a city, but felt like she had just left her Papa all over again.

Part V—Edwin and Lucy Dowling, Cont'd.

Edwin Joseph Dowling
Born: February 17, 1862, East Machias,
Washington County, Maine
Died: April 10, 1928 (age 66), Everett, Snohomish County,
Washington

Lucy Delia Cook Dowling
Born: November 27, 1872, Maine
Died: April 6, 1910 (age 37), Everett, Snohomish County,
Washington

ALL CHILDREN OF EDWIN AND LUCY DOWLING

Warren Henry Dowling
1893–1966
Born: April 30, 1893, Lowell, Middlesex County, Massachusetts
Died (age 73): February 27, 1966, Snohomish, Snohomish
County, Washington

Bertha Etta Dowling Troy Donker
1895–1989
Born: January 18, 1895, Lowell, Middlesex County,
Massachusetts
Died (age 94): March, 1989, Everett, Snohomish County,
Washington

Loring Estes Dowling
1898–1930
Born: May 26, 1898, Lowell, Middlesex, Massachusetts
Died (approx. age 32): sometime after 1930, in the
Bering Sea, Alaska

Louisa Marion Dowling Swanson
1900–1994
Born: August 24, 1900, Lowell, Middlesex, Massachusetts
Died (age 94): August, 1994, Tacoma, Pierce County,
Washington

Edith Hill Dowling Olson
1906–1970
Born: April 2, 1906, Lowell, Middlesex County, Massachusetts
Died (age 74), February 22, 19970, Tacoma, Pierce County,
Washington

Roy Arnold Cole (adopted out at Lucy's death,
at age five months)
1909–1982
Born: November 26, 1909, Everett, Snohomish County,
Washington
Died (age 83): December 16, 1982, Seattle, King County,
Washington

Part V

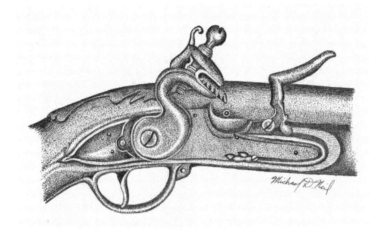

WARREN HENRY DOWLING
1893–1966

BERTHA ETTA DOWLING TROY DONKER
1895–1989

LORING ESTES DOWLING
1898–1930

LOUISA MARION DOWLING SWANSON
1900–1994

EDITH HILL DOWLING OLSON
1906–1970

ROY ARNOLD COLE (Adopted out of the family)
1909–1982

Chapter 1

Homecoming

Lucy spent the following weeks with Sarah and her husband on the riverside of Everett. Sarah, who had hoped for children for so many years, seemed to bloom as she took on her role as aunt to Lucy's children. Lucy felt as if she had finally arrived somewhere to call her own. The schools and the churches were a dream. She had never imagined the Wild West could be like this.

The summer of 1907 whisked by as Lucy found a house to rent on Walnut Street, hoping that one day she could find the money to buy it. It was a far cry from the small wood house she had left behind. This house had been built in 1900 and had modern conveniences: running water, a wood cookstove, and a coal-burning parlor stove. Lucy had to beg and borrow to collect cast-off pieces of furniture from the neighbors, but she made it a home.

She enrolled the children in the new brick schoolhouse, Garfield Elementary, which had been completed in 1903. Warren had just turned fourteen and would soon graduate from the eighth grade, and he planned to find a job to help the family.

Mr. Sealey purchased a house on Colby Avenue on the Bayside, often inviting Lucy and her children for a Sunday dinner. Shortly after he arrived in Everett, he met a widow whom he hired as housekeeper to live with him and take care of the house. Lucy could easily see their relationship was more than that of simply a housekeeper and an employer, but she kept her suspicions to herself. She was glad the children had someone like a grandfather in their lives.

She was still far from home, but for the first time since leaving Lowell, Lucy felt like she could find a home here in the West.

⇑⇑⇑

"Edwin is coming home this weekend, Sarah," said Lucy. "I just got a letter in the mail yesterday."

It was that special hour in the afternoon when the older children were at school and the young ones were napping. Sarah and Lucy would sit with a view of the river, sometimes talking away, sometimes reading and responding to letters. Sarah gave Lucy a questioning look, trying to ascertain how her friend felt about her husband's return.

"When Edwin gets here," Lucy said resolutely, "I will finally be able to give him a piece of my mind. He just has to find work up here in Everett. He needs to find a place to hang his hat where he can come home more than once every eight weeks."

"I don't blame you, Lucy. You have to stick to your guns on this one. You can't be raising five children all on your own without a husband to help you. I have to be honest: that man makes me so angry I could just spit."

"I do love him. If I didn't, then it wouldn't matter in the least to me if he came home at all. But I miss him so when he is gone from me. I miss sitting down to a meal with him. I miss sharing the funny things that I get to share with our children every day. Being married is about sharing your life, and our lives are short enough as it is. What else do we have except our time together? I know he likes to be alone and talk to his horses, but I need him. I guess we are just two stubborn people. He likes the woods and the solitude, and I like the city and the crowds. I know I don't go to shows very often, but if I want to, then I can. But if you live in Napavine or Mayger, you've got nothing."

"There must be work here in Everett. Someone would hire him. I think the lumber mill is hiring. They can't find enough men, and I am sure they pay a fair wage."

"Unless they need a horseman, he will never agree."

"What day is he coming?" asked Sarah.

"He's coming in on the Northern Pacific Saturday evening, and he is staying for a couple weeks. I hope I can talk him into coming for good."

"Are you thinking of having another child? It seems like all you have to do is think about that man, and you get pregnant."

Lucy knew Sarah was using the joke to cover her own pain. No matter how hard she and Albert tried, Sarah remained childless.

"It's not what I think, Sarah. Children are a blessing from God, and if He allows me to have another, then I will accept whatever he wants for me."

"I am so desperate to have a child," Sarah murmured.

"Have you spoken to a doctor?"

"What would a doctor be able to tell me about how to sleep with my husband? Besides, that would be an indecent conversation to have with another man."

"I suppose you're right. I don't have a lot of faith in doctors. If God wants you to have a child, then it will happen."

"I have been praying, but I just don't know if God hears me. I think He is so busy with important things like the unrest in Europe or the recent outbreak of Bubonic Plague in San Francisco."

"I don't know if God gets distracted by world events and forgets about the lives of His people. I think He loves each of us and is involved in our lives, and wants to hear from us. Just because He does not give us what we think we want doesn't mean He has forgotten or is disinterested."

"That's probably a very good point, Lucy."

"Life is strange. Sometimes I think I am going to have a short life and that must be why God gave me such a strong faith. I just hope I can pass it down to my children, and I would love to see my husband wake up from his deep slumber."

"Edwin doesn't share your faith?" asked Sarah.

"We have had some discussions about God. Edwin is very stubborn. I think he is mad at God for taking his mother and father. He has a very hard time seeing the things of God."

"I understand not wanting to talk about God and faith. My mother always told me that what we believe should remain a very personal thing."

"I would never pry into your personal life, but we are best friends, and best friends share everything. Don't they, Sarah?"

Lucy could see that Sarah didn't want to go any further with the conversation, but to her surprise, her friend responded.

"I think sometimes I am afraid to find Him because I know He will be angry when He finds me."

"Oh Sarah, that's silly. What would He be mad at you for?"

"Believe me, Lucy, He has plenty to be angry with me about."

"Like what?" Sarah sat quietly as her eyes welled up, and Lucy could see that something in her friend seemed terribly wrong.

"I can't bring myself to say it. I know God could never forgive me."

"Oh, that's just silly, Sarah."

"I can't tell you; you will think I am a terrible person."

"You don't have to tell me."

Sarah paused, trying to force the words off her lips. She whispered her secret into Lucy's ear.

"That's it?" Lucy smiled reassuringly at her friend. "I was afraid maybe you murdered someone."

"Oh, Lucy, for heaven's sake, no, I didn't kill anyone."

"That's a relief," laughed Lucy.

"Do you think God can forgive me?"

"Have you ever asked Him?"

"No, I've been afraid."

"Don't ever be afraid of God. He created you, and He loves you more than you love yourself. He knows our sin, and He even sent His son to give His life for ours. I am not a priest, Sarah, but when you come to my church again, the preacher can pray for you."

"You see Lucy, that's what I mean. I will never have somebody else pray for me like that."

"Then it will be our secret, and we can pray right now."

"But what if God says no, and He refuses to forgive me?"

"That's not in His nature. He made a way for all of our sins to be forgiven. If He didn't intend to forgive us, then Jesus wouldn't have died on that cross."

⭡⭡⭡

That Saturday, Lucy had a skip in her step. The Great Northern, if the schedule remained true, would be carrying Edwin from the fields of Napavine. She had spent most of the morning fixing her hair and had even bought a new hat, just for the occasion. She had made all the preparations for his arrival and had cleaned and dusted the house and made everything perfect. She wanted him to see the life she had created in Everett for their family. She wanted him to stay.

She had written him, urging him to make this his final trip from down south, hoping he could find work here so they could live as a proper family. In his letter back to her, Edwin had been non-committal, with little enthusiasm for the idea. But she knew if she could just show him a good time during his stay, then she just might have a chance to bring him home. At least she knew he loved her, but as to how he showed it, that was another matter altogether.

"I hear the train whistle, Mama!" shouted Loring as he and Louisa came sprinting in from the back porch.

"He's coming!" squealed Louisa. "Papa is coming!"

"That whistle means the train is leaving the Snohomish station," said Sarah. "Looks like we will get there just in time."

"That's fifteen miles away," said Etta. "That's impossible."

"You will see, the train will be here in twenty-five minutes," answered Sarah.

"That's more than enough time for us to get to the station. Isn't Albert coming?"

"No, he had business to attend to, and he will be home late. It's Saturday evening, and the train will be busy. Best to get there early to find a place to put the surrey."

"C'mon children, go get in Sarah's buggy, and I will be right behind you."

"Will you drive the horse, Lucy? I just don't have the same confidence you have." As Lucy slapped Tilly's back with the reins to get her going, she could feel that familiar pit in her stomach—a little bit of excitement to see Edwin mixed with a whole bunch of worry about what sort of mood he would be in. There was room in Sarah's buggy for a trunk and she wondered if Edwin had brought his with him.

As they made their way down Hewett Avenue on that Saturday evening, some folks stared at the sight of two women and a gaggle of children piled in a buggy heading across town. Lucy could imagine what they were saying. The train whistle became louder as it approached the outskirts of town and blew at every crossing, but when Lucy started down the hill toward the harbor, the noise faded. They parked the buggy and tied the horse. Louisa was the most excited, but then again, Louisa had gained much favor with her Papa and they had built a special bond on their train ride across the country.

As they stood at the terminal, a warm summer breeze blew off the bay, and the sun began its approach toward the horizon of the distant Olympic Mountains. The work had started for a new tunnel going under the city's business section, just a thousand feet from the terminal. As for now, the train came overland across the city. People waited with great anticipation for the black steel monster to come barreling over the hill, breathing smoke and steam, bringing loved ones from faraway places.

The locomotive broke over the hill and rumbled down the track with the bell ringing. The engineer let out a long blast that unsettled the nearby horses, and they nearly knocked an older woman standing next to them off her feet and two men had to catch her from hitting the bricks. The breaks squealed, and the steam hissed and chugged as it slowed coming in. Louisa held her ears from the noise, and Loring gritted his teeth with excitement. The engine went right on by where they were standing, and they began to watch the coach windows. Strangers gazed out with blank faces while others waved with smiles. Coach after coach passed with no sign of their father.

"Papa!" shouted Louisa as she spotted Edwin coming off the train with a satchel, and she and Loring bolted across the platform and into his waiting arms. Edwin laughed and picked them up in his arms, half carrying them back to where the rest of the family was staying.

"Oh, darling," said Edwin. "I do miss you so when I am away." Lucy kissed him on the lips, then stepped back to take another look.

"My horseman; it will be good to have you home finally."

Chapter 2

Edwin's Return

Edwin stepped back and began brushing the bread crumbs off his jacket and then smoothed out his mustache with the palm of his hand. He took his hat and hit it against his pants, trying to make himself presentable, then formed the brim of his hat and put it back on his head.

"That's better," he said and reached out his hand toward Sarah.

She greeted him warmly. "I don't know if you remember me. I'm Sarah Bowers."

"Weren't you at our wedding?" asked Edwin, looking up from a crouched position and removing his hat.

"Yes, sir, and I was not just 'at' your wedding," said Sarah. "I was *in* your wedding."

"Yes, yes, of course, you were," he replied good-naturedly.

"Oh, Papa, can you stay this time?" asked Louisa. "We miss you awful when you are gone." Edwin gave Lucy a guarded look, suspicious that she had put little Lou up to the question.

Lucy hadn't noticed a lone buggy pull to the curb, but she saw Edwin's attention had been drawn away from their conversation.

"Nice-looking horse he has there," said Edwin.

"What do you suppose it is?" asked Lucy, taking a second look.

"That's a Tennessee Walker all right, a beautiful coat and well taken care of too. Whoever that is paid a pretty penny for her." Lucy brightened up as she recognized the owner of the buggy.

"That's Mr. Sealey!" she shrieked, trying to get his attention. He looked up and waved. "I thought that horse looked familiar. I wrote to him about you coming in today. Come on," she said, taking Edwin's hand. "You've got to meet him."

Lucy knew Edwin all too well, especially his reluctance to meet new people, but she always tried to help him get over his inhibitions. She took his hand with a death grip and tugged him up the street as Henry began to walk in their direction.

"Mr. Sealey," said Lucy. "You came down here just to meet my husband, didn't you?"

"I wanted to meet the lucky man. Besides, if he is married to you, then he is worth coming across town just for the handshake."

"Nice-looking horse you have there," remarked Edwin.

"Thanks," said Henry extending his hand. "Nice-looking family you have there."

"Lucy told me you have been just like a father to her. I want you to know how much I appreciate you looking after her."

"So, you like my horse, do you?" asked Henry. "She is a beauty, all right. I bought a house up the hill, and the horse and buggy came with it. I wanted to buy a horseless carriage, but I think if I wait a couple years, the price will come down."

Edwin folded his arms across his chest and tightened his lip. Henry continued, "They say they are making strides every year perfecting them and the people I know say we should wait till they make their improvements, and then they will catch on a little more. The people I know who have them say there are plenty of bugs to be worked out."

"Yeah, they can keep their bugs," said Edwin. "As far as I am concerned, I hope they never catch on. The whole damn world seems to be in a hurry. It just don't make no sense to me because when you hurry, you just end up waiting on somebody else."

Lucy hesitated to butt into the conversation, but she just had to know if Edwin would be staying or going back right away. "We should get the rest of your things," said Lucy.

"No dear, this is everything," he said, holding up the leather satchel he had carried off the train.

"That's it? How long are you planning to stay?"

"Now, Luce, let's not get into this right now." Lucy bit her lip to hold back the anger to the point she could taste blood. She fought back her tears and emotions that almost overwhelmed her.

"I can hardly wait for you to see our house," she said, trying to lift her spirits. Lucy caught Sarah's glance, and she knew Sarah had seen her disappointment.

"What are your plans, Mr. Sealey?" asked Edwin.

"Oh, it's Henry, please call me Henry. I should probably get back home before dark. I told my housekeeper I would be home for supper. I wanted to let you know I have a line on some work here in Everett if you are interested."

"That would depend on how much they are paying," said Edwin.

"We can get together this week, and I can introduce you to some of my friends."

"That is very kind of you, sir, but I have horses down in Lewis County and very good employment."

"Never hurts to look," said Henry. He turned to Lucy, "I have to say it is always good to see you, but I must run."

"Thanks for coming, Henry," said Lucy. She wanted to hug him but hesitated because of her husband and the crowd of people. Henry took her hand, feeling that she wanted to show her affection, saving her from any public embarrassment.

"Let's plan on getting together this week."

"Why don't you come to Louisa's birthday on Tuesday?" asked Lucy.

"That would be perfect. What time?"

"Come around five."

"Five it is; I will see you on Tuesday." Henry reached out for Edwin's hand, and the men shook, both looking in the other's eye, trying to size up one another. Edwin always had suspicions about people and their motives. He didn't trust people, and he remained cautious about those he didn't know.

"He seems like a nice fellow," said Edwin as he drove the horse up Hewitt Street back to the riverside of Everett with Lucy on his right and Sarah on his left.

"He is a very nice man; he's been like a papa to me. I hoped you would like him."

"I know that is what you said in your letter, but you only have one papa. It somehow just don't make no sense to have two."

"I don't think you can have feelings for too many folks. Our lives are not so small that we can't let others in."

"You can invite them in all right, but you don't have to let them take up residence."

"He's not moving in with us. He has a beautiful home; he just needs someone to look after him, and someone who cares for him."

"I know you put him up to helping me find a job up here in Everett."

"I don't know if I put him up to it, but I know he believes that you need to put your family first."

"You know I put my family first," snapped Edwin. "It's on account of the kind of money I can make running a team in the woods that I have sacrificed everything for my family. Don't I send nearly every penny I earn home to you? Aren't these children kept in food and clothing and a roof over their heads because I work like a dog six days a week and nearly fourteen hours a day? Isn't that putting your family first? You think I like being away for months on end?"

Edwin could feel Sarah squirm in her seat, feeling uncomfortable with the tone of their conversation. Lucy looked over her shoulder at the children sitting quietly in the back seat with big round eyes. Their conversation went silent, and over the noise from the clip-clop of the horse hooves on the brick street, they could hear the occasional laughter from the street corners from isolated conversations as the day began to dim into the night.

"You know we might have stayed in Lowell if Old Dan hadn't died," said Edwin.

"Who is Old Dan?" asked Sarah.

"His name was Dan Gage," said Lucy. "He was like a father to Edwin."

"He was about to make me one of his lead men, but his daughter, Martina, and I never saw eye to eye."

"He owned a very successful ice, coal, and wood company, and Edwin was his favorite employee."

"She was his only daughter and always jealous that I was the son Old Dan never had," explained Edwin. "After he died of pneumonia, she was bound and determined to cut me out of everything, then called me in her office and let me go. That's when I went back to the woods."

Lucy had finally gathered enough courage to confront Edwin about his constant absence, and she had gotten the exact response she knew would come from his lips.

⚲⚲⚲

The next day after the children had left for school, Lucy and Edwin sat on the front porch with a cup of hot coffee, enjoying the fresh air, and watching the neighborhood. Edwin gathered his thoughts carefully as he tried to explain his work situation.

"Lucy, this is how it is. I am the same man you married fifteen years ago. I am not a banker or writer, a ship captain, or some big-time rancher. I don't own a logging company, and I never will. I am just a horseman, and I will always be a horseman. Lots of men have to work away from home to support their families. If I were a seaman, I would be gone for months on end, and you wouldn't even get a letter. I could have been lots of things, but I chose to be a horseman. Right now, I am making a good living, probably the best I have ever done with my own team. I have earned a reputation for being one of the best horsemen in the country. People come to me for advice, Luce. Can you believe it? They come to me. Don't ask me to give this up to come up here to Everett and fight for a job. I'm telling you, Luce, people in those parts know the name Edwin Dowling, and that name means something."

"Maybe we could bring your team up here on the train?"

"Did you even hear a word I said? Somehow I knew you would ask me that, and so I checked into it. I suppose if I had thoroughbreds worth a couple of thousand bucks, that might make sense to someone with money. But what I have is a couple of run-of-the-mill log draggers. People say I could make a silk purse out of a sow's ear. Some other bloke wouldn't get half the pull that I get. I can't explain it, other than I just know horses. These horses drag because they love me, on account of how I am with them. Besides, you know how I am around a crowd. Seems like I get nervous just being next to an anthill."

"We will make do, Edwin. I think I have been putting too much pressure on you to be something you're not. I know I am stubborn; heck, I admit it. I am a city girl; that's just who I am. There is a lot of things I am not sure of in my life, but that is one I know for sure. The other thing I know for sure is that I love you with all my heart. I just want to make a good life for our children, and I don't think Napavine is the place for them."

"Lucy, I agree, and I think our children will have many more opportunities here in Everett, and I want them to grow up here. So I will make this commitment to you to try harder to come home more often and to write more often too. But I will make this commitment to you as well. I will work just as hard as I can to make just as much money as I am able, and if that means staying in the fields and pulling every stump I am able, so every penny I earn will put food on your table and a roof over your head, then that is what I will do. What I won't do is come up here and have to grovel for work.

"Luce, I have found my niche in life, and it suits me. I am comfortable in what I do, and I'm respected for how I do it. I have a good team, and they work well for me. If I got injured on the job, I don't know what we would do. We live nearly hand to mouth, and month to month. If I were to be killed in the woods, you would have to find someone to marry right off the bat to support this family."

"Same goes for me, Edwin. If something happened to me, you would have to come home and raise the children."

"Don't even talk like that, Lucy. If anything ever happened to you, I would just curl up and die."

"Neither of us is exempt from death. I just want to make sure that if I go first that you will promise me you will take the children to church every Sunday."

Edwin folded his arms across his chest and wrinkled his brow at the thought of losing his wife.

"Yea, I promise," he said. "But that ain't gonna happen, Luce. Besides, you are healthy as a horse, and if there is a God as you claim, then He will protect you because of your faith."

"Well, that isn't exactly how it works, my dear husband. I believe God knows exactly the number of our days before we were born. I don't get how all that works, but it gives me peace to know that there is something bigger in this world than man and governments. And when someone dies, God is at work, because greater is He that is in you, than he that is in the world."

Edwin took a sip of his now-warm coffee and they both grew silent.

🌲🌲🌲

Edwin stayed in Everett for a week, celebrating Louisa's sixth birthday. By the time he left, Lucy could see he had become agitated and was ready to get back to Napavine. When he left, he promised to return every three or four months, and stay longer in the summers if he could.

Chapter 3

News

In April of that year, Lucy received one of her mother's regular letters, opening it quickly with a kitchen knife and hoping for good news from home. Her eyes followed the words as they floated off the page and drifted into her heart.

April 10, 1909
My Dearest Daughter,

If only I were there to put my arms around you as I share this news. If ever I had a twin sister closer to me, it would be you, my darling, and you know it too. We have always had a special relationship that is undefinable by any means.

I am writing this morning with a heavy heart as I don't know how to break this news in a gentle way other than to tell you outright that your dear Papa has passed on.

Yesterday, while getting ready to go to work, almost in the middle of our conversation, he collapsed on the floor. I knew it the minute he fell from the look on his face that he was gone forever. I summoned the doctor, and they said it was a cranial hemorrhage, which caused him no suffering or fear from the immediate passing from this life to the next.

I know when you read these words I shall feel it in my spirit as you grieve this terrible loss. I know that you wanted so much to have him come and visit you in your new home out West. I know that you said on several occasions that he was the best papa a girl could ever have and I know it to be true, my darling. I am so sorry that you have to hear such news in a letter and I wish I could be there with you now, as I am sure your tears are falling on the page, as are mine.

Lucy paused from the letter and noticed that her tears had indeed dripped from her eyes, as her mother predicted, and the wetness had scattered the ink on several words. She could barely see the page, her eyes were blurry from the moisture, and she wiped them with her sleeve. Lucy dabbed at the wet spots on the page, trying not to smear the ink, then picked up where she left off.

I know we talked about me coming to visit you this summer. I have been in such ill health, my darling, and it nearly makes my heart ache to say my doctor told me I needed to give it some time before I would be ready to make such a trip as that. I know you will be disappointed with this news, and I don't mean to trouble you twice in one letter, but I promise you that within the next year I will come to see you and stay just as long as you like.

Well, my darling girl, don't lose faith on account of this setback. If you are seeking a life where there is no heartache, disappointment, or pain, it is not here in this world but in the next. I would suppose if I go on, I will only be rambling about the same things again, so I will close.

May God's peace be with you,
Your forever loving Mama and Grammy

Lucy went back to the first page to read the part again about her father, just to verify she had read it right. She wished she had known that day at the train station that she was saying goodbye to him for the last time.

⇑↑⇑

After Lucy wrote to Edwin about her father, he came home to Everett just as quickly as he could. Even though he was a man of few words, Edwin had great compassion for his family, knowing from his youth the sting of losing his mother. Edwin knew how much his children loved their grandfather, and he had loved the man too. Simeon had always been there for Edwin's young family in all of his absence during the long winters working in the woods up in Maine. He knew that his boys would be hit hard by the news, as their Grampa had been like a second father to them.

⇑↑⇑

By the time Edwin prepared to leave Everett and go back to Napavine in mid-July of 1909, Lucy had begun to show, five months into a new pregnancy.

"I heard they are pulling stumps up in Snohomish," said Lucy as the family waited on the platform at the train station. The early morning sun began to poke its nose over the horizon in the summer blue sky. The children stood in silence, waiting for their father to respond to their mother's comment.

"Is that right, my dear? Are you going to go dragging this log back in the woods so you can drag it out again? I thought we had this all settled."

"Just a last-minute hope, that's all."

"You always do have to have the last word, don't you?" Lucy tried not to make a scene in front of her children.

"Okay, I suppose we don't need to go dig this up again if you say so. I know that you know how we all feel, and we will leave the subject right where it lays."

"And that is where it will stay. I will be home in the fall. I am sorry to miss your ninth birthday, Louisa, but I will be here for your mother's in November. I should think that would make you happy, Lucy."

"I'm always happy when you come home. My birthday or not."

"Let's see," he said, scratching his chin. "Your birthday is on the 27th. I will catch the Friday train and be here in Everett late Friday evening. I'll plan on staying until the week before Christmas when I will have to go back to work."

"Do you have to be gone at Christmas again?"

"Luce, for heaven's sake!" Edwin squinted then tightened his lips as he looked her square in the eyes.

"Did you hear the whistle?" said Warren.

"You have to be here when the baby comes," she said.

"Whose baby?" he answered. "You didn't tell me your friend Sarah is finally pregnant?"

"Oh, Edwin, you are so clueless. Look at me. I am five months pregnant, and you never even noticed."

"Our baby . . . what? You didn't tell me."

"I shouldn't need to tell you when you can see it plain as day."

"You're having a baby, Mama?" asked Louisa with a squeal.

"I've been trying to hide it, but now it is starting to show. I was going to let you come and see my condition on my birthday. That is if I don't have him or her before you get home. But I thought you should know before you left for another four months."

Now they could hear the shrill whistle from the train, blowing again at the crossing on Hewett as it made its way to the waterfront.

"I'm glad you told me." Edwin took her hand in his and shook his head with a smile. He turned to his oldest son, who was now almost as tall as he was.

"You are growing into a fine young man, Warren. Remember, I expect you to act like the man of the house while I'm gone. You buckle into that job at the mill and make something out of yourself. Remember, hard work is the key to success. The bosses like a hard worker, and if you work hard, they will notice, and they will move you up. You won't always have to work pulling green chain."

"He comes home pretty tired, don't you, Warren?" said Lucy.

"What time did you say you had to be to work today?" asked Edwin.

"It's shift change. I have to be to work at three o'clock, and I get off at one in the morning."

"Ten hours, that's a fair day," said Edwin. "But I think if I tried to do that, it would kill me. You know, at forty-seven, I can feel my age catching up with me."

"You're right, Edwin. I think this pregnancy is going to be different this time. You know how I've been feeling lately. Doctors, what good are they? You tell them you have a pain in your side, and they just look at you with a blank stare and scratch their chin. I tell them I think my skin is turning yellow, and they tell me to stop eating so many tomatoes and carrots."

"They ain't never done much for me," said Edwin. "Seems like all they can do is fool you into thinking you are going to get better. They are nothing but a bunch of quacks trying to take your money. I think sometimes you'd be better off drinking snake oil."

"Maybe I'll have to find some of that, but I don't think you drink it. I think you rub it on your skin. I might have to find something to get me through my pregnancy."

"You'll be fine, Lucy," said Edwin as the train broke over the crest of the hill and came rumbling down and rolling up to the station. The whistle blew, screaming about its arrival, and the bell clanged as it chugged in and then came to a halt. Everyone held their ears but Edwin.

"You are young and healthy."

"You take care now, Papa," said Loring, reaching out to shake his father's hand.

"Give your horse a kiss from me," said Louisa.

"I don't usually kiss my horses, but for you, my girl, I would kiss a horse."

"How about me?" asked Etta.

"For you, darlin', I would kiss 'em both."

The doors on the coach burst open, and the hordes began to fill the boardwalk as passengers greeted loved ones, and their conversations filled the air. The engine let out a blast of steam as it settled in, as if letting out a deep sigh of relief.

"Don't forget your lunch, Papa," said Etta holding out the satchel. "I'll be content if you just kiss *me*."

"I wouldn't have forgotten," said Edwin, taking it from her and kissing her on the forehead.

"Looks like they are boarding now, Papa," said Loring.

"I don't have to be the first one on; I'll give them some time. I want you to study hard in school now, son. If you are going to be a ship's master, you will need good grades. You hear me?"

"I will, and I will be a ship's master, just you wait and see."

"Well, I suppose I should find my seat. Come on, Pumpkin, give me a proper goodbye." Edwin dropped to a knee and let Louisa throw her arms around his neck.

"I love you, Papa," lisped little Edith, who had just turned three in April, as she wormed her way in to get some attention.

"Yes, you too, baby," said Edwin. "Your Papa loves you." Edwin stood back up and reached to shake the hand of his oldest son. "You take care of them, Warren. I'm counting on you, boy. You too, Loring." Edwin shook Loring's hand, who was eleven. Then, holding the handrail, he hoisted himself aboard, looking back to take one last look at his family.

🌲🌲🌲

Edwin arrived home just in time for Lucy to deliver the family's newest member. Lucy's birthday fell on November 27th, and little Roy came the day before—a perfect birthday gift for a woman on her thirty-eighth birthday.

The final months of Lucy's pregnancy had been different from the others; pain had gripped her nearly every day. But the baby had been born healthy, so she thought nothing more of it as she bid Edwin farewell once again, her belly still swollen from childbirth, and prepared for another Christmas without her husband.

Chapter 4

A Turn

A few months after she gave birth, Lucy's health took a turn for the worse, and her skin began to turn noticeably yellow. She returned again and again to the doctor as her pain grew worse, but just as she suspected, they did nothing for her. "Muscular rheumatism in the neck," they told her, and the solution offered was morphine and cocaine, to ease the pain.

Lucy disliked being medicated so heavily, but couldn't seem to get out of bed or function without it. When her condition only worsened, the doctor finally visited her at home and said the dreaded word out loud: *cancer.*

"I'm afraid you've probably had it for years, my dear," he told her kindly but soberly. "There's nothing we can do, I'm afraid."

Lucy, having long lived with physical pain, now swallowed the fierce, emotional pain that rose in her throat. She must be strong.

After the doctor left, she pulled out ink and paper and wrote to Edwin, though she could not bring herself to write the word "cancer."

Dearest Edwin, she wrote. *I am sick. Please come home. I hope you will come in time for Edith's fourth birthday party. It would mean so much to us all . . .*

⬆⬆⬆

When Edwin arrived in Everett on Saturday night, sixteen-year-old Warren came to meet him.

"Where is your mother?" asked Edwin as he stepped off the train. The sun lay low over Puget Sound, and the snow-capped Olympic Mountains poked up in the distance into the clear evening sky.

"She is down in bed," he answered, shaking his head. "I don't know, Pa."

"What do you mean?"

"She has been in a terrible way; the doctor won't talk to me."

"Has Henry Sealey been to visit her?"

"Just last week."

Edwin grabbed his mustache with the palm of his hand and pulled the hair down straight over his lip.

"Shall we try to get a cab, or do you want to walk, Pa?"

"I need to stretch my legs after that train ride; it's not that far. Not much more than a mile. I walk further to work every day. Now that you are sixteen, have you thought about coming to join me out in Napavine?"

"I don't think it's a good idea to pack up right now with Mama being so sick. Besides, the doctor said the baby has something. Mama needs her rest to get her strength back, and she doesn't need to be worrying about me moving. Do you think it's a good idea?"

"I don't know what to think anymore, son. I'm just trying to support all of you. Not that I don't enjoy my time at home, but a man has to do what a man has to do."

"I understand, Pa, but the family is having a difficult time."

"Yeah, women are always complaining about something, aren't they? If you handed them a gold bar, they would complain it was too heavy."

"I suppose," said Warren, but he didn't think his father understood the gravity of the situation. He would see soon enough when he got home.

As they walked, a woman from the church Lucy attended stopped them to inquire after Lucy's health.

"How is your wife?" asked the woman. She wore a white apron over a grey dress and nurse's white bobbed hat.

"Oh, I don't know rightly." said Edwin. "The doctors don't know."

"So she is under a doctor's care, then."

"For what it's worth."

"What's her symptoms?" she asked, and Edwin shrugged his shoulders.

"The doctor said its rheumatism, but I think it is something more serious," said Warren. "She seems awful sick to me, and her skin is yellow."

"Is it cancer?" the woman asked.

"Now hold on," said Edwin. "Nobody has suggested she has cancer. If that were the case, then she is going to die."

"I'm just asking, that's all. I am not suggesting your wife is going to die. If you will excuse me, I have to get on to work." The woman turned and then stopped in her tracks, and wished them good health before walking away.

As Edwin and his son made the turn on Walnut Street, Edwin had a pit in his stomach. Louisa saw them make the corner and came running off the porch with her arms open.

"Oh Papa," she said, tossing herself at him. "Mama should perk up now that you are home."

"You know I can't stay, Pumpkin," he said, setting her down, eager to get into the house.

"Yes, I know," she said, tightening her lip. "But you'll be here long enough for her to brace up, won't you?"

"How is she?" asked Edwin as he came up the porch.

"The doctor has her on morphine," answered Warren.

"All she wants to do is sleep," said Louisa. "Etta and I have to do all the chores, besides taking care of the baby." Edwin opened the front door and walked into the back bedroom, where Lucy lay on the bed.

"Edwin, you came!" said Lucy, trying to sit up.

"How are you, my darling?"

"Oh, don't you worry about that. But wouldn't you know, the doctor suggested that I should pack up and move to Napavine." She let out a short laugh, but the sound was hollow and mirthless. Edwin realized how much her condition had deteriorated since the baby had been born.

"No," he said quietly, "I think maybe I should sell my horses and move up here to Everett and find a job."

"Edwin, you can't do that. You love those horses."

"I can get more horses; it's you I can't replace. So, if that means letting them go and taking care of you, that's just what I will have to do."

"We can talk about this later, Edwin. I am just so happy to see you. Have you had dinner? You must be famished."

"Papa . . . Papa!" shouted Edith as she came running into the bedroom, followed by Etta, who was carrying the baby.

"We are all here but Loring," said Lucy.

"Where is Loring?" asked Edwin.

"I think he is at the neighbor's house," replied Etta.

"He is usually on the dock watching the boats," said Lucy. "I can't control him."

"An eleven-year-old boy has no business down at the docks by himself," said Edwin.

"You tell him, then," said Lucy, "I have been harping on him, and he won't listen to me. Louisa, go fetch your Papa something to eat."

"Come on, Papa, let's go find you something," she said, taking his hand.

"Etta baked a birthday cake for Edith. I swear someday she is going to own a bakery."

"Today is my birthday, Papa," said Edith. Her hair had grown into long, blonde curls and she looked up at him adoringly with her big round eyes.

"That's why I came home, little honey. Just for you."

"And Mama too, right?" she said.

"Yes, I came home for all of you, but just special for you because of your birthday." Edith looked at Louisa and gave a big wide grin.

"See, you are not Papa's only special girl," she said, putting her hands on her hips.

"You are all special to me," said Edwin. "Why do you think I work like a dog?"

"Come on, Papa, you are going to waste away if you don't get some nourishment," said Louisa, pulling on his arm. "You can't just have cake; you are a growing boy, you know."

Louisa laughed as she tugged on Edwin to follow her, and he finally pulled himself away from his wife to allow Lucy some time to put herself together. Louisa scurried around in the kitchen and set her father at the table while she poured him some hot coffee. "Do you want a little something special in your coffee, just how you like it?"

"You know me, don't you darlin?" Louisa got a stool and stepped up in the top of the cabinet over the washbasin to reach her father's whiskey bottle.

"Not too much now; just a shot to take the edge off the day.

"Here you go, Papa, just how you like it."

"Wait, let me look at that bottle," said Edwin, taking it and holding it up. "Someone has been in my whiskey."

"How can you tell?" asked Louisa.

"Because I bought it new when I was home in January, and look, it's almost empty."

The back door flew open and in walked Loring. His eyes brightened when he saw his father sitting at the table.

"Have you been in my whiskey bottle, boy?" Edwin bellowed, his anger getting the better of him. To his surprise, Loring's face grew pale and his voice was just a whisper when he responded.

"It's not me. Mama has been sipping on it just to get through the day."

Edwin wouldn't know until later that the combination of morphine and alcohol was a lethal concoction.

That night, they celebrated Edith's birthday in Lucy's bedroom. After the cake, Edwin poured each person a glass—alcohol for him and Lucy and hot chocolate for the children. Warren was permitted a splash of whiskey in his. They raised their glasses as Edwin gave a blessing.

"This blessing was passed down through our generations from my great-grandfather, John Dowling. He was a true Irishman who fought for the freedoms we enjoy in this country.

May the most you wish for be the least you get.

May the good Lord take a liking to you, but not too soon.

May you have rye bread to do you good, and wheat bread to sweeten your blood,

Barley to do you no harm, and oatmeal to strengthen your arm.

May big headaches and little fevers be always far away,

May the doctor never take a penny any single day.

May your glass be full and ever big,

May the joy in your life cause your feet to do a jig.

May you be in heaven a full half-hour before the devil knows you have slipped away.

And may you live as long as you want, and never want as long as you live.

Edwin took his cup, and everyone raised their glass of juice, and then they took a drink to their sister.

"Where did you learn that poem?" asked Etta curiously.

"I was just a boy. Funny how I've remembered it all these years. I suppose it's not word for word, and I might have embellished just a bit, but it still fits for a little girl who loves her family."

"And a family who loves her," said Lucy.

The family sang happy birthday and ate birthday cake. Finally, they were all together, laughing and enjoying each other.

Lucy put on a good face, trying not to dampen the mood with her pain and weakness. But the unspoken tension was there, and everyone knew the seriousness of it. By Tuesday morning, when Edwin should have been catching the train back to Napavine, it was quite apparent that he would be staying indefinitely to care for his wife.

Chapter 5

Psalm 22

Edwin had risen early and made coffee and read the newspaper, and then around eight o'clock, he went into the bedroom to check on Lucy.

"Here you are, Edwin, needing to leave to go back to work, and I am so sick I am getting in the way of your plans." Lucy put her hand out and coaxed him to sit on the edge of the bed.

"Don't say another word about me leaving you right now. I will stay as long as you need me."

"Edwin, I need to be honest with you. I don't think I will make it much longer."

"Don't talk like that," he snapped.

"I need to be honest with myself," she answered in a weakened voice.

"There is too much good living ahead for you to die. Why, there are more birthdays, Christmases, weddings, and such. This family needs you; you just can't die."

"We are all going to die, my dear husband. You will die someday too. So, it's not about if, but when, and my time is drawing short. I can feel it in my bones. I know you want to hold on, but I have known for several years now that something was going on in my innards. I have been going hand over hand down this rope, and now just a small bit is dangling below me, and I don't have far to go." Edwin gritted his jaw to hold back his emotions.

"No . . . I won't let you go this way. You hear me, darlin'? I need you. The children need you."

"I won't last the week, Edwin. We have to talk about this now while we still can." Edwin began to weep, but Lucy continued.

"This is what I want you to do. Listen to me because this is my wish. You know full well that Sarah has never been able to have any children. When I pass on, I want you to give Roy to her to raise him as her own and care for him. Her husband does very well, and they have plenty to provide to raise our son in a proper way. And he will be loved and nurtured and grow to be a fine man. Not that I don't doubt that you and Etta could do it, but it would be one less mouth for you to feed. Promise me, Edwin."

"Are you afraid?" Edwin whispered.

"No. I will be with Jesus. Nothing could be better than that. Besides, my Papa is there waiting."

"You are delirious." Edwin buried his face in his hands.

"Edwin . . . no . . . this is a reality. I know you have always had trouble believing in God. I know you felt betrayed when you were a young man, having to deal with the death of your mother."

"If God can raise someone from the dead, then why do people have to die anyway? If God is the great healer, as they say, then why can't He just snap His fingers and make you well right now? It is hard to believe in something that people say is so miraculous when miracles never seem to come your way. Where is my miracle?"

"Edwin, just look at your children, and you will see God's miracle. Look to your horses, and they will tell you. You claim to be able to talk to them, but you don't listen. If you did, they would tell you. All creation knows there is a God in heaven."

Edwin sat quietly, not knowing how to respond and mulling over everything she was saying.

"You know you are my gift in this life. If our families had not been rooted in Machias and Whiting, we would not be together, and our children would have never been born. The generations beyond would never come to be. I pray every day for our children and their spouses, and their children and their children, that they will come to know God as I know Him. And I pray every day for you too, Edwin."

"What did I do to deserve you?" Edwin choked through his tears.

"What I don't want to happen is the same thing that happened last time, when you came to resent God for taking something precious away from you. I will be fine in a place where I will be completely content—a place called home where we were all meant to be since the beginning of time. But you will never get there unless you give up this life to God and acknowledge Him, just as your horses have done."

"Really?"

"Yes, that's the secret to life. Letting go of yourself and giving the life to God. A man without God lives in fear of the darkness of the grave. But a man of faith walks with confidence and purpose; he is an eternal soul and a friend of God."

"I wish I had faith like yours, my dear wife."

"You can, Edwin." Lucy gave him a sweet smile and reached for his hand. "You can, and you will. I want you to bless your family as they grow. I want you to usher our grandchildren into the world, and I want you to become a man of faith."

Lucy slept most of the day, and by the late afternoon, Edwin sent for the doctor to come and make a house call. She was so very, very frail. Her eyes had become foggy, and her speech very slow. By the time the doctor arrived, she had slipped further into death's clutches, and Edwin couldn't get her to open her eyes.

"It's time to call your family in, sir," said the tall and slender white-haired gentleman. "I am so sorry to tell you, but I am afraid your wife is dying."

Edwin felt as if a baseball bat had hit him in the stomach. He had suspected the worst, but hearing it from the doctor made it a reality.

"I don't know what else to do for her at this point. I suppose more morphine to make her comfortable."

"What do you think it is?"

"Most likely cancer of the liver or the pancreas. Us doctors can only guess at these things most of the time. But with her yellowing skin color, it's a pretty darn good clue as to what is making her so sick."

"Nobody survives cancer, do they, Doc?"

"Not so much, son. Oh, I suppose I have seen a miracle or two in my day," he said, rubbing his chin. "But in your wife's case, it would take a big miracle to save her."

"How long does she have?" asked Edwin.

"No one can predict how nature will take its course," he said, putting his hand on Edwin's shoulder. "I don't suppose you have more than a few days, maybe only hours." Edwin couldn't believe his ears. He wanted to run and hide or go back to the time when he had spent all those long months away from her, taking life for granted.

"I'm afraid I failed her; I don't see how I can go on alone!" Edwin put his hands over his face to cover his emotions. "What are my children supposed to do without a mother?"

"These are questions for the Reverend, not your doctor. Do you know if Lucy has one?"

"She does," said Edwin.

"Well, I don't claim to be a preacher, but I can tell you this. It's not whether your glass is half full or half empty, but it comes down to being thankful that you have a glass at all. You have a big task ahead of you now, raising a family as both a mother and father, but don't lose heart and don't give up. You will have to tap into your divine purpose and come to the realization that God has had a plan for your life from before time began. Take this moment and make the best out of it. This can destroy you mentally and physically; it's what your enemy, the devil, wants. But God has a greater purpose for you if you will only allow Him to work."

Edwin looked up and dropped his hands to his side, letting the doctor's words come over him like a warm rain straight from heaven.

"This is a huge task," said Edwin. "Larger than life itself . . . that's for sure."

"I lost my dear wife ten years ago now, and I think of her every day. We had the world by the tail in a new city and a new grandchild just born to our oldest son. I don't know how to tell you this, and I am sure it's nothing you even want to hear right now, but it has made me into a better doctor, a better father, and a better friend to those around me. I would never have been like this before I lost my Olivia. But most of all, I have been given eternal hope where none existed before. I now have something in heaven to keep my eye on where before I had nothing."

Edwin tried to wrap his mind around the doctor's advice. He felt so out of his depth. The guilt of this seemed to be crashing in around him and he didn't know if he could become the better man the doctor believed he could be.

"I'm sorry I can't do more for Lucy, but my advice is for the living, my son. Your job now is to let her go and let her be with God. Oh, don't stop praying until she has taken her last breath. God can do a miracle, even now."

The doctor left, and Etta and Warren poked their head into the bedroom, and Edwin waved them in.

"Is Mama going to be okay?" asked Etta. Edwin paused, thinking he would lie to her and say she would be fine, but then hesitated as the words began to form on his lips.

"I don't know how to tell you, but Mama is dying." Etta gasped and put her hand over her mouth as the tears began to flow. Warren wrinkled his nose, turned to his sister, and then dropped to a knee and put his hand on his mother's arm as she lay motionless.

"Mama, wake up, Mama," he implored as Lucy's eyes moved and then parted in slits as she peeked out to see the people in the room. "Don't leave us, Mama."

"Go get the rest of them, Etta," said Edwin. "Bring them all in." Etta turned and opened the door, and the rest of the family filed in and surrounded the bed.

"Where I am going, you cannot come with me," said Lucy, trying desperately to say the words as they escaped her lips like feathers in the wind. "I can see it, and it's beautiful. So many of our family are there waiting for me. I can see their faces, so many I have never met." She paused, a smile on her lips. Then she lifted her head to look at each of her children.

"You are so precious to me, each and every one of you. I am so sorry I won't be here to share your lives. I won't be able to make your wedding dresses like we planned. Girls, I won't be there to hold your hand when you bring a child into the world. I won't be here to encourage my sons and meet my new daughters. I want you to obey your father and help him. Help him to be a father like the one I had. Encourage him and support him; he will need your help." Lucy paused, closing her eyes as she took a deep breath to find her strength.

"Read to me, Louisa."

"Yes, Mama. What shall I read?"

"My Bible, sweetheart, on the nightstand. Psalm twenty-two. Just the first part."

"Edwin, come find me when you leave this world. Where I am going, we will finally be together."

"I won't know how to find you, Lucy."

"By heart, Edwin. You can find your way back to me by heart."

Louisa opened the Bible and found the Psalms, turning to the twenty-second, and there began to read. Lucy closed her eyes and took a shallow breath, then struggled to open them.

"Come close to me, Edwin," she whispered as Edwin dropped his ear to her face to hear the faint words. "The curio shop." Edwin thought she was delirious and passed off the comment as nothing.

Louisa began to read, "My God, my God, why hast thou forsaken me? Why art thou so far from helping me, and from the words of my groaning?"

Louisa paused and looked up from the page to see what looked like eternal peace on her mother's face. She focused back on the page and continued to read.

"O my God, I cry in the daytime, thou does not answer; and in the night season, and am not silent. But thou art holy, O thou that inhabits the praises of Israel. Our fathers trusted in thee: They trusted, and thou didst deliver them. They cried unto thee, and were delivered: They trusted in thee, and were not put to shame."

Louisa looked up from the page and saw that her father's eyes were red, with tears welling up in them.

"She's gone; our dear Lucy is gone."

Lucy had a smile on her face as she passed into eternity. To Louisa, it seemed as if a candle had been blown out on a birthday cake as her mother lay motionless on the bed. Etta began to cry, and Warren took his mother's hand. Loring dropped to his knees, putting his hands over his face. Little Edith frowned, turning toward Louisa, seeming not to understand anything about what had just happened. Louisa closed the Bible and laid it at the foot of the bed. The room became blurry as the tears formed in her eyes, and she began to cry. She took her little sister by the hand and pulled her out of the bedroom.

"What's wrong with Mama?" asked Edith. "Why is everyone crying?" Louisa took a deep breath, trying to control her sorrow and form an explanation of the unexplainable to her four-year-old sister.

"Mama is gone, Edie."

"She is not gone; she is in bed."

"Mama died. Where she has gone, she is never coming back from. You will understand when you are older. People just die, and they go away. It's just how life is."

"She is never coming back?"

"She is never coming back," said Louisa. "She is gone from this life."

"Who will be my mama," said Edith as she started to cry. "Who will take care of us?"

Louisa put her arms around her little sister to comfort her. "Don't worry, my precious sister. I will always be there for you, and I will always take care of you."

Chapter 6

The Curio Shop

Edwin sent a telegram to Lucy's mother and got an immediate response that she would be coming out on the train in two weeks, just in time for Warren's seventeenth birthday. Edwin had a chill go up his spine, wondering how he would be able to remember all of his children's birthdays, all the details Lucy had taken care of that he had never been a part of. Then the thought about baby Roy came to mind, and what Lucy had said. He decided to call his children together and come up with a plan.

The following morning, he gathered his children in the parlor after his girls had served breakfast and cleaned the kitchen.

"What are we going to do, Papa?" said Louisa. "Are you going to leave us to go back to Napavine, or will you be taking us with you."

"No, I am staying in Everett. I have sold my team there, and there is no reason to go back."

"Where will Grammy stay when she comes?" asked Etta.

"I will take the couch, and she can have my bedroom."

"When will she be coming?" asked Loring.

"She said she would be here for Warren's birthday."

"What about me?" said Edith. "What about my birthday?"

"We just had your birthday."

"I know, but I wanna change it. It's too close to Mama dying. Every time I have a birthday now, it will make me sad."

"Your mama is gone, and we are all going to have to make sure we just make the best of it. I am not going to know all these kinds of details. Etta, I am putting you in charge. You're fifteen now and old enough to run the house. We will be giving baby Roy to your Aunt Sarah. I know she is not your aunt, but that's what you all call her. Mr. Sealey is helping me to find work, and I hope it involves what I know best, which is horses."

↟↟↟

Edwin knew what he had to do to make his son's birthday a special day and thought long and hard about what to do. The following day, he took a walk uptown. As he strolled up Hewett, his heart felt heavy, knowing how much Lucy loved to window shop. He passed her favorite dress shop and wondered what she would say about the white dress with frills on the collar and the big red bow tied around the waist, hanging in the front window. Again her words echoed in his head as he wondered what she meant when she said he would have to find his way back to her by heart. Then he spotted it, the curio shop. He knew she visited here regularly, and was almost certain she had been delirious as she uttered her final words. He grabbed the door handle and stepped into the shop. The shopkeeper, wearing overalls and a white apron, came around the counter to greet him.

"What can I do for you, sir?"

"I'm just looking," said Edwin as he gazed across the store at all the trinkets stacked on shelves and piled on the floors in wooden boxes. Tapestries and pictures hung from the walls, and dishes, plates, and teacups of every color and pattern imaginable were everywhere. The owner had put the women's jewelry safely under a glass case. There were children's dolls, old furniture and chairs, and mixed and matched items of every size and shape.

"You sure have a lot of stuff."

"Mostly other people's old junk, but treasures to those who are looking and a gem when you find it." The shopkeeper had thin graying hair and a thick white beard. "Sure I can't help you find something?"

"Looking for something for my seventeen-year-old son's birthday."

"Well, that ought to be easy. What does he like?"

"That's my problem. You see, I really don't know the boy all that well. I have been working in the woods ever since he was born, and the boy grew up before I could get a handle on him."

"Any chance you are Dowling?"

"Edwin Dowling," he said, extending his hand.

"What a treat indeed," said the shopkeeper taking his hand in a firm grip. "Why, I know your wife, Lucy. I am so pleased to finally meet you. She hasn't been in the shop for a month or so now, but she is a delightful woman." Edwin's throat tightened as he stood stunned, not knowing how to respond. "You tell her that Sam sends his greetings and wishes her well. You tell her I still have that item she put on hold."

"She is dead, Sam."

"What?" exclaimed Sam wrinkling his brow and tightening his lip. "What happened?

"Cancer. She succumbed to cancer on Wednesday last."

"Oh, my God. I can't believe it; she was just in last month, and we had such a nice chat. Oh, this darn life is cruel. What a shame and with all those children and a baby."

"What is it she put on hold?" asked Edwin. "I suppose it was a teacup or something of the sort."

"Wait here; it's in the back," said Sam disappearing through a doorway. When he came walking out with it. Edwin couldn't believe his eyes, and his jaw nearly hit the floor.

"I can't believe it!" Edwin blinked, just to make sure his eyes weren't playing tricks on him. He wanted to pinch himself to make sure this wasn't a dream.

"Here, take it," said Sam handing Edwin the flintlock Brown Bess musket. Edwin took it in his hands, which were trembling at the thought of what Lucy had done.

"Where did you get it?"

"A woman brought it by last winter and said her husband had it. Said she had no use for it since his death. I tried to pay her for it, but she just gave it to me. I had it leaning against the counter when Lucy came in last month. She did say, if she didn't make it back, then her husband would be coming in. It makes so much sense now," said Sam, shaking his head.

"What do you want for it?"

"She put ten bucks on it to hold it; I couldn't take a nickel more now."

"It's worth much more than that." Edwin looked at the fine wood stock with hardly a scratch on it. "He certainly took good care of it, whoever he was."

"If you want to haggle over the price, I can start higher," laughed Sam.

"But ten bucks? That's just nonsense."

"I'm making you a deal because of Lucy. I loved her smile, and I am sure whatever you decide to do with it, she will be smiling down from heaven. Besides, I owe her my life."

"How is that?" Edwin still had trouble believing he was holding a Brown Bess, probably used in the American Revolution, in the palm of his hands.

"She told me about her faith, and I caught it like a sunrise coming over the Cascade Mountains on a sunny day."

"Ten bucks?" confirmed Edwin as he extended his hand, and the two men shook.

"It's the least I can do for your dear Lucy."

"That's still a full week's pay for most men, any way you slice it." Edwin picked the rifle off the counter and pulled the hammer back, hanging on to it with his thumb. He pulled the trigger and let it down easy to see if it still worked. "Lord knows it is probably still loaded with a charge," he said as he tucked it under his arm.

"Don't be a stranger," said Sam. Edwin tipped his hat and headed out the doorway, not wanting to look back just in case Sam changed his mind. He chuckled to himself, feeling a little bit like he had just robbed the place.

⚶⚶⚶

On Saturday, April 30th, Ida Gardner came in on the train to Everett. Warren and Loring met her at the station, and they hired a horse and buggy to bring her back to the house.

"Grammy!" yelled Louisa as she ran off the steps, followed by Etta and Edith. Ida stepped down from the cart and held out her arms to catch Louisa as the other two girls crowded around.

"My lands, how you have grown, little one. Last time I saw you, Edith, you were just a baby," said Ida as she parted from Louisa and took Edith in her arms.

"Papa said he is coming home early from work today," replied Etta.

"We put all fresh linens on the bed, and the room is all ready for you," announced Louisa.

Warren paid the cab driver, and Loring retrieved his grandmother's luggage. The two boys followed their grandmother and the girls into the house.

"Look, Grammy, me and Etta baked Warren a birthday cake," said Louisa, pointing to the chocolate cake sitting prominently on the dining table.

"Do you need help making dinner?" asked Ida.

"Oh no, everything is ready. All we need now is Papa." It seemed so odd to be with all these children and not share the time with her daughter. The house seemed cold; it was as if a spirit had been torn away. Everyone tried to put on a good face, but Ida could tell that tears were lurking just under the surface.

That evening, Edwin arrived home early, and they all sat down to a beautiful dinner. They tried to avoid talking about death, but both Edwin and Ida knew the events over the last year were like a sharp knife in the guts with Simeon and now Lucy released from the cares of the world.

After dinner, it came time to give Warren his gifts. Grammy Ida put her gift on the table, and everyone admired the beautiful gold cross on a chain.

"Lucy wore this as a young girl. I didn't expect that you would wear it, but I am sure this will mean a lot to you just to have it. Maybe someday you will have a little girl, and you can pass it on to her."

"Where is your gift to Warren, Papa?" asked Louisa.

"Your mother always took care of all that. Now someone else in our family is going to have to step up and take care of those kinds of details for me."

"You mean you didn't get him a gift?" asked Etta.

"You of little faith. Wait here, and I'll go get it," said Edwin as he ducked away to the other room and then returned. Warren's eyes brightened up, and his mouth dropped open as he saw his father holding the musket.

"Pa, you didn't," exclaimed Warren. "Where did you find it?"

"I didn't find it. Your mother did."

"Papa, you didn't wrap it," said Louisa.

"You never gift wrap a firearm. That is just the tradition as I know it."

"How did Mama find it?" asked Warren.

"It was the last thing she whispered in my ear. All she said was 'curio shop.'"

"Sam at the curio shop, of course," said Etta.

"Anyways, Sam took in the musket and was saving it for your mother. That's all I know." Louisa looked at Edith, and she shrugged her shoulders. Etta shook her head, and everyone came up speechless.

"No matter, Lucy found the musket, and so here it is, and I am giving it to you, Warren, because we all know how much the story of the old family musket meant to you as a boy. It's not the same musket, but it's more about what it represents." Edwin held it up and handed it off to Warren, who took it in his hands as if it were a piece of precious china.

"I know what it represents, Pa. It means freedom. Without it, the United States of America would not exist at all. The stars and stripes would not fly in the wind. How do you know if it is loaded or not, Pa?"

"That was the same question I asked when I picked it up. So I took the ramrod and put it down the barrel. It goes all the way to the end, so you know there is nothing in it."

"Without a charge in the barrel, then it would just be a flash in the pan," said Warren.

"That right, you put the powder in the pan, and when this piece of flint hits the steel striker, it sparks and ignites the powder, and that ignites the charge in the barrel, and the musket fires."

"A flash in the pan," said Louisa. "That is sort of like our Mama's life—just like a musket without a charge, her life was a flash in the pan."

Everyone in the room began to cry, and Warren buried his face in his hands to hide his emotions. Ida broke down and sobbed uncontrollably, and Edwin bit a hole in his cheek to stop the tears.

"That's right, Lou," said Edwin. "She came into this world, grew up, married, and had a bunch of kids." He grinned at them all. "She was a daughter, a wife, a friend, and a mother. She was gone in a flash. But that flash will never be forgotten." Slowly their tears turned to smiles as they remembered Lucy, sharing memories and stories.

As Edwin gazed at their faces, he savored the moment like a piece of candy melting in his mouth. Suddenly, the heartbreak over what he had lost disappeared in a flash, replaced by the sweet memories of Lucy. The sweetness of her life and love lingered still, and her incredible legacy could not be denied.

Final Epilogue—Edwin and Lucy Dowling and Their Descendants

Louisa always kept her promise she made the day Lucy died. Even though they were only five years apart, Louisa took on mothering her younger sister, Edith.

Edwin blamed himself for his wife's death. On several occasions, he voiced that none of it would have happened if only they had stayed in Lowell. He had so many regrets about not spending more time with Lucy. He struggled with depression for the rest of his life.

Eventually, he sold his team in Napavine, never returning to Lewis County, and found a job at a local mill in Everett, making lumber deliveries with a horse and wagon. This kind of work began to dry up for horsemen with the advancement of motorized vehicles after 1910. By 1920, you couldn't even find a horse and buggy on the streets of an American city. Men like Edwin found themselves obsolete and out of work. He could see it coming at the turn of the century and tried to avoid it, but there was no escape.

When Ida Cook heard the news about Lucy's death, she got on a train and came out to Everett, arriving after the funeral. She stayed for a month and then made the long trip home again to Lowell. She died of a broken heart just three weeks later, on June 14, 1910 (sixty-seven years to the day, that our daughter, Susanne, was born).

Edwin lived a quiet life, raising his children as a widower, and never remarried. Louisa remembered growing up that if things got too loud, her father would rustle his newspaper. Louisa loved to dance, and a dashing young man named Nate Swanson kissed her on the dance floor one night in Everett. She was nineteen years old when she married Nate, ten years and four days after her mother died.

Loring became a seaman and the captain of a tugboat in Alaska's Bering Sea in the 1940s. He never returned, and the family always suspected some scoundrel might have pushed him overboard.

Warren bought a farm in Monroe, Washington, where he raised gladiolas. He and his wife had a son, Roy, who became a doctor in Seattle, likely named after Warren's little brother. Edwin honored Lucy's request to give their infant son, Roy, away to her good friend, who couldn't have children, and she adopted Roy as her own.

Etta eventually took over as a mother figure in the family. Family history related that this never went over very well with the sisters!

Nate and Louisa had two children, Rodney Dean and Barbara Jean (my mother). Nate worked as a lineman on high towers, with no harnesses and no hardhats. In the early 1940s, a man working above him dropped a wrench and hit Nate on the head, nearly killing him. There was no such thing as worker's compensation or sick leave in those days. If you couldn't work, you didn't get paid. Barbara had to go live with her Aunt Edith (Dowling) in Cashmere, Washington.

Aunt Edie, as Louisa always called her, married a big Swede named Earl Olson, who was a Washington State Trooper. Earl and Edith had three boys: Loring, Don, and Warren, Edith naming two of her sons after her grandfather, Warren Loring Dowling.

Louisa never knew why she had the middle name of Marion, or that it was a place three miles north of Gardner Lake in Washington County, Maine. Born Marion Louisa, she always went by her middle name, just like her father did. All of Lucy's children thought their mother had been born in Lowell, Massachusetts, but Lucy was born in East Machias, Maine.

Louisa occasionally wrote back and forth to her cousin, Helen Cates Seavey, who lived in Conway, New Hampshire. Helen was three years old when her mother, Allie Bell Dowling Cates (Edwin's sister), died of cancer in 1909. Helen kept records of the family history and had everything in a book. In a letter to Louisa, Helen said there were archives in a vault in the Machias bank. To date, that book has never been located—or any of the family records, for that matter.

Edwin always favored Louisa, and they had a special relationship together because she reminded him of Lucy. Of course, they never forgot the train ride they took across the country together, and the six months they spent in Mayger, Oregon before the rest of the family arrived. Louisa said she cut her hair when she was a teenager, and her father cried when he saw her. She also shared that she would ride along with him when he made his deliveries with his horse and wagon.

After my mother, Barbara, was born, Edwin took a walk uptown with Louisa, who was twenty-eight at the time. My grandmother remembered how proud he was to push the baby carriage with his one-year-old granddaughter.

Edwin died of cancer in 1928 when my mother, Barbara Jean Swanson, was just one year old. She never knew her grandparents; however, her mother, Louisa, always kept her parents alive by telling stories about them. As a little girl, my mother remembered visiting their graves with Louisa in Everett, cleaning the headstone, and leaving flowers behind.

Lucy left a big footprint on our family because of Louisa Dowling. I remember seeing her on a horse when she was sixty-eight, at Goose Prairie, where my Uncle Rod owned a cabin, and thinking to myself, *How in the world did she learn to do that?*

At the age of eighteen, Roy Cole (Lucy and Edwin's youngest, who was adopted by the Cole family) attended the funeral of Edwin Dowling with his mother. Warren Dowling asked him why he came, and he said his mother was a friend of the Dowlings. Warren said, "My mother, Lucy, died of cancer eighteen years ago. She loved your mother so much that she gave him her baby up to raise as her own, since she couldn't have children. That was you—and that would make you our brother."

Understandably, this created quite a stir, and everyone at the funeral was furious with Warren for spilling the beans. In the probate records from 1928, since Edwin had no last will and testament, the siblings split evenly the $6500.00 in his estate, receiving $1300.00 each except for Roy Cole, who got five bucks.

My Uncle Rod, my mother's brother and Louisa's oldest child, was like a second father to me—not because I did not have the most wonderful father in the whole world, but because my Uncle Rod and my father were inseparable. I don't think I have ever seen or heard of two brothers-in-law who loved each other as much as they did.

My father, Lloyd Jesse Neil, was a "Junior." His father, Lloyd Senior, worked selling cars in Colville, Washington. Lloyd Sr. met a young girl in Seattle while attending school there, and they both had to leave the school after being found talking in her room. She had been born and raised in Addie, Washington, so they made their home in Colville. Lloyd joined the local sportsman's club, and one night they had a speaker from the newly formed two-year-old State Game Department, who was recruiting for a State Game Protector. The club president made everyone laugh when he said, "Get Neil to do it; he is the biggest poacher here."

Lloyd applied, and became a State Game Protector in 1934. Several years later, he met a new State Trooper, Earl Olson (who was married to Edith Dowling). The two would have a lifelong friendship even though their careers took them to different places. Earl transferred to Cashmere, working in Chelan County. My mother remembers how she loved Earl Olson and how he loved her. Earl never had a daughter of his own. She would spend the day with him in his patrol wagon, and they would stop somewhere and have a picnic lunch along Blewett Pass.

Earl and Edie ended up in Tacoma, where Earl became a Sergeant in 1940 with the State Patrol, then promoting to Captain in 1942. During the war, he worked at keeping the balloons carrying fire bombs from Japan a secret. If the papers had reported it, the Japanese would have launched more, but they thought they were a waste of time because newspapers were not reporting the fires.

Lloyd and Arvella had a son, Lloyd Jr., and a daughter, Alverna. On the Fourth of July, 1937, Lloyd Sr. threw a firework off the porch. His son, age ten, who stood nearby, was hit in the eye with a fragment and blinded. My grandfather never forgave himself for that costly mistake. My father wanted to become a pilot, but his eyesight held him back. He came home from high school one day and announced he wanted to go to law school and become an attorney. My grandfather took a dim view of attorneys, having had to fight them his whole career, and the idea of his son being a lawyer went over like a lead balloon. "No son of mine is going become a damn attorney." My father decided it would be better to become a Game Protector.

After he graduated from Ellensburg High School in 1945, Dad joined the Army. He would have been part of the planned Japanese invasion if the Atomic Bomb had not forced Japan into surrender. His parents moved to Tacoma, where his dad was promoted to District Supervisor for Pierce and Thurston Counties with the Game Department. His old friend Earl served as Captain for the State Patrol. The Olsons invited the Neils to a family Christmas party in 1946, where Lloyd Jr. formally met the Captain's niece, Barbara Swanson. Louisa and Edith were neighbors living on the same block on 19th and Union in Tacoma.

Their sister, Bertha Etta, whom they now called Bert, lived in Edwin's house in Everett. After her divorce, she had taken in a boarder named Steve Donker. Steve lived there for years before her sisters got suspicious. They pressured her to get married, but Steve held the cards. It would have been scandalous for a couple to live out of wedlock in the 1940s. They hounded her so severely that, finally, she vowed that she would get married to Steve, but they would never know if she did. She always used the last name of Troy because she ran Troy's Bakery. It wasn't until many years later, when I found Bert's gravestone, that my mother finally realized her Auntie *had* gotten married ,because her name is engraved as "Bertha Donker." Bert's son Bob Troy lived on Lake Stevens and married Gladys, who died of cancer as a young mother of two daughters and one son. Lake Stevens is near a little town in Snohomish County named Machias. (I wonder if Bob ever knew the origins of that name or its significance for his roots?)

My father, Lloyd, worked on fish hatcheries for several years but never liked the work. He arranged a meeting with the Chief Game

Protector, begging for a job as a protector, but at age twenty-three, the Chief said he looked too young, and they couldn't hire him until he was thirty-five. Twelve more years of grinding fish food did not appeal to him. My father quit and took a job as an Apprentice Optician just before I was born. My grandfather was furious that he would walk away from state employment.

In 1961, my grandfather was tragically killed, unloading a tractor from the state game farm off a flatbed truck. At age ten, I remember the day of his funeral, seeing the throng of game wardens in their campaign hats, telling my father I would be a Game Protector one day.

My mother always told me I should have been born a hundred years before my time. Maybe that is why when I traveled to Machias, Maine, in 2016 with my wife, Susan, to search for Warren and Louisa Dowling's graves, I felt as if I had arrived home on the shores of Gardner Lake.

Unless you look back to find out where you came from, there is nothing to measure to see how far you have come. My mom and dad met because of a friendship between a Game Warden and a State Trooper. Now I am the Senior Chaplain of the Washington State Patrol and Washington Department of Fish and Wildlife Police.

Looking back for me has enriched my life and given me more of a foundation than before. Most genealogies are just a math problem: date born, date married, and date died. You have to do the math to learn more about the thirty-two great-great-greats and the sixty-four great-great-great-great-great grandparents. Today, there are thousands of people related to those in my family tree.

I hope you have enjoyed this story and that my search has inspired you to learn more about your family history. Every person who has ever read this book or talked to me about the story always tells their own. May God bless your family history. I hope you look back off the boat of life and see the waves and ripples fade into the calm waters of eternity and emerge like a vision of *trees in the mist*.

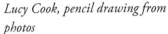
Lucy Cook, pencil drawing from
photos

Edwin Dowling

This photo is from probably sometime around 1903. I found it on the internet on the Patten Lumbermen's Museum website from Maine, after looking through hundreds of photos. I was stunned when I recognized the man in the back row, standing third from the left, as Edwin Dowling. He is holding an axe over his shoulder. After looking at his sweater, I could see it was the same one he is wearing in the ice cart photo. This is the same sweater he referred to in a letter to Lucy, saying, "It is very cold, but I have my warm wool sweater."

This is Edwin in Lowell, Massachusetts, delivering ice for the Dan Gage Ice Company. Note the sweater is the same one he is wearing in the logging photo in the woods. This photo was found among other family photos.

Lucy Dowling with Warren, Louisa, and Loring in Lowell, Massachusetts about 1905

Edwin Dowling dragging logs with his horse team in Lewis County, sometime prior to 1910

Louisa Dowling, three years old, 1903

Louisa Dowling, 15 years old, 1915

Louisa Dowling Swanson,
50 years old, 1950

The Dowling sisters: Edith, Louisa, and Bertha on Thanksgiving of 1954

ACKNOWLEDGMENTS

The greatest thing about writing this book has been the opportunity to meet my ancestors. My Grandmother Louisa was a significant influence on my life. When you are young, you don't appreciate the pathway that older people have been on throughout their lifetime. I remember her wit and how she loved to laugh. She loved her grandkids and Goose Prairie, where my Mom's brother, Rod Swanson, had a cabin in the mountains near Yakima, Washington. As a kid, I never realized that my grandma lost her mother when she was nine years old or that my grandfather nearly died in his thirties when a guy on a power pole high above him dropped a wrench on his head.

My mother never had grandparents growing up, and Louisa always talked about her mother, Lucy, as being larger than life and sharing stories she remembered. My mother said they visited her grandparents' grave often when she was a little girl, with her mother. They would clean the stone and put out fresh-cut flowers.

I want to acknowledge my mother, Bobbe Neil, devoted wife, mother, grandmother, and great-grandmother. She was an artist and writer in her own right, an encourager and mentor, and a woman filled with so much love, it dripped from her soul. She was not spared from the gripes of life and the stress of living; she had her struggles as we all do. She dealt with them the best she could in a way that seemed right for her. My mom was with me every step of the way in writing this novel, telling me the stories she remembered. When I would find out something in my research, she became excited and was always interested to hear where the story was going. During the process, I would write and then call her to read it over the phone. This story is a collaboration between her and me. She died three years before it was finished.

ACKNOWLEDGMENTS

I know it is not customary for an author to thank his characters. Nevertheless, the characters in this book were real people who lived their lives here on earth. I want to acknowledge the courage it took for John Dowling as a young man to come on a sailing ship to an unknown world and start a new life in New England. He would find himself in an English colony, filled with hope, in a place crushed by taxes and suppressed by the control of a foreign and powerful government. It is a common thought that courage is facing a dangerous situation without fear. Actually, it involves facing danger despite fear. Courage is not the absence of fear, but it is the absence of self. It is because of men like John Dowling that we enjoy the freedoms in our country.

As we live our lives, we don't think about our descendants because many haven't come to life yet. We wonder about our ancestors, not spending much time at it because life is filled with enough pain and elation to keep us focused on the now. We let the past be obscured in a blur or a mist, and live our life focused on what matters to us the most. Having lost two children with my wife, Sue, in our lifetime, I want to acknowledge Louisa and Warren Dowling for surviving the loss of their twins, Willie and Addie, in 1856. When you lose a child, you lose your hopes and dreams. It is your hopes and dreams that drive your life.

If anyone in this book had courage, it was Lucy, who was a devoted daughter to her parents, Ida and Simeon Cook. Lucy loved her husband Edwin enough to follow his dreams and leave her parents behind, knowing she would never see them again. I can only imagine what fortitude it took for her to get on that steam train bound for Oregon. With a stiff upper lip and determination in her step, she had to make the best of a bad situation. A woman living in a man's world had to swallow her pride and cast off her dreams to make a better life for her children. A woman in that time had to make her husband successful and use his talents. There were very few options for a single woman to make a living wage and support her children.

ACKNOWLEDGMENTS

I want to acknowledge my editors, Arlyn Lawrence and Kerry Wade, for their hard work in making this into a novel. I want to thank them for believing in my story and for encouraging me along the way. The book was much too long, and Kerry did a masterful job cutting it down and taking out the fluff. This has been a difficult book to write because it relays a time when both men and women had a different perspective about family and marriage, and they helped me navigate that shifting paradigm and portray it accurately and sensitively.

Finally, I want to recognize the most significant person in my life, the one who has loved me more and encouraged me more than anyone else, my best friend and life partner: my wife, Susan Newschwander Neil. This year, as I write this (2021), is our forty-eighth year of marriage, and the fifty-fourth year of her being my girlfriend. We had three children together and have lost two of them. Tragedy, it seems, has a way of making you stronger if it does not kill you first.

Susan has made me into the person I have become by nudging me when I needed it and helping me to see clearly when my vision became obscured. She has put her foot down to stop me from doing something rash, and picked me up and dusted me off after a fall when I needed her the most. She has always shown interest in everything I have done and been the one to encourage and love me every step of the way. Without Susan, this book would not exist. Lord knows who I would be without her. Our trip back east searching for graves on Gardner Lake had to be a team effort, and the team we have together has been made stronger by our life challenges. You cannot put a price on enduring love and friendship; it is worth all the money in the world.

The first time we met, I was eleven; Sue was ten. My family stopped by to visit her family at her beach house, and we became close family friends. She was like a little sister to me. We went to the same school together, and our older sisters were best friends. I remember the day I saw her at the Puyallup Fair; she had just gotten her braces off that day, and I said, "Whoa, man." She was sixteen, and I was seventeen.

We started dating that Christmas after we kissed in the backseat of a friend's car. We dated steadily through high school; she went to college, and I went into the Navy. We got married in June of 1973. Over our fireplace reads a placard I made, ***"Of all the great love stories ever told, we like ours the best."*** That sums up our life together. I like to shock people when I tell them I live with my girlfriend.

ABOUT THE AUTHOR

Mike Neil is an author and artist whose first novel, *The Miracle of Africa,* was published in 2014. A retired State Fish and Wildlife Officer, Mike currently serves as a national leader in the field of Police Chaplaincy, and is the founder and president of the Washington State Chaplain Foundation. Additionally, he is the cofounder of the National Police and Fire Chaplain Academy, and Regional Director for Region 2 of the International Conference of Police Chaplains. As the Senior Chaplain for the Washington State Patrol and the Department of Fish and Wildlife Police, Mike leads a statewide team of professional police chaplains who support officers in various aspects and stages of their career. He is a recognized speaker and a Northwest pen and ink artist. He lives with his wife Susan in Gig Harbor, Washington. *www.mdneil.com*